Disasters Without Borders

To Ruth, as always

Disasters Without Borders

The International Politics of Natural Disasters

JOHN HANNIGAN

polity

First published in 2012 by Polity Press

Polity Press
65 Bridge Street
Cambridge CB2 1UR, UK

Polity Press
350 Main Street
Malden, MA 02148, USA

ISBN-13: 978-0-7456-5068-5
ISBN-13: 978-0-7456-5069-2 (pb)

A catalogue record for this book is available from the British Library.

Typeset in 9.5 on 12 pt Swift Light
by Toppan Best-set Premedia Limited
Printed and bound in Great Britain by the MPG Books Group

For further information on Polity, visit our website: www.politybooks.com

Contents

Acknowledgments

Disasters Without Borders began with a note from Louise Knight, Senior Acquisitions Editor at Polity Press. Louise said she would like very much to commission a really good introduction to the international politics of natural disasters and I had been recommended as someone who could potentially write on or advise her on the project. I was immediately intrigued. After many years of operating in separate realms, disaster studies and environmental scholarship were finally starting to seriously engage with one another, prompted in particular by events during 2004–5 surrounding Hurricane Katrina, and by the Indian Ocean tsunami. As an established urban and environmental sociologist with a background in disaster research theory and methods, I concluded that this would be a wonderful opportunity to explore and interpret disaster politics through a fresh set of eyes.

Over the course of the last three years, a number of people have contributed to the success of this project in ways large and small. At Polity, Louise deputized Assistant Editor David Winters to see the project through to completion. David has been unfailingly encouraging, courteous, and helpful at each stage of the publication process. Two anonymous referees, one an expert in international relations, the other a veteran in the disaster management field, provided extensive and detailed comments on the first draft. These were very useful in undertaking a revision of the manuscript. During a visit to England in 2011, Mark Pelling, a geographer at King's College, London and author of a seminal book on disaster risk reduction, kindly spent an hour with me and sent me home with an armful of required reading. Mark Baker, a Toronto risk and insurance consultant with a degree in disaster management from Royal Roads University, opened my eyes as to the frequently unacknowledged but significant contribution of the private sector to natural disaster recovery and assistance. Viviana Jimenez, who is researching the impact of changing climate on Colombian coffee growers, sent me some useful reports and web links. Of course, the views expressed in the book are entirely my own.

As was the case with my previous two books, I couldn't have done this without the help and support of my immediate family. Maeve, now launched on a career in corporate communications and public affairs, helped me to do the footnotes and to set up the diagram in chapter 8. I benefitted greatly from ongoing discussions with Tim, a doctoral student at Oxford, about innovation, publics, and organizational fields. T.J. and Olivia have been uniformly interested and supportive. Most of all, I want to acknowledge my wife of nearly 40 years, Ruth. Over the course of this book coming together, we spent many wonderful hours viewing television documentaries, reading, and talking about geologic phenomena, from the catastrophic Laki volcano in the eighteenth century to the threat of 'super-volcanoes' in the twenty-first. Thank you Ruth for your love and support, sage advice, and constant enthusiasm for this book project.

Finally, as I was completing the first draft, Andrew, our first grandchild, was born in Princeton, New Jersey. Immensely curious about everything new he encounters, especially music and the natural world, I pray that he will grow up to witness the advent of that safer world, which so many of the academics, bureaucrats, politicians, and humanitarian workers that you will encounter in *Disasters Without Borders* have worked so tirelessly to bring about.

Glossary of Abbreviations and Acronyms

ADB   Asian Development Bank
ARC   American Red Cross
ASEAN   Association of Southeast Asian Nations
CBDM   community-based disaster management
CCA   climate change adaptation
CCDR   Centre for Climate Change and Disaster Reduction
CERF   Central Emergency Response Fund
CFCs   chlorofluorocarbons
CIDA   Canadian International Development Agency
CRB   Commission for Relief in Belgium
CRED   Centre for Research on the Epidemiology of Disasters, Université
          Catholique de Louvain in Brussels, Belgium
DARTs   Disaster Response Teams (OFDA)
DFID   Department for International Development (UK)
DFRI   Disaster Risk Financing and Insurance
DRR   disaster risk reduction
FAO   Food and Agriculture Organization of the United Nations
FEMA   Federal Emergency Management Agency (US)
GFDRR   Global Facility for Disaster Reduction and Recovery
IADB   Inter-American Development Bank
ICRC   International Committee of the Red Cross
IDNDR   International Decade for Natural Disaster Reduction
IFIs   international financial institutions
IFRC   International Federation of Red Cross and Red Crescent Societies
IGY   International Geophysical Year
IMA   International Meteorological Association
INGO   international nongovernmental organization
IPCC   Intergovernmental Panel on Climate Change
IRU   International Relief Union
JBIC   Japan Bank for International Cooperation
MDGs   Millennium Development Goals
MEAs   multilateral environmental agreements
MSF   Médecins sans Frontières
NATO   North Atlantic Treaty Organization

NGO	nongovernmental organization
OFDA	Office of US Foreign Disaster Assistance
OFOA	Office of Emergency Operations in Africa
PAHO	Pan-American Health Organization
PONJA	Post-Nargis Joint Assessment
PPCR	Pilot Program for Climate Resilience (World Bank)
PVO	private voluntary organization
RADIUS	Risk Assessment Tools for Diagnosis of Urban Areas against Seismic Disaster
TCG	Tripartite Core Group (Myanmar/Burma)
UNCRO	United Nations Centre for Regional Development
UNDP	United Nations Development Programme
UNDRO	United Nations Disaster Relief Office
UNEP	United Nations Environment Programme
UNFCCC	United Nations Framework Convention on Climate Change
UN/ISDR	United Nations International Strategy for Disaster Reduction
UNROD	United Nations Relief Operation in Dacca
UNU-EHS	United Nations University Institute for Human Security
USAID	United States Agency for International Development
WB	World Bank
WFP	United Nations World Food Programme
WHO	World Health Organization
WMO	World Meteorological Organization
WSSI	World Seismic Safety Initiative

Text Boxes

Introduction

On the morning of June 8, 1783, the earth split open along a 16-mile fissure in southern Iceland called the Laki volcano. Over the next two years, the Laki volcanic eruption killed an estimated six million people worldwide. The immediate, horrendous damage to Iceland caused by the molten lava flow, and by a vast plume of acid rain formed when volcanic gases dissolved in the vapor of clouds, was followed by a much greater trail of destruction that was eventually to "reach halfway around the world, from the Altai mountains of Siberia to the Gulf of Mexico" ("The summer of acid rain," 2007: 133). A persistent dry fog, followed by several freakishly cold winters, contributed to devastating crop failures in France and to the destruction of the rice harvest in Japan, where as many as one million people died. Ice floes floated down the Mississippi river, past New Orleans.

The Laki eruption and its global trail of destruction is an early illustration of the notion of "disasters without borders." In dramatic fashion, it established that a natural event originating in one geographic locale is capable of triggering thousands of other events miles away. Meteorologists and oceanographers have long acknowledged this, employing the term "teleconnected" to describe how world weather and ocean currents are linked in a network fashion. For example, *El Niño* conditions off the coast of Peru mean that there will be a drought in India and Australia.

A second meaning of "disasters without borders" is more sociological in nature. In this interpretation, we unquestionably accept the moral responsibility to help citizens of other nations who have fallen victim to the ravages of natural disasters or complex emergencies. It echoes a common theme in the research literature on the study of transnational civil society, which identifies transnational advocacy as "efforts to solve problems that span borders in the absence of border-spanning governments" (Florini and Simmons, 1999: 6). In this spirit, Keck and Sikkink (1988) title their seminal book on advocacy networks in international politics *Activists beyond Borders*.

The *sans-frontièrisme* (without borders) movement originated in France at the end of the 1960s among several international aid organizations, most notably a group of activist physicians who christened themselves *Médecins sans Frontières* (Doctors Without Borders) (Siméant, 2005). Four decades later, the movement has migrated across the social and political spectrum. Occupational groups who have adopted the "without borders" name now include architects, engineers, firefighters, journalists, lawyers, nurses, reporters, teachers, and even clowns. Most of these organizations contribute to humanitarian and development work overseas, although not exclusively in the disaster sector. More broadly, "without borders" has become shorthand for "transnational politics." For example, a Canadian newspaper, *The Globe and Mail*, recently headlined its editorial about German Chancellor Angela Merkel's decision to make joint campaign appearances with Nicolas Sarkozy in the French presidential election in April 2012 "Merkel sans frontières" (*Globe and Mail*, 2012). Furthermore, the phrase has penetrated mainstream commercial culture, where "without borders" simply denotes global consumer appeal. There's even a franchised Mexican fast-food chain in the United States that calls itself "Burritos Without Borders."

In humanitarianism and global politics, a central policy discourse has emerged and solidified around the notion of "disasters without borders." In spite of a host of normative, ideological, and strategic differences, all of the players/actors in the international politics of natural disasters acknowledge to a greater or lesser extent that what happens in one part of the globe resonates elsewhere. As Adger et al. (2009: 150) put it, the "vulnerabilities of local systems, peoples, and places are networked or teleconnected in their social and economic implications." Even those in the military and intelligence sectors, who are in the forefront of realist politics, understand the normative power and appeal of the phrase, and draw from its logic. Nonetheless, as I discuss in chapter 3, the assertion that natural disasters, and particularly their first cousins complex emergencies, are borderless continues to provoke considerable controversy, especially with reference to the moral and legal justifications for humanitarian intervention.

Over the last century, there have been two contrasting ways of imagining natural disasters within the framework of international relations and international law. As Fidler (2005) explains, the first equates natural disasters with other problems such as transboundary pollution that have the potential to cause friction among nations. Here, national states have favored multilateral treaties (hard law) to institute regulatory regimes designed to control the proliferation of nuclear weapons, landmines, ozone-depleting chemicals, and the like. By contrast, natural disasters have been treated as episodic, short-lived events that are optimally handled as humanitarian matters rarely connected to the fundamental material interests that states have in international relations. That's not to say that humanitarian assistance hasn't from time to time been used as a cover for achieving foreign policy or national security objectives. Nonetheless, rather than looking to a set of international legal rules, natural disasters (wartime emergencies are somewhat different) were routinely relegated to the vagaries of what international lawyers sometimes call "soft law" – non-binding actions and activities (Fidler, 2005). In the absence of a strong multilateral presence, natural disasters fell under the influence of an uneasy alliance of the Red Cross, United Nations development agencies, and humanitarian nongovernmental organizations (NGOs). While they had different agendas and frequently held conflicting views about disaster management, the three partners did share a conviction that citizens in the developed world have a moral responsibility to help, and even save, their less fortunate compatriots in the South. The cornerstone of this international relief system (Cuny, 1983; Green, 1977; Kent, 1987) was (and still is) a tangled web of donor and host governments, the military, NGOs, UN bodies, and private charities and firms. Humanitarian disaster relief operates within the broader context of development assistance and politics, and is guided by the prevailing international political situation (van Niekerk, 2008: 358).

In the 1980s, a new *disaster risk reduction* (DRR) paradigm emerged and began to assume a visible presence. This approach differs markedly both from the "business as usual" operation of international politics, and from the humanitarian intervention model that still predominates in international disaster planning and relief circles. In contrast to "sustainable development" and "global warming," DRR is not a concept that resonates widely in the media and in popular discourse. Nevertheless, it has ascended to the top of the agendas of many agencies and donors who deal with disaster mitigation and protection. Despite being embraced by a number of key humanitarian and development agencies such as the Red Cross/Red Crescent and Oxfam, DRR activities still only account for a relatively minor proportion of the total money donated to and spent on overseas relief and recovery. Furthermore, action to reduce risk and build resilience does not seem to be trickling down to those at a grassroots level who are most directly impacted by natural disasters (Mercer, 2010: 260; Views from the Frontline, 2009).

Most recently, the political economy of disaster risk reduction has become part of a wider dialog about global climate change, poverty, and international development (chapter 5). Disaster risk reduction and the various multi-actor initiatives and partnerships that it has nurtured are increasingly popular at the World Bank (see chapter 2). On a positive note, this provides an unparalleled opportunity for DRR to reach a much larger global audience and to access sources of bilateral and multilateral financing than would otherwise be possible. At the same time, it carries a potential risk that DRR discourse could be co-opted by the much better funded and politically connected climate change adaptation (CCA) network. This is problematic for several reasons. CCA tends to be top-down, much like traditional humanitarian disaster relief. By contrast, DRR has been steadily moving towards a more consultative, grassroots model that values local knowledge and initiative. In addition to this culture clash, skating in the slipstream of CCA exposes DRR proponents to the multiple uncertainties and conflicts that characterize the politics of global climate change.

This odyssey of natural disaster aid, mitigation, and prevention over a period of more than half a century, from humanitarianism delivered straight-up to a mixed cocktail of risk management, poverty reduction, and climate change adaptation, is fascinating not just on its own terms, but also as a case history in the politics of transnational advocacy and institutional change. As I discuss in chapter 8, this trajectory is not adequately explained by turning to existing theories in political sociology, comparative politics, or international affairs. Change has not followed Kuhn's model of scientific (and political) revolutions, wherein a challenging paradigm unseats and replaces an established one after a brief, intense period of conflict. Neither is it fully explainable by a world polity model that features a global diffusion of values with minimal opposition; nor by a global norm dynamics model that high-lights the importance of cognitive framing, advocacy networks, and norm entrepreneurs. Unlike in the environmental field, there have not been influential epistemic communities of scientists who successfully spearhead the adoption of multilateral agreements or international agreements. In fact, there have only been two binding treaties, 70 years apart; the first failed and the second is narrowly technical.

The international politics of disaster takes the shape of a "global policy field" with nine major categories of organizational players (chapter 2) who populate four overlapping discursive realms: hazard, risk, and safety; international development; humanitarian aid; and environmentalism and climate change (chapter 8). These realms both engage and collide. Elements from each have been woven together to form the disaster risk reduction paradigm, but the field remains fluid and unsettled.

In the final chapter, I draw upon Ansell and Gingrich's (2007) concept of *emergent institutionalism*, which they introduced in a study of how BSE ("mad cow disease") was officially dealt with in Britain. By emergent institutionalism Ansell and Gingrich mean that the emergence of a new and uncertain problem requires the mobilization of a particular and possibly unique configuration of people, knowledge, and resources. Once an incipient institution has crystallized around an interpretation of a problem, it claims jurisdiction and rebuffs other attempts to engage in sense making. Unfortunately, what can occur is a serious mismatch between emergent problems and emergent institutions.

I conclude the chapter by proposing that a new wave of emergent institutionalism is currently unfolding in the international politics of disaster. This is located at the juncture of four trends (which I have labeled the SCPQ configuration): securitization, catastrophic modeling and scenario building, privatization, and quantification. Among its major players are international financial institutions, insurance (or more precisely reinsurance) companies, catastrophe modelers, defense policy analysts, and geospatial intelligence gatherers. Escalating concern over global climate change and its threats to economic prosperity and national security has prompted this shift in thinking about natural disasters. Whereas they were once viewed as epiphenomena, today, disasters are increasingly acknowledged as having important strategic and financial implications. Insofar as it attracts more resources, notably money and legitimacy, this newfound concern is welcome. However, there's a downside. Insurance logic and security concerns will crowd out humanitarian concern. The language of disaster management will shift, with phrases like accountability, era of results, measurable outcomes, economic viability, cost efficiency, return on disaster risk reduction investments, disaster proofing, and willingness to pay becoming paramount. More broadly, a new humanitarian framework that focuses on strengthening the local community's ability to prevent, prepare for, and respond to natural disasters may be derailed by strategies that are more oriented to a calculus of risk, profitability, and long-term global catastrophe mitigation.

CHAPTER ONE

The Disaster Politics Nexus

As the second decade of the new millennium dawned, a plague of natural hazards visited the Southern hemisphere, triggering multiple disasters. From early December 2010 to mid-January 2011, heavy rainstorms and flash floods – an "inland instant tsunami" – swept across the Australian state of Queensland, spreading over an area the size of France and Germany combined (Rourke, 2011). The flooding obliterated small towns in the Lockyer Valley and overwhelmed low-lying suburbs and parts of the central business district in Brisbane, Australia's third largest city. This followed earlier flooding in the northeast part of the state that resulted in an estimated C$1 billion in lost agricultural production.

During the flood emergency period, Australian Prime Minister Julia Gillard was criticized in the media for appearing stiff and emotionally distant from the problems confronting disaster victims. By contrast, Queensland State Premier Anna Bligh, a descendant of Captain William Bligh of *Mutiny on the Bounty* fame, was praised for striking the right note of steady determination. Bligh saw her public approval rating skyrocket from 25 percent in November to 83 percent in mid-January (Dagge, 2011).

After the waters subsided, Gillard introduced a legislative package that included a temporary flood tax levy on higher income earners, the promise of fast visa processing for skilled migrants wanting to work on the reconstruction, and a A$2 billion payment to the Queensland state government. The third of these ignited a political firestorm, especially among members of the Australian Greens Party. To raise extra money for disaster relief, Gillard proposed abolishing various environmental programs: cleaner automobile initiatives, solar rebates, and the establishment of a Global Carbon Capture and Storage Institute. Speaking on Radio Australia, Richard Denniss, director of The Australia Institute, a progressive think tank, opined that Gillard was probably using the Queensland disaster as a smoke screen for getting out of carbon abatement policies that were ineffective, poorly designed, and had been widely criticized (ABC International/Radio Australia, 2011).

In a mountainous tourist region an hour's drive from Rio de Janeiro, devastating flooding and mudslides precipitated by heavy rains buried several towns, killing over 700 and leaving more than 15,000 homeless. According to the daily newspaper *Folha de Sao Paulo*, this was the worst natural disaster to hit Brazil in four decades (RTE, 2011). Recalling all too well the political fallout from President José Sarney's reluctance to conduct an on-site inspection of Rio's slums in the 1988 floods (see chapter 6), newly elected president Dilma Rousseff – in only her second week in office – donned black rubber boots to walk the streets of Nova Friburgo, one of the worst impacted communities, and pledged "firm action."

Official response to the disaster played out politically in the context of international pressure to ensure safe and adequate facilities for the 2014 World Cup and 2016 Summer Olympic Games. As the *Homeland Security News Wire* (2011), an American e-information service, points out, "Should a disaster strike during one of these events, the response by the Brazilian government could have the potential to create an international incident." A second Brazilian daily newspaper, *Estado de S. Paulo*, questioned Brazil's ability to successfully stage these mega-events given its poor track record, "A look at public policy . . . or the lack thereof . . . reveals a long chain of unpreparedness, administrative incompetence, technical incapacity, and political irresponsibility" (cited in Hake, 2011). Rousseff, who was attempting to secure finance for a major upgrade to Brazil's infrastructure in time for the World Cup, readily acknowledged that this was "not only a natural disaster" but a problem caused by irregular land occupation and reckless development, "Housing in risky areas has become the norm in Brazil and no longer the exception" (Fick and Prada, 2011).

In this book, I view disaster events such as those that have recently plagued Australia and Brazil through the lens of international politics. Surprisingly, this analytic perspective has been slow to develop. With some notable exceptions, political theorists and researchers interested in global affairs have not traditionally been involved in doing disaster studies (McEntire, 2005: 2). This is indicative of political science and international affairs in general, where disaster research has tended to be marginalized and largely invisible. Those political scientists who are active in the disaster research field tend to publish in specialized places, and focus primarily on security and terrorism issues. This contrasts with several other social science disciplines, notably anthropology, geography, and sociology, where research on disasters has been published both in leading journals and annuals, as well as in multidisciplinary journals such as *Disasters* since the 1970s. To be fair, there is an extensive literature dealing with the history and politics of humanitarianism. Natural disasters are often included here, but not always distinguished from other emergencies such as civil war.

Rather than just a matter of benign neglect, there are more complex reasons why the disaster-politics nexus was overlooked until relatively recently. Of particular importance is the tendency to treat disaster and disaster response as essentially *non-political* in nature, or at least ideally so. Disasters are depicted as occurring in a liminal space beyond the pale of normal politics. There are two versions of this, one applicable primarily to community disasters in America, the other to international disaster management.

Post-disaster Utopia and the Altruistic Community

In the 1950s and 1960s, North American disaster researchers routinely characterized the period immediately following the impact of a flood, tornado, hurricane, or other natural disaster as a time of community consensus and solidarity where partisan conflict and political dealing are temporarily suspended. People are said to roll up their sleeves, pull together, and put prior political and social divisions on the shelf. This is sometimes described as a *post-disaster utopia*, wherein formal rules and regulations are set aside, the usual distinctions between rich and poor are disregarded, and people feel an unselfish concern for the welfare of others. Especially influential has been sociologist Alan Barton's (1969) concept of the "altruistic community," the tendency of citizens to selflessly help others in the immediate aftermath of a tornado, hurricane, or flood. As such, natural disasters are viewed as a "consensus-type crisis" with only limited long-term trauma for its victims (Picou et al., 2004: 1495).

This period is distinguished by the emergence of what Taylor et al. (1970) call "the ephemeral government." By this they mean a period of radical revision where one finds "an ephemeral governing structure, different in form, action, and capability from that which had gone before" (1970: 129). In their case history of a tornado that struck Topeka, Kansas on June 8, 1966, the researchers found that community leaders, ordinarily unrelated in any formal sense, came together quickly to plan, coordinate, and expedite effective action, only to disband when the period of crisis ended.

According to this explanation, as the disaster impact recedes, the divergence of interests typical of everyday community life slowly reappears, especially with reference to the politics of reconstruction and the allocation of emergency relief (Quarantelli and Dynes, 1976; Hannigan, 1976). In contrast to sharing of common tasks during the utopian period, the long-term tasks of recovery require "a specialized bureaucracy with specialized roles and rationalized procedures – insurance adjusters, claim investigators, street crews and so forth" (Taylor et al., 1970: 160). This usually creates disillusion, strain, and conflict.

In her best-selling book *A Paradise Built in Hell: The Extraordinary Communities That Arise in Disaster*, Rebecca Solnit (2009) revives and modifies this notion of the post-disaster utopia. Solnit, a San Francisco writer and activist, believes that calamity brings out the best in people and provides a common purpose. "In the wake of an earthquake, a bombing, or a major storm," she says, "most people are altruistic, urgently engaged in caring for themselves and those around them, strangers and neighbors as well as friends and loved ones" (Solnit, 2009: 2).

Solnit introduces a second, related idea in her book. Not only is the imme-diate post-disaster period characterized by selflessness and consensus, but it also represents a time of extraordinary innovation and grassroots democracy. Solnit mixes Barton's "altruistic community" and Taylor's "ephemeral gov-ernment" with the contemporary idea of "civil society," yielding a utopian notion of an emergent, temporary, disaster society that operates *outside of* institutional politics and constitutes "the acting decision-making body – as democracy has always promised and rarely delivered" (2009: 305). If anyone can be found to be behaving badly here, it is the community "elites" and their foot soldiers (politicians, bureaucrats, police, firefighters, soldiers), who "panic" because they sense that their legitimacy and power are being under-mined.[1] In proposing this contemporary version of an emergent disaster community outside the limits of normal politics, Solnit is clearly reacting to events following Hurricane Katrina.

As I discuss in chapter 6, radical political and social change as a direct consequence of natural disaster is relatively rare, and even then most often occurs where disasters act as a catalyst of processes already under way. Solnit's claim that a kind of "Arab Spring" spontaneously arises among disaster victims is more boilerplate than reality.

De-politicizing Emergencies

In the arena of international affairs, the historical reluctance of sovereign states to engage directly with disaster relief and governance beyond their borders has created the impression that such activities effectively lie beyond the limits of normal politics and legal jurisdiction. Fidler (2005) contrasts the extensive use of international law in the contexts of war, epidemics, and industrial accidents to its almost total absence in peacetime natural disasters. He describes the latter as episodic and short-lived with minimal impact on the material interests of national states in the theater of international rela-tions. Whereas the international response to wars, epidemics, and accidents is based in "hard law" (multilateral treaties), the center of gravity in disaster response is situated in "soft law," that is, the non-binding actions and activi-ties of international nongovernmental organizations (INGOs).

Citing an alleged comment by the late Maurice Williams, a US presidential coordinator for major disaster relief efforts before heading up the United Nations World Food Council, that "disaster relief is above politics," Kent (1983: 708) observes that disaster relief is rarely regarded by practicing dip-lomats as a political weapon that can be utilized to gain advantages over an adversary or serve geopolitical interests. Three decades later, Williams' comment seems naïve and out-of-date, but it does point to one reason why the political dynamics of disaster was previously downplayed in the study and interpretation of world affairs.

In the 2004 Sorokin Lecture, presented at the University of Saskatchewan (Canada), sociologist Craig Calhoun argues that a discourse of *emergencies* is now central to international affairs. The term "emergency," Calhoun says, implies that a well-oiled, smoothly functioning normal system of global processes in which business, politics, and the weather all interact properly occasionally goes off the rails. When this happens, quick action is recommended in order to restore equilibrium, ideally through external intervention. International emergencies "both can and should be managed" (2004: 375). This "managerial" perspective is de-politicizing, Calhoun believes, because it skirts democratic decision making. So too is a humanitarian response, insomuch as it "involves precisely trying to alleviate suffering without regard to political identities or actions of those in need" (Calhoun, 2004: 392). Calhoun is not suggesting that this "emergency thinking" is inherently apolitical, but that an emergency informs both managerial and humanitarian perspectives in a way that conjures up the illusion of being situated outside of "normal" politics.

The illusion that natural disasters lie beyond the purview of normal politics has been officially acknowledged by humanitarian agencies, permitted to deliver aid only on the assurance that they remain strictly neutral. This prohibition is enforced both by the United Nations[2] and by individual nation states. In its "Code of Conduct for NGOs in Disaster Relief," the International Red Cross/Red Crescent stipulated, "When we give humanitarian aid, it is not partisan or political and should not be viewed as such." Note, however, that this position increasingly came under fire after the end of the Cold War, "when the political causes of many emergencies were more widely and openly acknowledged" (Buchanan-Smith, 2003: 6).

Nevertheless, some elements within the humanitarian aid community continue to have a marked aversion to all things political, which they equate with "nonfeasance, malfeasance, incompetence, corruption and/or obstructionism" (Drury et al., 2005: 454). Ironically, the agencies and institutions with whom these humanitarian NGOs must regularly deal rarely hesitate to take a political stance. Kent (1987: 118) cites a vignette in which former UN Secretary-General Kurt Waldheim recalls, "Four years ago (1974) I believed that humanitarian relief was above politics. Now I know that humanitarian relief is politics." Among others, the UN, the World Bank, the International Monetary Fund (IMF), the World Trade Organization (WTO), and USAID (United States Agency for International Development) all link their political objectives to interventions in humanitarian disasters. Middleton and O'Keefe (1998: 157) describe this as being both paradoxical and problematic:

> Yet many INGOs, including some who work with one or more of these and similar institutions, seem to regard what they do as somehow apolitical, as having no political agenda of its own, or even, except by accident, of having no political effects. Their philanthropic ancestry, their close connections with "donor" governments, their disbarment from overtly political activity within their parent countries, their existence

within that culture of political world-weariness all conspire towards this self-defensive, but ultimately irresponsible reaction.

At the same time, individual practitioners working for humanitarian agencies usually come to accept that politics is central to disasters and that neutrality is largely a mirage. As Nick Leader (1999) points out, "A recent study of British agencies reported that the Red Cross/NGO code, a short and general code, is a statement which has 'not been internalised by organisations and remains unused as a means of guiding and auditing their work.'" As one referee for the manuscript of this book commented, "I think this [the belief that disasters are apolitical] is a very rare view indeed ... it's long been accepted that weak governance underpins almost all disaster." Nonetheless, disaster managers are usually smart enough to recognize that articulating an apolitical or neutral position facilitates cooperation with host governments, whereas a more politicized approach might jeopardize it. Thus, humanitarianism "is a form of politics in which it is useful to assert that one is non-political" (Volberg, 2005/2006: 63).

It's fair to say, I think, that those who affirm the apolitical dimension of natural disasters are not so much stating that this is *actually* the case so much as they are expressing the fervent wish that it *might be so*. As Drury and Olson (1998: 153) observe, "Indeed, the end argument for most practitioners as well as academics concerned with disasters and disaster response is essentially normative: In this dominant outlook, it is expected that disaster management be apolitical or at least as non-political as possible."

The Disaster–Politics Nexus

Alas, there is a wide gap between what should be and what is. "Every scholarly study of disasters documents that prevention, preparedness and response are determined by political factors," insists Alex de Waal (2006: 129), a veteran observer of famines and other slow-onset crises in sub-Saharan Africa. His observation is echoed by numerous other disaster practitioners and scholars of sundry ideological and methodological stripes. Fuentes (2009: 100) describes post-disaster reconstruction as "fundamentally a political event that can have very discernible political outcomes." Kathleen Tierney (2008: 135), a leading American sociologist of disaster, observes, "Disaster scholarship has long noted that decisions regarding hazard and disaster management are fundamentally political." Political forces, she explains, drive decision making across the entire hazard/disaster spectrum: framing hazards as social problems requiring governmental intervention, political agenda-setting, crisis planning and response, the issuance of presidential disaster declaration, and the provision of disaster assistance. Lee Clarke (2006: 101), an expert in the study of risk communication, argues that politics and power are intertwined; and power "is exceedingly important in talk about disaster, the production of disaster, responses to disaster, and how people make sense of disasters after they happen." Rather than temporarily receding during disasters, social conflict and political struggle are part of the fabric of disasters. Based on her participant observation and in-depth interviews with international aid workers, government officials, and local NGO representatives in Aceh, Indonesia several years after the 2004 Boxing Day tsunami, Lisa Smirl (2008: 236) concludes, "Humanitarian reconstruction after a large-scale natural disaster has become a key site of international politics; a site where global assumptions, relationships, and responsibilities are negotiated, solidified and questioned." This being so, there is considerably less consensus over the breadth, strength and direction of the link between politics and disasters. Essentially, there are two versions of this relationship.

According to the more moderate version, politics and disaster are frequently intertwined, but one should never assume a cause and effect relationship. Thus, in a Harvard Business School working paper, Cohen and Werker (2008: 2) argue that natural disasters aren't exclusively driven by politics, but neither are they immune; rather, disasters *occur in a political space*. In similar fashion, Welsh (1996: 409–10) proposes that the environment "needs to be understood as a site within which a number of social, cultural, economic and political forces intersect, compete and co-operate."

In this spirit, economists, political scientists and public policy researchers have privileged an approach that treats disasters as a space/site/sphere *within which political activity occurs*. In an early example, Abney and Hill (1966) studied the effect of Hurricane Betsy on voting in the 1962 city election in New Orleans (they found that the hurricane was not a decisive factor in voting decisions, with "wet" precincts no more likely than "dry" ones to vote against the incumbent mayor). In *Disasters and Democracy: The Politics of Extreme Natural Events* (1999), one of the better known books on this topic prior to Hurricane Katrina, Rutherford Platt, a geographer and land use lawyer specializing in public policy concerning urban land and water resources, spotlights the increasing involvement of the US government in domestic disasters. By being overly eager to issue a presidential declaration of a "major disaster," thereby making the stricken area eligible for federal emergency relief funds, the government removes incentives for individuals and local communities to protect themselves.

By contrast, the strong version asserts that natural disasters are *direct products* of their surrounding social, political, and economic environments. This strong model is most strongly associated with scholars in anthropology, cultural geography, and development studies. Pelling and Dill (2006) state that they see disasters both as political events in and of themselves, and as potential producers of secondary political events. An acceptable political reading of disaster, they claim, "requires the situating of political action within the wider national and global socio-cultural and historical contexts in which they occur." Researchers who embrace this approach take "an acknowledged political stance which more 'traditional' hazards researchers have tried to refuse or downplay" (Fordham, 2003: 59). Typically, they call for the adoption in Southern hemisphere countries of policies such as "land reform, enforcement of building codes and land-use restrictions, greater investment in public health, provision of a clean water supply and improved transportation to isolated and poorer regions of a country" (Wisner et al., 2004: 7).

Defining Disaster

Several authors (Bolin and Stanford, 1998; Oliver-Smith, 1996) have suggested that the disaster literature has become divided into two general camps, the behavioral and structural. The former paradigm conceives of disasters as events caused by physical hazard agents such as hurricanes and tornadoes. The central task of the disaster researcher is to focus on the social consequences of and responses to these impacts. In contrast, the structural paradigm conceptualizes disasters not as single, discrete events but as "part of the larger patterns and practices of societies viewed geographically and historically" (Bolin and Stanford, 1998: 27). This view is consistent with the "strong" version of the relationship between politics and disaster.

Key differences between the behavioral and structural are embedded in conflicting definitions of what constitutes a disaster. This has constituted an important ongoing debate in disaster research and has even generated an entire book (Quarantelli, 1998a) devoted to the question, "What is a Disaster?" One reason why these definitional disagreements are so important is the insistence by the behavioral school that disasters are something apart from normal social and cultural processes. This has led to an "ongoing concern with defining unique features of disasters and how they differ from other types of social phenomena" (Bolin and Stanford, 1998: 27).

While this debate has many, varied strands, a central difference arises over whether or not to include chronic, diffuse, and long-term situations such as famines, epidemics, and droughts (FEDs), which in contemporary parlance are called "complex emergencies." According to E.L. ("Henry") Quarantelli, co-founder of the University of Delaware Disaster Research Center and "dean" of American disaster researchers, with the exception of some applied disaster researchers in England who are primarily interested in international relief, most scholars in the disaster area have more or less ignored FEDs. Quarantelli gives several reasons for this. First of all, most established disaster researchers are from the First World where FEDs are less common. Second, leading FED scholars are not part of the same scholarly and social circles as disaster researchers.[3] Third, there are valid conceptual reasons for excluding FEDs from the disaster rubric.

Quarantelli favors this third explanation. "My general inclination," he says, "would be to exclude FEDs from the disaster category and to treat FEDs as social problems, involving chronic stress settings rather than crisis occasions"

(1998b: 260). He gives two reasons for this exclusion. First, FEDs lack the suddenness of conventional disasters, such as those triggered by earthquakes and tsunamis. Furthermore, they can only be identified in terms of response, since the agents involved are complex and diffuse. Second, there is minimal overlap between the empirical data and theoretical ideas on famine and droughts and those relating to sudden-onset disasters. The two may have more in common than has heretofore been evident, but until a systematic point-by-point comparison is undertaken, "a good case can be made that the stressful kinds of FEDs discussed should not be conceptualized as disasters, and probably not even as instances of crises" (p. 261).

In an "invited comment" published in the *Natural Hazards Observer*, Russell Dynes, co-founder of the Disaster Research Center, covers some of the same terrain as his longtime colleague, Quarantelli, but, rather unexpectedly, arrives at a radically different conclusion. Dynes observes that existing theories of disaster are not at all helpful in helping to understand "disastrous events" such as forced migration, famine, and HIV/AIDS. Traditionally, the focus has been "predominantly Western, community-based, urban, and deals with sudden-onset agents from natural causes." By contrast, these contemporary emergencies are "principally African, involve displaced populations, are predominantly rural, and deal with conflict or slow-onset events." Dynes insists that it's vital that we expand our research horizons,

> Otherwise, the field of disaster research will be truncated into a catalogue of responses to natural hazards . . . Indeed, the lack of research attention to disaster events that result in enormous human costs in developing countries perhaps makes our current research an example of trivial pursuits (Dynes, 2004).

Dynes' comments notwithstanding, the behavioralist viewpoint has been sharply challenged. As Oliver-Smith (1998a: 22) explains it, starting in the 1970s many anthropologists and social geographers started to broaden the focus of disaster research and embed it in deeper time frames. In doing so "they opened up new theoretical and practical (political) questions and began to reconsider disasters as less the result of geophysical extremes (earthquakes, hurricanes, droughts, etc.), and more as functions of ongoing social orders, human-environment relations, and historical structural processes." Thus, a famine should not be treated as the inevitable outcome of a lack of rainfall and/or of crop failures, but instead of the political failure of the state to deliver food to its citizens (Sen, 1981). It can even transpire that a famine is deliberately engineered by power-holders for tactical military purposes. According to David Keen (2008), this is what occurred in Sudan in 1988, where the Khartoum government deliberately funded ethnic militia groups to create famine in parts of the country. This mode of understanding is consistent with those political-economic approaches to society–environment relations, now commonly labeled *political ecology* (Bolin and Stanford, 1998: 40).

Several pages later, Oliver-Smith explicitly links this discussion to the cause–effect issue or, as he terms it, the "what-why" question. Traditional disaster researchers, he says, label the task of the definition as clarifying what disaster is or what disaster does rather than explaining *why* a disaster takes place (1998a: 24). This exclusion reflects their belief that disaster is a behavioral phenomenon that occurs at a specific moment in time and always in the context of societal disruption. At the heart of this controversy is a profound difference of opinion over whether a disaster is an event or a process (Bankoff, 2002: 155).

Anthropologists involved in disasters particularly object to the established paradigm because it renders the concept of "vulnerability" as irrelevant in defining disasters. Disasters do not simply happen, they assert, but they occur in the context of a specific set of human–environment relations. Thus, the root cause of famine can be attributed to the structural imbalances between rich and poor countries, as evidenced by the "high correlation between disaster proneness, chronic malnutrition, low income, and famine potential" (Oliver-Smith, 1998b: 74). What sociologists of disaster regard as antecedent or underlying conditions, political ecologists interpret as a defining feature or characteristic of the disaster itself. Citing Hewitt (1983: 27), Oliver-Smith (1998b: 75) urges that the perspective of disaster research and analysis shift from an exclusive focus on "extreme events" to one that gives equal weight to those societal and human–environment relations that "prefigure" disaster.

Since Oliver-Smith wrote this in the late 1990s, application of the concept of vulnerability has broadened. Southern Africa's "current humanitarian emergency," Ailsa Holloway (2003: 30) insists, "illustrates almost unequivocally how disaster risk is driven upwards by often silent but intensifying conditions of political, socioeconomic and environmental vulnerability." Prime contributors to Southern Africa's vulnerability include rainfall failure, disruptions to food availability, failures of governance, extreme levels of prevailing poverty, and, especially, poorly managed responses to HIV/AIDS. In a 2009 report entitled *The Right to Survive: The Humanitarian Challenge for the Twenty-first Century*, Oxfam International makes this quite clear, "Vulnerability to threats such as conflict or environmental hazards like floods and earthquakes is a direct result of poverty; the political choices, corruption, and greed that cause it, and the political indifference that allows it to endure" (Oxfam International, 2009: 4).

Consider the case of Nicaragua, a country that has been described as existing "in a permanent state of emergency." Between 1972 and 1996, Nicaragua suffered 11 disasters that seriously affected its socioeconomic development, nine of which were caused by natural phenomena (Rocha and Christoplos, 1999). The situation here more closely resembles a chronic FED than it does a series of sudden, one-off disasters in North America, Western Europe, or Australia. The high human toll exacted by these earthquakes, hurricanes, tropical storms, tsunamis, and volcanoes – 77 percent of the country's population were variously killed, hurt and injured, evacuated, displaced, and/or left homeless – is understandable largely in political and institutional terms. Since poor Nicaraguans have no choice but to build their houses and cultivate their crops on poorly irrigated mountain slopes, they tend to be especially vulnerable to severe floods. Rather than undertake measures to reduce this vulnerability, the federal government has wrongly opted for broad economic development initiatives, on the assumption that natural disasters are first and foremost a sign of underdevelopment and, therefore, only affect the poor. Cases such as that of Nicaragua clearly illustrate the folly of trying to conceptually isolate natural disasters from the everyday practices of politics and power relations.

Conclusion

In this chapter, I argue that the global politics of disasters has consistently been downplayed compared to other aspects of disaster management. Rather than just a matter of benign neglect, this reflects a lingering belief that disasters suspend and transcend normal politics. This is evident in the notion of the "post-disaster utopia" in local emergencies; internationally, it takes the form of a humanitarian disaster politics in which it is desirable to assert that one is non-political. However, over the last decade or so, this view has changed. Most disaster scholars and practitioners now readily concede that prevention, preparedness, and response are determined by political factors; in particular, humanitarian reconstruction after a major disaster has become an important venue of international politics.

Two versions of the relationship between politics and disasters can be identified. According to the more moderate version, politics and disasters are frequently intertwined, but one should never assume a cause and effect relationship. Rather, politics is a space or site where political activity occurs. By contrast, the strong version asserts that natural disasters are direct products of their surrounding social, political, and economic environments. This view is predominant among anthropologists, cultural geographers and development studies scholars. These differences in perspective also play out in the ongoing debate in the disaster research community between proponents of the behavioral and structural paradigms over what constitutes a disaster. The latter assert that a disaster constitutes a process rather than a single event, and is primarily traceable to "vulnerabilities" caused by chronic poverty, inequality, corruption, and government inaction. As we will see in later chapters, this emphasis on vulnerability has become a central tenet of most current thinking on international disasters and the politics that suffuse them.

Further Reading

Craig Calhoun (2004) A world of emergencies: fear, intervention, and the limits of cosmopolitan order. *The Canadian Review of Sociology and Anthropology*, 41, 373–95.

Anthony Oliver-Smith and Susannah Hoffman (eds.) (1998) *The Angry Earth: Disaster in Anthropological Perspective*. Routledge, London and New York.

Ben Wisner, Piers Blaikie, Terry Cannon, and Ian Davis (2004) *At Risk: Natural Hazards, People's Vulnerability and Disasters*, 3rd edn. Routledge, London and New York.

CHAPTER TWO

The Global Policy Field of Natural Disasters

In her book, *The Environment and International Relations*, Kate O'Neill traces "the evolutionary arc of *global environmental governance* from when it first emerged as a coherent system in the early 1970s up to the more contested and disillusioned years of the early twenty-first century" (2009: 3). Initially, the international community sought to govern the global environment through cooperation among nations and the creation of multilateral environmental agreements (MEAs) or regimes. However, in recent decades, this has been supplanted by other collective actions outside of the community of nations – most notably private agreements (e.g. carbon trading schemes).

In mapping this evolving landscape of environmental governance, O'Neill (2009) identifies five main "actors": nation states; international organizations (specifically the United Nations and its associated agencies, and international economic institutions such as the World Trade Organization (WTO), the World Bank, and the International Monetary Fund (IMF)); corporations and the private sector; scientists, expert groups, and knowledge holders; and the global environmental movement. In similar fashion, Newell (2006) devotes a chapter each to four main "non-state actors" in his book on the global politics of climate change: the scientific community; global warming and environmental pressure groups; the fossil fuel lobby; and the mass media.

As will become evident in my historical overview (chapters 3–5), it is not entirely accurate to refer to a "landscape of disaster governance." While there have been scores of conferences, declarations, strategies, global platforms, and UN disaster agencies over the years, virtually none of them has translated into a binding treaty, convention, or other multilateral agreement.[1] For example, adherence to the principles laid out in the *Hyogo Framework for Action 2005–2015*, a touchstone for advocates of disaster risk reduction, is entirely voluntary, with no specific targets, timetable for action, or sanctions against nations that fail to achieve a substantial reduction in disaster losses. While this document has symbolic status, it is not legally binding, and has not led to the emergence of a mechanism with the same legal status as the UNFCCC (United Nations Framework Convention on Climate Change) (Schipper and Pelling, 2006: 32). Nonetheless, collective efforts to respond to, mitigate, and prevent natural disasters are by no means random without the visible presence of any transnational institutions or discursive structures. Indeed, some of the same actors identified by O'Neill (2009) for environmental governance, and by Newell (2006) for the global politics of climate change, are also central to the global policy field of disaster politics.

Past attempts to map the structure of international disaster politics have tilted toward the concepts of "system" or "network." In the 1970s, Green (1977) observed that the "international disaster relief system" at that time consisted of four major elements: the United Nations, private organizations (including the Red Cross), donor governments (through their development agencies), and the international media. Six years later, in his book *Disasters and Development*, Fred Cuny (1983) enumerated a five-tier "international relief system," consisting of a variety of different types of "donors" (those who collect and channel resources to those active in the field) and "intervenors" (organizations that carry out relief activities in the impacted countries). The first three tiers, Cuny noted, represent the international level, the fourth the regional or country level, and the fifth the project level. Into these five tiers "are fitted a complex network of organizations, each of which has a specific role or resources to offer following a disaster" (Cuny, 1983: 107).

More recently, West (2001: 18–23) describes an "international humanitarian system" which is composed of specialized humanitarian agencies that work with humanitarian issues (including those related to natural disasters) in conflict regions or at the international level. Additionally, there are those "who are not authentic humanitarian actors" but are indirectly linked to the international humanitarian system: government donor agencies, the International Committee of the Red Cross (ICRC), the military, the media, and some international governmental organizations (IGOs). These actors play a number of roles, "They grant resources to humanitarian agencies, shape the discussion on humanitarian issues, inform the public about humanitarian crises and assist aid operations on the ground" (p. 18). West acknowledges that this system is "more conceptual than legal." It is loosely held together by "some basic drives toward common action and cooperation" in specific geographic areas or regions (p. 23).

Randolph Kent wrote about a loosely coupled "international disaster relief network" in the 1970s and early 1980s. This cannot be called a "system," Kent argues, since it lacks structural interdependence (i.e. a change in one unit ricochets among the other units); lacks a boundary which separates it from the world beyond; only weakly displays a consistent pattern of relationships among the components; and rarely shares a set of common institutional goals (1987: 68). Instead of a system, Kent described the international relief network as "an amalgam of non-binding contacts, sustained by various channels of communication and by an awareness of who is around" (1987: 69).

Kent underlines the ad hoc nature of the international relief network. Most of the time, it forms "a body of diverse actors tenuously linked by a host of informal contacts and temporary commitments." During a crisis, relief operations often exhibit "spasms of ad hoc coordination." Many "islands of coordination" emerge in the field during a single relief effort, most linked in some fashion to the ongoing relief network. In addition, hundreds of private agencies and ad hoc committees raise funds and collect relief supplies. These "cannot be regarded as either a permanent or predictable actor in the relief network" (1987: 73).

A dozen years later, Aldo Benini published a case history of a 1998 earthquake that devastated a number of villages near the town of Rostaq in a remote area of northern Afghanistan, killing an estimated 2,223 people. Quite a few outsiders descended on the area, including the Red Cross/Red Crescent, Doctors without Borders, and many foreign journalists (during the critical mobilization period, the media outnumbered the aid workers). Benini labels the organizational network responding to the earthquake as a *network without center*. That is, it constituted "a temporary alliance from a pool of partners, each capable of contributing something valuable to a short-term project" (1999: 46). Less than two months after the Rostaq quake, the *ad hoc* network disbanded, only to be re-activated later on by a second earthquake in the region.

In another, more recent case study, Comfort (2007) examined the networks of interaction among organizations participating in Indonesian response operations following the December 2004 Sumatran earthquake and tsunami. She identifies 372 organizations from local, provincial, national, and international jurisdictions. Comfort's analysis reveals both clusters of communication exchange and gaps among participating organizations at different jurisdictional levels of operation.

As helpful as they are, these snapshots of international disaster systems and networks tend to focus almost entirely on relief operations. There is minimal recognition here of other key activities, notably, disaster prevention, preparedness and mitigation. In contrast to the earlier era, disaster risk management[2] can no longer be accurately described as an ad hoc network or network without a center. At the same time, the relationships among various actors engaged in disaster risk management are sufficiently fluid and contested that they still do not constitute a system, as defined by Kent (1987). Rather than labeling the disaster-politics nexus as either a system or network, I have chosen instead to depict it in this book as a *global policy field*.

Although he does not pursue it at any length, Barnett (2008) suggests that a new humanitarian sector has emerged over the last two decades that possesses all of the characteristics of a "field." Referencing DiMaggio and Powell's (1983) oft-cited article on institutional isomorphism and organizational fields, Barnett argues that the humanitarian network has transformed itself into a "community of practice," where the members "have regular interactions, exchange information, rely on specialized knowledge, and understand themselves to be part of a common enterprise" (2008: 253). This leads to increasing rationalization, bureaucratization, and professionalization.

As Barnett has recognized, in the academic specialty areas of economic sociology and management studies, the *organizational field* is a well-established concept. According to Hoffman (1999: 351–2), an organizational field forms around a central issue such as the protection of the natural environment and becomes the center of debate. Multiple and competing interests (i.e. field constituents) negotiate over the definition of issues and forms of institutions that will guide organizational behavior, within an arena of power relations. "[F]ew fields are completely 'settled' or 'institutionalized' . . . Instead, multiple and often contending logics inhabit a field or its peripheries" (Ventresca, 2002: 28).

In the sociological literature on social movements, the analog of the organizational field is the *discursive terrain* or *discursive field*. Snow (2004: 402) says that discursive fields emerge or evolve in the course of discussion and debate about contested issues and events. The various sets of players that populate a discursive field include the social movement in question, countermovements, targets of action and change, the media, and the larger public. Drawing on a longitudinal media content analysis of debates over welfare reform in the United States during the 1960s and 1970s, Steensland (2008) describes the changes in policy framing that occur in a discursive field as constituting an "ecology of competing frames."

Marc Ventresca, a sociologist who teaches in the Said School of Business at the University of Oxford, has been in the forefront of institutional scholars who have analyzed discursive fields and policy framing at a *global* level. In his case study of the historical development of the global policy field of official statistics (i.e. the modern census), Ventresca (2002) identifies a field as "a methodological tool, an heuristic that *links broader social structures, discourse and activity and outcomes*" (emphasis added). Citing theoretical arguments by Wuthnow (1989) and Spillman (1995), he stresses that a field is a venue for oppositional ideas and practices, and new forms emerge from this struggle. The modern census, Ventresca says, "developed in the context of how a global field of talk, attention, and organization took shape," and this international activity "was an important source for 'global' meanings, models, motives and mechanisms that provided authoritative prescriptions for state-level census activity." To structure his account of the global field of official statistics, he employs the method of *comparative episodes*, episodes being "pivotal" moments in the historical narrative that "enable us to see key conflicts, contradictions and institutional settlements."

Ventresca's understanding of what constitutes a global policy field fits nicely the case of the international politics of natural disasters. In particular, it integrates elements of discourse, structure, and power relations in a fluid and dynamic manner. Addressing O'Neill's (2009) concerns about the "state-centric" nature of realist and neoliberal explanations of environmental politics, the construct of the global policy field allows for the introduction and interplay of new ideas into the politics of the environment in a way that the concepts of system and network do not (see chapter 8). Furthermore, it avoids the insider-outsider distinction introduced in West's (2001) discussion of the international humanitarian system, whereby some actors are considered more "authentic" than others.

In later chapters, I argue that the global policy field of natural disasters is becoming considerably more crowded and turbulent, with important implications. In the 1980s and 1990s, the influx of thousands of new NGOs into emergency and disaster operations in Africa and Central America triggered urgent efforts by the larger, established organizations to rationalize and reform the system. Among other measures, this produced the Humanitarian Charter, the Sphere guidelines, and the sectoral cluster approach. More recently, the courtship between DRR (disaster risk reduction) and CCA (climate change adaptation) scholars and policy analysts has further expanded the field (chapter 5). As I discuss in the concluding chapter, the emergence of a new cluster organized around militant humanitarianism, political disaster management, national security, insurance, catastrophe scenario building and risk modeling, remote sensing, and geospatial intelligence has the potential to significantly transform the landscape of the global disaster field.

Architecture of Global Disaster Politics

Although some overlap exists, basically, there are nine main categories of organizational[3] actors or players (see Christoplos, 2003; Christoplos et al., 2005; Coppola, 2011; World Bank, 2006: 65–6) in the global policy field of international disaster politics. In no special order, they are: national states and local governments; regional organizations; international finance institutions (IFIs); United Nations disaster agencies and other international governmental organizations (IGOs); nongovernmental organizations (NGOs); multi-actor initiatives and partnerships; scientific, technical, and academic communities; private actors; and the mass media.

National states play a somewhat ambivalent role here. Most of the time, they attach limited importance to disaster-related issues and activities offshore, focusing instead on disasters within their own borders. This is quite evident from the anemic financial support given over the years to the United Nations Disaster Relief Office (UNDRO), the International Strategy for Disaster Reduction (ISDR), the International Decade of Natural Disaster Reduction (IDNDR), and earlier on, the International Relief Union (IRU). Nations that have been among the most active in campaigning for a global infrastructure of disaster prevention and mitigation are of two types: those such as Japan, the Philippines, and Mexico that are highly vulnerable to natural hazards such as earthquakes, volcanoes, cyclones, and tsunamis; and those such as Canada, Norway, Sweden, and Switzerland that have relatively low disaster probabilities but are deeply involved with overseas development issues.

One special case is the United Kingdom, where discourses of disaster relief and humanitarian aid policy (Galperin, 2002) have had a relatively high profile in policy circles for quite some time. In particular, the (Parliamentary) Select Committee on International Development and the Department for International Development (DFID)[4] are influential voices in shaping overseas development discourse, and, by extension, disaster policy. DFID is a significant donor of both development aid and disaster relief assistance, and has been one of the major sources of financial support for the ProVention Consortium. DFID's "Multilateral Aid Review" is taken very seriously and a low rating here can even lead to an underperforming agency being de-funded (see chapter 4). Another indicator of DFID's influence is its success in selling the idea to the humanitarian community of CERF (Central Emergency Response Fund), a global stand-by fund established by the United Nations with the purpose of jump-starting action in sudden-onset emergencies and responding to needs in countries neglected through the normal allocation of donor government, UN, and NGO resources ("Revitalizing Humanitarian Reform," 2011: 4).

When a mega-disaster occurs, political leaders suddenly take a more direct and sometimes intrusive interest. In the case of donor governments, most notably the United States, the flow of international disaster aid generally follows existing foreign policy imperatives and strategic considerations (see chapter 6). The Office of US Foreign Disaster Assistance (OFDA) acts as the main conduit through which emergency supplemental funds allocated by Congress flow to crises developing overseas (Stoddard, 2006: 49). In the 1990s, OFDA established Disaster and Response Teams (DARTs), small squads of relief workers who assess the situation on the ground, determine what resources are required, and deliver supplies and funding to disaster victims via NGOs such as the Red Cross and CARE. In addition to providing valuable information about disaster damage and relief requirements, the DART situation reports are an "exceptional source of information for Washington policymakers" (Norris, 2007: 5) about the developing political situation in foreign locales. Note, for example, that the "Disaster Cable" transmitted back to Washington from OFDA officers in the field goes to the appropriate State Department desk and to the National Security Council (Stoddard, 2006: 50).

However, exceptions may occur when the disaster event is so massive (e.g. Haiti earthquake, Indian Ocean tsunami) that a failure to respond would be perceived as churlish and politically unwise. In the case of recipient states, domestic considerations play a more central role. Political leaders must balance the advantages of receiving transfusions of aid and expertise from abroad with the political fallout that may ensue if this is seen to indicate incompetence and subservience. Especially in states that have been cut off from the international community, one finds complex relationships between national political pride, legitimacy, disaster management, and international isolation (Pelling and Dill, 2010: 26).

Until relatively recently, one glaring absence among national states in the international politics of disasters was China. During the Tangshan earthquake emergency in 1976, the Chinese government refused international aid, although it later invited a scientific mission to tour the disaster site. This evidently echoed a power struggle in a period of political transition during the last days of the Cultural Revolution (Pelling, 2011: 100).

Three decades later, China appears to have finally joined the world community. In what has to be seen as a reflection of official policy, a 2008 article in the *China Daily* sounded the bells to proclaim support for both the Hyogo Action Plan and for a regional disaster prevention and reduction system. The author (Liu, 2008) praises Japan, with whom China has not enjoyed the best of relations over the years, for providing relevant seismic data, as well as professional rescue and medical teams, to Wenchuan in Sichuan province immediately after the massive earthquake that struck on May 22, 2008. Additionally, the author notes that China co-organized and hosted the Third World Conference on Disaster Reduction in the northeastern port city of Harbin in August 2007. This followed on from an earlier International Conference on Disaster Reduction held in Beijing, May 25–27, 2004. Finally, in a surprising gesture, in 2005, China allegedly offered the United States $5 million in aid and rescue workers, including medical experts, as part of the international response to Hurricane Katrina (CNN, 2005).

According to Pelling and Wisner (2009: 43), the actor with the greatest potential to mitigate urban disaster risk is the **local or municipal government.** Local governments have access to local knowledge, as well as national government support and influence. Ideally, they are advocates for local needs and priorities, and are directly accountable to the population through elections and everyday contact with local leaders and community actors. In theory, at least, local governments should have "the authority to negotiate with international humanitarian NGOs and to connect aid packages to pre-disaster development goals" (Pelling and Wisner, 2009: 44–5).

In reality, local governments often disappoint. Too often, local politicians are beholden to powerful political and economic interests, engaged in controlling and manipulating planning and development regulations, and extracting rent for private gain (Pelling and Wisner, 2009: 45). More often than not, they lack the money, expertise, and authority to be lead responders in disaster situations. Another endemic problem in some parts of the world is that the local government changes every time the national leadership changes, thereby orphaning ongoing disaster mitigation and prevention projects. This is made worse by the fact that municipal governments do not always have professional civil servants to ensure continuity (Select Committee on International Development, 2002).

Regional organizations play a more significant role in the global policy field of natural disasters than they are usually given credit for.[5] This is particularly the case in Latin America and the Caribbean, where national governments have established regional entities to help them define needs, share information and training opportunities, and elaborate projects (Fagen, 2008: 5).

One of the leading regional disaster agencies in Latin America is the Coordination Center for Natural Disaster Prevention in Central America (CEPREDENAC). The largest, oldest, and most active intergovernmental regional organization dealing with disaster, CEPREDENAC has been described as "a platform for bringing together state, civil society and donors to address risk" (Christoplos et al., 2001: 188). Headquartered in Guatemala, whose government contributes to staff support, its major achievement has been the development of a Regional Plan for Disaster Reduction in 1993, which forms the basis for contemporary national disaster policies across Central America. CEPREDENAC has a permanent secretariat and its statutes have been ratified by its member states (Fagen, 2008: 8). Most recently, it has been managing the coordination of regional projects supported by Germany and Norway that seek to strengthen local capacity to mitigate disaster impact and strengthen seismological risk analysis capabilities (Coppola, 2011: 611).

Asia-Pacific countries typically account for up to half of the world's total deaths, damage, and loss from disasters, and up to 90 percent of the total number of people adversely affected (O'Donnell, 2011). This should not be surprising given that Asians make up a considerable portion of the world population. For this reason, the level of regional collaboration and activity is also high compared to other parts of the globe. Of particular importance here is ASEAN (Association of Southeast Asian Nations). ASEAN played a vital role in coordinating the response to Cyclone Nargis in 2008. Nargis killed an estimated 140,000 people, many of them in the nation of Myanmar (Burma). A particular difficulty in Myanmar was the reluctance of the ruling junta to allow foreign aid workers into the country (see chapter 6). ASEAN was instrumental in organizing a meeting (ASEAN-UN International Pledging Conference) on May 25, 2008 to establish a Tripartite Core Group (TCG) comprising representatives of the Government of the Union of Myanmar, ASEAN, and the United Nations. It was TCG's responsibility to coordinate relief efforts and provide a forum for resolving issues affecting the delivery of relief assistance. With ASEAN's support, TCG was instrumental in fostering cooperation among the three parties. Especially notable is PONJA (Post-Nargis Joint Assessment), a collaborative undertaking tasked with identifying humanitarian needs in the stricken areas of the country and coordinating the overall response (OCHA, 2008). In December 2009, the ten members of ASEAN ratified the ASEAN Agreement on Disaster Management and Emergency Response, the first binding regional mutual assistance pact. The agreement included drawing up a set of standard disaster relief and recovery operating procedures; setting up early warning systems; preparedness and response; and recovery, rehabilitation, and reconstruction (Coppola, 2011: 270).

Aside from government-affiliated donors such as the US Agency for International Development (USAID) and the Humanitarian Office of the

European Community (ECHO), **international finance institutions (IFIs)** are the main institutional funders of recovery and reconstruction after major disasters. I have chosen to place them in a separate category from other international organizations on the grounds that this funding role gives them a distinctive and powerful role. The World Bank is the largest. Between 1984 and 2006, the Bank financed 528 projects that addressed natural disasters, representing more than US$26 billion in lending (Parker, 2006: 11). Others of note include the Inter-American Development Bank (IADB), the Asian Development Bank (ADB), the African Development Bank (AfDB), the Development Bank of Southern Africa (DBSA), the Caribbean Development Bank (CDB), the Council of Europe Development Bank (CEB), and the Japan Bank for International Cooperation (JBIC).

In the past, the World Bank's involvement in natural disasters has been channeled through a wide array of lending and non-lending services. Loans range from a few thousand dollars for fire detection towers in a forestry project to a US$500 million loan for post-earthquake reconstruction (Parker, 2006: 12–13). These take the form of funds that are reallocated from existing Bank loans, and the Emergency Recovery Loan (ERL), a three-year lending instrument that allows for expedited processing and quick disbursement. Non-lending services can include convening of donor meetings, provision of assistance with post-disaster assessments, study preparation, and technical assistance (Parker, 2006: xx).

The increasing engagement of the disaster risk reduction realm with that of climate change adaptation has led to the disbursement of funds through the Pilot Program for Climate Resilience (PPCR), administered through the World Bank. As I discuss in chapter 5, this has injected a measure of controversy into the global policy field for natural disasters, insofar as PPCR loans are bitterly contested by a coalition of civil society groups in the countries of the South. Additionally, the World Bank founded, funded (partially), and initially hosted the ProVention Consortium, a partnership initiative that is designed to mainstream commitment to disaster risk reduction (see below).

A third conduit for World Bank funds to disaster-prone Southern nations is the International Finance Corporation (IFC). IFC, a member of the World Bank Group, was created to support private sector development, mobilize private capital, and provide advisory and risk mitigation services in developing countries. IFC is not centrally involved in disaster relief and reduction activities, but it does direct funds in this direction from time to time. For example, in March 2011, Guy Carpenter & Company, LLC, a leading global reinsurance intermediary, announced that it was to receive a US$1 million grant from IFC to help develop a market for weather, index-based microinsurance in Mozambique. This was designed to assist farmers to survive catastrophic exposure to floods and droughts. At the end of 2011, IFC disclosed a proposed credit line of US$50 million to TMB Bank Public Company, Limited, a wholesale bank in Thailand, for flood relief purposes.

Since 1987, the Asian Development Bank has implemented more than US$12.3 billion in projects related to disasters, with much of the investment in the context of supporting post-disaster recovery activities (O'Donnell, 2011). For example, in 2005, the ADB responded to the Indian Ocean tsunami with a US$290 million grant to Aceh, Indonesia under the Earthquake and Tsunami Emergency Support Project (Steinberg, 2011: 4). The Bank's Disaster and Emergency Assistance policy, approved in 2004, promotes an integrated disaster risk management model with three pillars: disaster risk reduction, climate change adaptation, and disaster risk financing.

One advantage possessed by IFIs is that they already have the attention of national governments, since they are engaged in ongoing negotiations with ministries of finance about major investments. This entry point is generally unavailable to intergovernmental organizations operating under the umbrella of the United Nations (Christoplos et al., 2005: 16). The IADB, for example, which has formulated a Disaster Risk Management Policy aimed at reducing risks and vulnerabilities before disasters occur, communicates regularly with the Ministries of Finance and Planning in 14 Latin American countries (Fagen, 2008: 12).

On the other hand, IFIs sometimes come to the table with some decidedly unpopular views. In particular, their unwillingness to sanction debt forgiveness to disaster-impacted nations, and their insistence on "structural adjustment" policies, do not go well with many civil society activists. For example, in May 1999, the World Bank and the IADB organized a conference in Stockholm to facilitate funding for post-Hurricane Mitch reconstruction efforts. Whereas the NGOs and some donor governments argued for confronting poverty, marginalization, and the vulnerability of the weakest sectors, the IFIs and Central American governments favored rebuilding infrastructure such as roads and dams, while expressing doubt that debt cancellation could help the affected countries to recover (Mowforth, 2001: 7, 18). At the end of the day, the World Bank did establish a Central American Emergency Trust Fund to help countries affected by Mitch continue to make debt repayments, thus enabling Honduras to channel the millions of dollars normally spent on repaying foreign loans to relief and emergency work (Fuentes, 2009: 107). Nevertheless, despite pressure from civil society groups, the Honduran Congress passed a comprehensive set of laws allowing privatization of airports, seaports, and highways; and fast-tracked plans to privatize the nation's electricity utility, telephone company, and parts of the water sector (Bello, 2006). Allegedly, this was undertaken under pressure from the World Bank and the International Monetary Fund (Bello, 2006; Klein, 2005).

If one were to draw a formal network diagram of the international politics of disaster, the **United Nations-affiliated intergovernmental organizations** might seem to be focal points. Indeed, between 1971 and 2005, there were ten UN disaster units created, each "exerting its claim to be treated as a contact point, fund-raiser, coordinator and assessor" (Richter, 2005: 290). This first became evident in the 1970s with the creation of the United Nations Disaster Relief Organization (UNDRO), although UNDRO ultimately faltered (see chapter 3). Additionally, most major international agencies within the UN family (UNICEF, FAO, WHO, WFP) instituted departments or offices that dealt solely with disaster relief, preparedness, and prevention (Kent, 1983: 699). When the disaster risk reduction paradigm started to gain traction two decades later, this soon came under the UN auspices through the International Decade for Natural Disaster Reduction (INDNR) and its successor, the International Strategy for Disaster Reduction (ISDR).

As I demonstrate in chapters 3 and 4, United Nations agencies devoted specifically to disaster management and prevention have struggled mightily. To a large extent, they have been victims of chronic underfunding by member nations, many of whom fear that a strong centralized administration would intrude on their sovereignty. As Forsythe (2009: 66) notes, the nation states that control the UN system "get the type of United Nations they authorize and pay for." At the same time, UN disaster agencies have drunk deeply from the poisoned United Nations chalice, with its characteristic mix of political infighting and bureaucratic gridlock. As Richter (1995: 290) phrases it, the problem with the UN response to disasters is "its incoherence, timidity toward governments that obstruct relief operations, interagency feuds, reliance on paper commitments by pool funds and expertise that have repeatedly broken down just when the need is greatest."

While the United Nations disaster agencies have generally underperformed, **nongovernmental organizations (NGOs)** have consistently been the heavy lifters in the global field of disaster politics. They work in disaster management, humanitarianism, and development, and are increasingly engaged in advocacy (Christoplos et al., 2001: 185). According to Coppola (2011: 484), "In the field of disaster management, NGOs are commonly defined as non-profit, civilian-based and staffed organizations that depend on outside sources of funding and materials (including funding from governments) to carry out a humanitarian-based mission and associated goals in a target population."

With the exception of the Red Cross/Red Crescent societies, which arguably constitute a special case,[6] this leading role in the global disaster field was rather slow to evolve. As I discuss in chapter 3, in the years immediately following World War Two, the main buzz in relief and development work came from several of the larger and better funded UN agencies, e.g. UNICEF and the WHO. Over the next quarter-century, NGOs steadily assumed a more important role here, in no small part because of their ability to effectively deliver aid on a grassroots level in a variety of situations. Their popularity with governments and official aid agencies was further enhanced in the 1980s in response to developments in economic and political thinking that pointed to the market and private sector as the most efficient mechanism for achieving economic growth and delivering welfare services (Benson et al., 2001: 202).

By the early 1990s, NGOs had gained a new prominence in development and had become the favored child of development donors. This reflected a number of trends, both in world politics and within the development industry: the end of the Cold War, which removed the polarization of global politics around the two superpowers; the emergence of a global media system which provides a platform for NGOs to express their views; a theoretical impasse within development theory that opened up spaces for new theory and practice, particularly in relation to environment, gender, and social development (Charnovitz, 1997; Korten, 1990; Lewis and Kanji, 2009: 39–40).

Today, there are thousands of NGOs involved in one way or another with natural disasters. In post-tsunami Aceh, Indonesia, for example, an estimated 170 international NGOs had descended on the province by mid-2005, in addition to 430 local NGOs (Telford et al., 2006; cited in Smirl, 2008). Four years later, more than 800 NGOs, multilateral agencies, and donor countries had spent a whopping US$6.7 billion on homes, clinics, and roads in Aceh (Gelling, 2009). Immediately after the October 8, 2005, South Asia earthquake disaster, "numerous national and local nongovernment organizations (NGOs) and over 100 international organizations – United Nations, international nongovernment organizations (INGOs), European Union, North Atlantic Treaty Organization (NATO), bilateral partners, etc. – arrived in the earthquake zone to aid the relief effort" (Hicks and Pappas, 2006: 43). The number of NGOs working in Haiti is even greater. Some of these have been there for a number of decades, but others are of more recent vintage; a few are even fronted by celebrity spokespersons.[7] It is worth remembering, however, that the NGO sector may be increasingly congested but it remains stratified. A decade ago, 20 US and European multinational humanitarian agencies at the top level of the humanitarian system received 75 percent of all public relief funds channeled to NGOs (West, 2001: 8).

This proliferation of NGOs is frequently problematic. As the authors of the 2005 United Nations *Humanitarian Response Review* note, "The use of search and rescue teams has become increasingly dysfunctional as a result of the massive number of teams arriving in a disaster area. Effective coordination is rarely accomplished though the means to achieve it are available" (Adinolfi et al., 2005: 36). Hicks and Pappas (2006: 43) point out that coordination was a major challenge after the earthquakes in Afghanistan (1998), Turkey (1999), Gujarat (India) (2001), and Bam (Iran) (2003); in most cases, "this was due to the involvement of large numbers of humanitarian organizations and multiple levels of government." Furthermore, there have been frequent complaints that some NGOs, flush with "easy money," and disinterested in any long-term reconstruction strategy beyond the immediate relief phase, have encouraged a "government-less approach" to the provision of disaster services that could lead to the significant disempowerment of the local community (Sridhar, 2006; cited in Bello, 2006).

In the international relief network of the 1980s, the communication and coordination among NGOs in the field during a disaster episode were spasmodic and largely of an ad hoc nature (Kent, 1987). Two decades later, this is still a problem. The 2005 *Humanitarian Response Review* contains a section on "Deployment Capacity" in which the authors observe that NGOs lack a sound, predictable international first-response system. Rather, they "function more in terms of a pragmatic, flexible, approach, bringing people and resources together whenever needed" (Adinolfi et al., 2005: 39). Alas, this works well only some of the time.

More recently, things have become somewhat more ordered, although there are still many gaps and glissandos. In some countries, the humanitarian community has finally recognized that a high level of overlap and competition can be dysfunctional, and have made efforts to work in concert. Just recently, five of the leading aid organizations in Canada (CARE Canada, Oxfam Canada, Oxfam-Québec, Plan Canada, Save the Children, Canada) formed the Humanitarian Coalition. Described as a "one-stop-shop for all Canadians during times of humanitarian disaster," the Coalition offers a single phone center, website and communications team. In addition, the members share information gathered by field personnel at the crisis site. The Humanitarian Coalition is modeled on other successful national humanitarian funding umbrellas: the Disasters Emergency Committee (UK), Aktion Deutschland (Germany), Agire (Italy), Japan Platform, SHO Netherlands. Not all NGOs have agreed to participate in the Humanitarian Coalition in Canada. Two of the major holdouts are the Canadian Red Cross and World Vision Canada.[8]

A sixth major player in the global policy field of international disasters is what I have called **multi-actor initiatives and partnerships**. These bodies take on a variety of roles: research, coordination, and advocacy. While they owe their existence to efforts by other institutional actors, they do tend to take on a life of their own. Some examples are the ProVention Consortium and the Global Facility for Disaster Reduction and Recovery (GFDRR),[9] both associated with the World Bank. It is also possible to include some *coordinating organizations*, "NGO associations that coordinate the activities of tens to hundreds of preregistered organizations to ensure response with maximized impact" (Coppola, 2011: 485). They function both outside of and during disaster operations. InterAction is an example of a coordinating organization with strong partnership ties.

Arguably, the leading multi-actor partnership initiative today, at least in terms of policy impact, is the ProVention Consortium (see box 2.1).

Scientific, technical, and academic communities constitute the seventh set of organizational actors in the global policy field of disaster politics. Compared to many other academic areas, the study of disaster management tends to be more practically grounded than academically directed. Thus, Holloway (2003: 31) notes, "Yet, despite an abundance of compelling literature, it is important

Box 2.1 ProVention Consortium

Established by the World Bank in 2000, the ProVention Consortium is a global coalition of governments, international organizations, academic institutions, private sector actors, and civil society organizations. Its goal is to reduce disasters in developing countries by sharing knowledge about disaster risk reduction practices, and by leveraging resources. If humanitarian and development actors are to provide effective support to poor communities, institutional barriers for understanding and cooperation must be broken down, and interdisciplinary and multi-stakeholder approaches established that are able to address the root causes of vulnerability. Among the original members of the ProVention Presiding Council were such luminaries in development economics as Amartya Sen and Muhammad Yunus.

For its first five years, Consortium offices were situated at the World Bank in Washington, DC; then they were strategically rotated to the International Federation of Red Cross and Red Crescent Societies (IFRC) headquarters in Geneva. Initial funding of US$5.3 million came primarily from the World Bank, Development Grant Facility, and from the UK and Norway governments. When the Secretariat relocated to Geneva in 2003, financial support from the World Bank ended, but additional funding was attracted from Switzerland and Canada, while the UK and Norway increased their contributions by about US$1 million per year (World Bank, 2006: x).

From 2007 to 2009, ProVention focused on four strategic objectives: strengthening partnering and networking among key actors and sectors for effective disaster risk management; promoting policy to advocate for greater attention to be given to disaster risk management by leaders and decision-makers; improving practice to promote the development of innovative approaches and applications for reducing risk; and managing knowledge and information on good practices, tools, and resources for disaster risk management (ProVention Consortium, 2008: 6–7).

Several of ProVention's initiatives recall past initiatives that never got off the ground (see chapter 3). For example, the Consortium's Global Risk Identification Programme (GRIP), with its natural disaster "hotspots," national risk atlases, and disaster loss observatories, evokes memories of UNDRO's "World Survey of Disaster Damage." Similarly, ProVention's support for projects that develop and test models for disaster insurance at a national level is cast in the same spirit as Giovanni Ceraolo's – the founder of the International Relief Organization – ill-fated scheme in the 1920s whereby individual nations were to establish disaster insurance plans for their citizens, as well as contribute to a mutual disaster insurance fund at a global level. With its extensive partnership network and more robust funding model, ProVention stands a better chance of succeeding here where others have failed.

to recognize that disaster-related policy and practice is a highly visible operational field." In Southern Africa, which she knows very well, disaster management "has been less informed by theoretical discourse" than it has been "driven by political exigency, humanitarian imperative, media pressure and 'on-the-ground' realities" (Holloway, 2003: 31). Indeed, to an aid worker who is desperately attempting to circumvent bureaucratic roadblocks or corrupt local politicians in order to secure fresh water or a field hospital, formal disaster management models may seem about as relevant as the debate among medieval theologians over how many angels can fit on the head of a pin.

In environmental politics, *epistemic communities* play a major role in the process of regime formation. According to Oran Young (1994: 96), epistemic communities are defined as "coalitions of scientists and policy makers – usually transnational in scope – who share a common understanding of the nature of the problem and the appropriate solution and who make a concerted effort to inject their point of view into the process of regime formation."

Peter Haas (1989, 1990) first introduced the term in his study of efforts to control marine pollution in the Mediterranean Sea. In this case, a group of like-minded ecologists and marine scientists successfully spearheaded a political effort to press governments in the region to cooperate actively and intervene domestically to protect the Mediterranean environment. In similar fashion, science was a driving force behind the elevation of stratospheric ozone depletion as an environmental problem, and in the negotiations that led to the signing of the Montreal Protocol, an agreement that aimed at protecting the ozone layer by banning the use of chlorofluorocarbons (CFCs). In the two decades of debate over ozone depletion, the focus was on scientific rather than political issues. Scientists consistently played a key role within national delegations and international scientific organizations were prominent advisors (Susskind, 1994: 73). Epistemic communities do exist within the international politics of disaster. However, as has also been the case with global climate change negotiations, they tend to be "fragmented" (Susskind, 1994: 75) and their influence is decidedly more muted than in the cases of Mediterranean marine pollution and ozone depletion.

As I discuss in chapter 4, the International Decade for Natural Disaster Reduction (IDNDR) (1990–9) was primarily, although not exclusively, the creation of a small group of earth scientists and meteorologists, particularly two eminent and politically connected earthquake engineers, George Housner and Frank Press. Housner, Press, and their colleagues saw a linear relationship between knowing and doing, wherein "scientific knowledge would simply be 'put into practice' to prevent disasters" (Christoplos, 2003: 101).

By the time the IDNDR came to an end, the influence of these earth scientists had waned considerably. Activists from within civil society were challenging their understanding of disaster vulnerability in purely physical terms, claiming that they were blind to the influence of social and political factors. By the end of the decade, an external evaluation of the International Strategy for Disaster Reduction Secretariat (ISDR), the successor to the IDNDR, reported that representatives from the scientific and technical community were feeling marginalized, even though they retained significant influence over some national platforms and networks (Christoplos et al., 2005: 17). At the Hyogo Conference on Disaster Reduction (2005), this dual track was evident. While NGO representatives and other delegates and observers from the development community were present in substantial numbers, it was a technical issue – how best to create a tsunami early warning system for the Indian Ocean – that dominated center stage and media attention. As for earth scientists, they may no longer be dominant in the disaster management field, but they continue to make valuable contributions, for example through low-cost earthquake-proof design and construction.[10]

In the new millennium, another epistemic community has emerged in the field of disaster politics. Emerging from the encounter between climate change adaptation and disaster risk reduction (see chapter 5), this group is populated by environmental scientists, geographers, public health experts, and international development scholars. For DRR, this has been advantageous, insofar as it opened a portal to global policy communities and practitioners that possess far more money, political legitimacy, media attention, and public support.[11] At the same time there is a risk of being absorbed into the more extensive and better resourced climate risk adaptation community.

If the **private sector** is not quite the elephant in the room, neither is it extraneous to the global field of disaster politics. Capitalism and its discontents have long been targeted by a variety of disaster and development scholars, ranging from those writing in a neo-Marxist mode in the 1980s (Hewitt, 1983; Susman et al., 1983) to present-day critics of neo-liberal economic policies that are supported by "corporate capital" (Wisner et al., 2004: 322). Individual industries and businesses appear more sporadically and anecdotally in the disasters literature. For the most part, they make up a motley crew of profiteers and crooks: Turkish construction contractors who evaded building codes and used low-quality materials, thereby contributing to the high level of damage inflicted on housing stock and commercial buildings after the 1999 Marmara earthquake (Ozerdem, 2003); commercial logging contractors and concessionaires in the Philippines whose activity, legal and illegal, contributed to the Ormoc flash-flood tragedy of 1991, which killed more people than in the Baquio earthquake, Typhoon Ruping and the eruption of Mt. Pinatubo combined (Bankoff, 2003: 72).

Rather less is written about the positive contributions of the private sector, especially in the provision of relief assistance. One example of this is Walmart, the American retail behemoth, which has a well-established, proactive emergency response operation. Following the Hurricanes Katrina and Rita, Walmart donated US$18 million to aid emergency relief efforts and dispatched 2,450 truckloads of supplies to communities throughout the Gulf States and Texas (Walmart, Disaster Relief Fact Sheet, 2010). While the main focus of its disaster relief efforts is in the United States, Walmart does contribute to major disaster relief offshore, mainly through its international affiliates. For example, the Walmart Foundation donated more than US$3 million for relief and reconstruction in the wake of earthquakes that impacted central China in the spring of 2008; and gave US$12 million in assistance to flood victims in the Mexican states of Tabasco and Chiapas in 2007 (Walmart, Disaster Relief Fact Sheet, 2010).

Another corporation active in disaster relief is Toyota. In April 2003, the Toyota Group companies came together and formed the Toyota Group Disaster V (Volunteer) Net. Working with the Japan Red Cross Society and Japan Platform, the network helps to coordinate reconstruction efforts and disaster relief money collection in stricken areas, in Japan and abroad. In recent years Toyota has donated funds towards disaster relief in many major international disasters, for example, Cyclone Nargis (Bangladesh, 2008), the Sichuan earthquake (China, 2008), the Pakistan flood disaster (2010), and the New Zealand earthquake (2011). In January 2010 at the onset of the earthquake disaster, the global express delivery and logistics company, DHL Express, deployed its Disaster Recovery Team (DRT) to Haiti and was one of the first organizations to provide on-the-ground logistics support to the international relief effort. DHL sent rotating teams of DRT volunteers from Mexico, Guatemala, Costa Rica, Panama and the US, deployed several relief flights and with its volunteers processed thousands of tons of relief goods for the people of Haiti (DHL Express, 2010).

Of course, it can be argued that these are relatively insignificant contributions for corporations whose annual profits outstrip the economy of some nations of the world. Nevertheless, Horwitz (2008, 2009) makes a valid point when he argues that, within limits, the private sector's contribution to disaster relief and recovery has the potential to represent a viable supplement, if not an alternative, to the often inflexible and centralized government-led response.

A decade ago, Christoplos et al. (2001: 187) drew attention to suggestions that the insurance industry "may provide a viable channel of resources for both dealing with the impact of disasters and for promoting risk mitigation through the power of the market." Insurance is the one commercial activity that plays a substantive role in the global disaster field on a continuing basis. Insurance company participation in disaster management is, of course, not wholly altruistic but strategic and financial as well. Salt (2003: 131) cites statistics indicating that the total economic loss due to weather-related events in the 1990s was US$480 billion, with an associated insurance loss of US$107 billion. To put this in perspective, the global reinsurance pool at any one time can amount to US$200–300 billion. Significantly, according to data supplied by Munich Re (2000), a decade ago insured losses were accelerating at four times the rate of growth of the world economy. Most recently, Swiss Re estimates the cost to the insurance industry of flooding in Thailand that began in late July, 2011, at US$600 million ("Thai floods," 2011).

The two large Northern European reinsurance companies, Munich Re (Germany) and Swiss Re (Switzerland), both maintain statistical databases that are widely consulted, not only by disaster researchers, but by everyone in the global field of disaster politics. Both participate as partner organizations in the ProVention Consortium, and Swiss Re contributed a modest sum towards its establishment. The Munich Re Foundation hosted a conference in 2005 for 100 participants entitled "Worldwide Disaster Prevention – Awareness is the Key." In April of the same year, Munich Re launched its "Munich Climate Insurance Initiative," whose stated mission is to "develop insurance solutions that address the consequences of climate change" through bringing "global insurance players to the same table as UN organizations, non-governmental organizations (NGOs), and leading scientists" (Höppe, 2007). This initiative was hosted at the United Nations University Institute for Environment and Human Security (UNU-EHS).

The Consortium has made special efforts to become involved with the private sector in the areas of microfinance and microinsurance. By the mid-point of the previous decade, the ProVention Consortium had established microinsurance schemes for Mexico, Turkey, India, Romania, Bulgaria, Colombia, Vietnam and the OECS (Organization of Eastern Caribbean States) nations (World Bank, 2006: 15). In no small part, what is driving this are efforts to devise insurance instruments to support climate change adaptation and thus meet the intent of Article 4.8 of the UNFCCC. Examples to date include the Malawi groundnut insurance initiative and Mexico's catastrophe bond (Linnerooth-Bayer, 2007).

The Global Facility for Disaster Reduction and Recovery (GFDRR) is similarly increasingly involved with the private sector in the area of disaster risk financing and insurance (DFRI), which they interpret as supporting the fourth "priority action" to reduce disaster losses, as stipulated by the Hyogo Framework for Action 2005–15 (see chapter 4). Its DFRI program falls into four categories: sovereign disaster risk financing, property catastrophe risk insurance, agricultural insurance, and disaster microinsurance. In April 2011, the GFDRR and the Geneva Association, an alliance of the largest global reinsurance groups, signed a Partnership Agreement "to develop agendas of common interest in the areas of disaster assessment, loss prevention, risk management and financing."

The **mass media** represent the ninth institutional actor in the global field of disaster politics. Since I have devoted an entire chapter to the topic of the media and disasters, I will comment only briefly here. As is the case with national governments, the media normally pay scant attention to foreign disasters, at least until a major hurricane, flood, tsunami, or famine occurs. Suddenly, the media engage in continuous and intensive coverage, often of a sensational, stereotypical, and ethnocentric nature. This is widely thought to give rise to the "CNN effect," whereby cable television coverage of disasters and other international emergencies shapes the direction of American foreign policy. As I will discuss in chapter 7, researchers have found that, in fact, this is rarely the case. Nonetheless, the media do make a difference, both in terms of putting politicians and bureaucrats in the "hot seat," and by inspiring the viewing public to send millions of dollars in financial contributions to NGOs and private charities. Among other things, this distorts the balance between disaster relief and disaster reduction. West (2001: 22) stresses that the international media "are not a unitary actor with fixed interests and a single pattern of behavior." Rather, they are composed of a cluster of actors who "have different audiences, constraints, interests and resources; they operate in different countries and linguistic regions."

Tensions in the Global Policy Field of Natural Disasters

While most of the actors in the disaster field share a broad set of normative principles, there are also multiple fracture points. One longstanding fault runs along the axis of vulnerability. As I discuss in chapter 5, a split has lingered since the 1970s between those who treat vulnerability as a material and technical problem that can be remedied by designing stronger buildings, more advanced monitoring and forecasting tools, and more timely early warning systems, and those who place more importance on the relationship between disaster risk reduction and social vulnerability. Another philosophical difference exists between disaster practitioners and managers in the field, who prioritize the necessity for rapid life-saving responses, and development experts who argue for the importance of planning and the collection of data (de Ville de Goyet, 2008: 32). A third fault line has opened up between those who believe that the delivery of disaster relief must be regarded as being politically neutral, and those who argue in favor of a more proactive, "human rights" approach to humanitarian aid. Finally, there are recurrent differences between those embedded in the international development realm, who are currently preoccupied with meeting the Millennium Development Goals (MDGs), as adopted at the United Nations in 2000, and disaster risk advocates, who would rather prioritize the mainstreaming of disaster risk reduction into development planning (see Schipper and Pelling, 2006: 23–6).

In recent years, several sharp differences have developed over how much standardization and coordination should or should not be introduced into disaster risk management. Specifically, two flash points have emerged in connection with the policy of clustering/lead organization, and with the adoption of the Sphere standards. Both of these have played out within the wider humanitarian sector, but are also applicable to the politics of disaster.

Clustering

The intertwined concepts of *lead organization* and *sectoral clustering* represent a concerted attempt to introduce better coordination into the disaster response process. Initially applied and interpreted by UNHCR in the mid-1990s, the idea of the lead organization initially did not gain much traction among humanitarian agencies working in natural disasters and complex emergencies (Adinolfi et al., 2005: 47).

The most recent initiative to promote clustering arose as part of efforts in 2005 to improve the United Nations response to humanitarian and natural disasters by establishing a more accountable, predictable, and reliable emergency response procedure with an emphasis on partnerships (McDonald and Gordon, 2008: 60). In this new approach, a lead organization, chosen primarily on the basis of its special competency and access to resources, is assigned to head each of ten critical sectors: shelter, food and nutrition, health, water and sanitation, camp management, logistics, protection, education, IT/telecommunications, and early reconstruction and recovery. During a specific emergency, the principle is extended to the disaster site, with a lead organization being chosen to coordinate the relief operation. The policy of clustering only demands accountability from non-UN actors to UN agencies where individual humanitarian organizations have made a specific commitment to clustering.

Just several months after the UN had approved this cluster-sectoral approach, an earthquake measuring 7.6 on the Richter scale struck Pakistan, Afghanistan, and India, with the epicenter located less than 100 kilometers northeast of Islamabad. The Office for the Coordination of Humanitarian Affairs (OCHA) decided to field test the new approach, and, if successful, roll it out globally. The South Asia earthquake of October 8, 2005, was "the first crisis where participating agencies, which continued to be separately funded and governed, found themselves under a single structure, in a single operation, having a single aim" (Hicks and Pappas, 2006: 43).

Alas, the lead/cluster system failed dismally in Pakistan[12] and "relief operations quickly devolved into the coordination of chaos" (Hicks and Pappas, 2006: 49). Some valuable lessons were learned from this experience. First of all, it is mandatory that local NGOs and governmental structures be involved in planning and decision making both before and during the emergency response. Second, the cluster approach should be more narrowly targeted to gap sectors rather than expanded to cover the entire humanitarian response. Third, donor agencies need to be given more input about how best to disburse emergency aid, especially during a disaster event. Fourth, there needs to be better information sharing and coordination between the clusters at a global level and those that operate on the ground. The former tend to be dominated by the UN agencies, while the latter operate within the NGO humanitarian network.

Since 2005, the cluster approach has been utilized in many different crises and disasters, with a fair degree of success. For example, the UN Inter Agency Standing Committee (IASC) cluster approach was implemented in February 2007, in response to the Zambezi river floods and Cyclone Favio in Mozambique. In its critical evaluation, the Emergency Nutrition Network (ENN) declared, "Overall, the cluster approach was a success in Mozambique. It encouraged a cooperative ethos between agencies that led to a better quality and more effective response" (ENN, 2007: 24). In a policy statement released the following summer, Oxfam International offered a more cautious assessment:

> The cluster approach initially failed to engage well with non-UN agencies, and to be adequately grounded in the field experience of UN or NGO agencies alike. Despite such early shortcomings, the basic approach is sound. Oxfam has critically engaged in the cluster approach across a range of sectors. Like every other initiative, its success depends on being owned by UN field offices, the International Red Cross Movement, international organisations and NGOs at every level. Its success will be judged by improved humanitarian responses, and reduced death and human suffering (Oxfam International, 2008: 2).

Van Wassenhove (2006) has observed, "Since disaster relief is about 80% logistics, it would follow then that the only way to achieve [results-oriented programs and accountability] is through slick, efficient and effective logistics operations and more precisely, supply chain management" (cited in Altay and Labonte, 2011: 85). Even Médecins sans Frontières, which has sometimes been critical of the humanitarian establishment, operates a supply chain that is "among the most agile in the humanitarian aid scene and has been copied by various other non-governmental organizations (NGOs) over the years" (Seipel, 2011: 216). The Logistics Cluster (LC), chaired by the WFP (World Food Programme), thus becomes a central component in any international disaster relief operation. Altay and Labonte (2011: 85–6) conclude that, in the five years and 36 country rollouts since the UN cluster strategy was established, the logistics cluster "gets high marks operationally for improving coordination between and among other Clusters; information and knowledge sharing; building systematic emergency response capacity; and clarifying leadership roles and accountability between Cluster actors." At the same time, they acknowledge complaints from some humanitarian actors that the LC, like the cluster approach as a whole, is top-down and UN-driven.

Sphere

Another effort aimed at greater rationalization is Sphere, a code of conduct/handbook/process of collaboration for humanitarian organizations that establishes a set of minimal standards for such things as water, food, sanitation, and medical care. The Sphere project emerged in the aftermath of the 1994 humanitarian crisis in Rwanda, which involved about 250 NGOs, making it the largest-ever humanitarian operation to date. While some NGOs performed impressively in Rwanda, others acted in an unprofessional, and at times even dangerous, manner. Within months, Study 3, an international multi-stakeholder evaluation of the humanitarian response, was launched. Study 3 made two sets of key recommendations specifically targeted at NGOs: that there be a set of standards aimed at improving NGO performance; and that there be some means of enforcing standards and codes of conduct

(Buchanan-Smith, 2003: 10). Initiated in July 1997, Sphere was initially promoted by a group of international NGOs and by some organizations within the Red Cross/Red Crescent movement.[13] The intention of the project was to help improve accountability and the overall quality of humanitarian response to those affected by disasters, as well as putting relief aid on a legal basis as set forth by international law. The latter was set out in the "Humanitarian Charter." Volberg (2005/2006: 23) describes the Humanitarian Charter as "the analytical foundation upon which the rest of the 'Sphere' handbook rests." He says that it is unique insofar as it combines human rights law, international humanitarian law, and refugee law. The Charter asserts three core principles, humanity, impartiality, and neutrality, which in combination "provides an ethical framework, which defines and delineates the humanitarian space within which NGOs operate" (Volberg, 2005/2006: 24).

Many in the humanitarian community believe that Sphere has had a very positive impact on aid delivery quality. Some donors really like these standards because they establish objective and measurable criteria (de Ville de Goyet, 2008: 33). Others are not nearly as enthusiastic. Christoplos (2003: 99) points out that there is a built-in conflict between the humanitarian imperative set out by Sphere – to save lives and address acute suffering – and disaster mitigation and preparedness. That is, a shift in resources to disaster reduction, a hypothetical long-term objective, is perceived by some humanitarian NGOs as conflicting with "their ethical commitments to immediate life-saving response." Others complain that the minimal standards set by Sphere are far above the standards being enjoyed by most of the rest of the population that is unaffected by the disaster or complex emergency. Similarly, the Sphere standards are more generous than those required to satisfy the needs to be addressed in a long-term recovery project (de Ville de Goyet, 2008: 33).

Fundamental opposition to Sphere has come from a number of Francophone NGOs, most notably Médecins sans Frontières (MSF). Initially one of the sponsors, MSF withdrew at the end of Phase 2 (November 1998–January 2000), citing its reservations that Sphere reduced humanitarian response to its technical aspects, leaving no room for non-quantifiable aspects of humanitarian action such as ethics and solidarity building (see Tong, 2004). Furthermore, MSF and some of the other agencies were concerned about the possibility of donor governments insisting that their NGO partners adhere to Sphere standards, thereby compromising the latter's independence and pushing them closer to political rather than humanitarian objectives (Buchanan-Smith, 2003: 15). In response, Volberg (2005/2006: 22) argues that MSF and other Sphere critics were overreacting. Sphere never meant, he says, to impose a set of rigid standards, nor to dictate to any organization what decisions to make. The Handbook makes quite clear, he notes, both variation in the identities, mandates and capabilities of humanitarian agencies, and the influence of local factors such as lack of access or security that may make the realization of global standards unattainable.

In 2011, the Sphere Handbook was significantly revised, with input from 650 experts from 300 organizations in 20 countries. The Humanitarian Charter was completely rewritten, the common standards were changed significantly, and a stronger focus on protection was introduced (Shelter Centre, 2011). In the latter instance, a new chapter – Protection Principles – was added which considers the protection and safety of populations affected by disaster or armed conflict as an integral part of humanitarian response. The revised Handbook also addresses several of the hot button issues in the development field: climate change and disaster risk reduction, civil military relations, and the adoption of state-of-the-art methods for improving accountability in foreign aid, notably cash transfer and early recovery (reliefweb, 2011).

Conclusion

In the 1970s and 1980s, scholars endeavoring to map the structure of international disaster politics opted for the concept of an international relief network consisting of donor governments, the United Nations, relief organizations (notably the Red Cross/Red Crescent), and the international media. There was general agreement that this network was temporary, informal, and loosely coupled; one researcher (Aldo Benini) labeled it "a network without a centre." By the 1990s this was changing. Humanitarian agencies, major players in delivering disaster relief, transformed themselves into a "community of practice" that was distinguished by regular interaction and information exchange, greater professionalization, and a shared identity.

I depict the current structure as "the global policy field of natural disasters." There are nine major actors or players in this field: national states and local governments; regional organizations; international finance institutions (IFIs); United Nations disaster agencies and other international governmental organizations (IGOs); nongovernmental organizations (NGOs); multi-actor initiatives and partnerships; scientific, technical, and academic communities; and the mass media. The locus of power and control in this field is fluid, but in recent years it has resided in a small group of IFIs and donor states, NGOs, and private sector organizations. While most of those in the disaster field subscribe to a broad set of normative principles, there are also multiple fracture points. These are located around issues of physical versus social vulnerability; rapid, short-term disaster relief versus longer-term development and sustainability planning; and, most recently, around the question of how much standardization and coordination should or should not be introduced into disaster risk management. Flash points have emerged in relation to two notable attempts to better rationalize and coordinate international disaster response: sectoral clustering and the Sphere project.

In the next section of the book, I present an historical overview of the evolution of international disaster politics from World War One up to the present period. This section is divided into three chapters, arranged in chronological order, but also according to the predominant disaster management discourse of the time.

Further Reading

I. Christoplos, A. Liljelund, and J. Mitchell (2001) Re-framing risk: the changing context of disaster mitigation and preparedness. *Disasters*, 25, 185–98.

R.C. Kent (1987) *Anatomy of Disaster Relief: The International Network in Action*. Pinter Publishers, London.

CHAPTER THREE

The Kindness of Strangers

International humanitarianism is defined as "the transnational concern to help persons in exceptional distress" (Forsythe, 2009: 59). As such, humanitarianism is fundamentally an *ethos* with a strong narrative that can generate constituencies for particular causes (Wilson and Brown, 2009: 2). In keeping with the title of this book, the delivery of humanitarian aid, including disaster assistance, cannot easily be confined within national boundaries. As Barnett (2008: 248) notes, "A commitment to humanity means a world without ethical boundaries."

Until the 1990s, when the discourse of disaster risk reduction (DRR) emerged, humanitarianism, which is fueled by a fervent belief in "the kindness of strangers," remained largely unchallenged as the preferred approach to disaster management. In this chapter, I trace the evolution of humanitarian disaster aid, from its origins at the beginning of the twentieth century up to the 1980s, when it both endured considerable turbulence and ascended to new heights as a result of political conflicts and complex emergencies on the African continent. First, however, I give a brief overview of humanitarianism, its essential nature, and the limitations constraining it.

Humanitarianism and its Discontents

Humanitarian narratives are more than just sentimental tales of individual suffering multiplied by hundreds of thousands. Rather, they are connected to political factors external to the narratives themselves. For example, the 2011 famine around the drought-stricken Horn of Africa is equally a story of "failed peace talks, violence, refugees, pirates, chronic underdevelopment, proxy wars, foreign invasions, clan conflicts, warlords, Islamic extremism and a growing terror threat from al-Qaeda-linked radicals" (Goodspeed, 2011).

Herein lies a thorny dilemma for humanitarians, including those wearing a disaster relief suit. For humanitarian sympathies to be elicited, especially among the general public, the narrative of suffering must strongly testify to the innocence of the sufferer (Wilson and Brown, 2009: 23). Yet, doing so demands that politics must be downplayed or excluded. This is very much in the tradition of the charitable humanitarianism of the nineteenth and early twentieth centuries, wherein humanitarians "pursued the mitigation of suffering, rather than the transformation of institutions" (Calhoun, 2010: 37). In a similar mode, Fassin (2010: 276) argues that the leadership of Médecins sans Frontières, the high profile French humanitarian organization, deliberately constructs a world of binary opposition in which there are two opposite camps: institutional political authorities who do not hesitate to sacrifice the lives of ordinary citizens in their march toward power and control; and humanitarians, who are dedicated to saving as many lives as possible. "In order for humanitarian agents to claim they are on the side of life," Fassin says, they "have to place political actors on the side of death."

Much has been written about the historical differences between humanitarianism and human rights. While both share a common view of humanity that acknowledges the existence of a "natural law" that resides with individuals and transcends national borders, they differ in their underlying warrants. As a rule, humanitarian action is undertaken on the basis of a moral claim, whereas human rights interventions are always based on a legal claim. This can be interpreted as meaning that humanitarianism's obligation to victims arises from the heart, while human rights confer entitlements that come from the head. Rights advocates sometimes critically seize upon this difference. As Wilson and Brown (2009: 8) observe, "Writers [see Rajaram, 2002] have commented on the antipathy of human rights activists to the language of humanitarianism, a language often perceived as laden with outmoded notions of charity, protectionism, sentiment and neocolonial paternalism." Nevertheless, human rights activism and humanitarianism have increasingly taken a parallel course in recent years. In part, this has occurred because the basis for intervention has shifted away from intervening states towards innocent individual victims of abuses, "In this way, modern humanitarianism has come to draw increasingly from the model of human rights in its conferral on individuals of rights hitherto reserved for states" (Wilson and Brown, 2008: 7).

Humanitarian intervention, rights advocates argue, is justifiable in situations where sovereign states lack the will or resources with which to protect their citizens from "avoidable catastrophes." In such an instance, the broader community of states has an obligation to step in to protect the rights of affected populations. This rights issue has split some prominent humanitarian NGOs, most notably MSF, where an ideological schism resulted in the formation of Médecins du Monde (Doctors of the World), which is dedicated to challenging human rights abuses as well as tending to the sick and wounded. Whereas Médecins sans Frontières looks to humanitarian law, Médecins du Monde is guided by human rights (Fassin, 2010: 277). It is worth noting, however, that once in the field, pragmatism often becomes the guiding principle. Thus, while MSF has from time to time articulated a more engaged form of humanitarianism compared to the Red Cross "discreet neutralism," this has not prevented it from entering a conflict situation under the ICRC rules of engagement – this is what happened in the Rwandan genocide in 1994 (Forsythe, 2009: 79).

The type of direct intervention preferred by human rights advocates such as Médecins du Monde is generally discouraged by international law. This has consistently posed a problem for those seeking to deliver disaster relief to countries other than their own. In particular, legal conditions that permit the delivery of humanitarian assistance only with the consent of the affected country and under the umbrella of political neutrality act as a firm constraint. Some legal scholars have attempted to skirt the sovereignty discourse by making a distinction between humanitarian *intervention* and humanitarian *access*. The former is restricted to sovereign states and certain intergovernmental organizations and usually involves the use of force. By contrast, the latter is open to a wider array of actors, notably NGOs, and "is focused on ameliorating the immediate humanitarian situation rather than addressing the broader political and military aspects" (Mills, 1998: 148). The legal peg for this is the 1949 Geneva Conventions and two Additional Protocols passed in 1977 under which the Red Cross has based its activities, and more recently, United Nations General Assembly Resolution 43-131.

Disaster Relief before 1950

Although this sense of obligation to distant strangers was visible in the eighteenth and nineteenth centuries, notably in the international movement to abolish slavery, it only began to inform the international provision of aid during and immediately after World War One. Prior to that time, response to national and natural disasters (as opposed to relief in times of international war) was still regarded as a local issue (Walker and Maxwell, 2009: 29). In those very few cases where disaster relief was delivered on a wider scale, it was strictly on a bilateral basis (van Niekerk, 2008: 357).

International Red Cross

A milestone in the growth of humanitarianism and relief was the founding and remarkable growth of the International Red Cross. The origins of the Red Cross in the nineteenth century are now legendary. In 1859, Henry Dunant, a visiting Swiss businessman from Geneva, organized local women to aid the battlefield wounded near the village of Solferino, in Northern Italy, during the French–Austrian war. Walker and Maxwell (2009: 22) describe this as a path-breaking moment, "By his actions, Dunant established some of the fundamental ideals and methodologies of humanitarianism. He negotiated access, he chose to act impartially, he used his position of neutrality, and he organized civil society in a voluntary, non-coerced fashion."

Upon his return to Geneva, Dunant proposed that army medical services should be supplemented in times of war by national relief societies whose volunteers would be regarded as "neutral" (McAllister, 1993: 5). Dunant's ideas struck a chord in Geneva, and a small band of citizens, the International

Committee for the Relief of the Wounded, came together. Just five years after Solferino (1864), the International Committee, now transformed into the International Committee of the Red Cross (ICRC), and the Swiss Government organized a diplomatic conference in Geneva at which 16 states were represented. The outcome was the "Geneva Convention for the Amelioration of the Condition of the Wounded in Armies in the Field," now known as the first "Geneva Convention." Ironically, more conservative elements on the Geneva Committee eventually forced Dunant out. Many years later, he was "rediscovered" and "rehabilitated," receiving the Nobel Peace Prize in 1901. However, in a foretelling of future conflicts in the humanitarian movement, some critics argued that Dunant should not have been selected because, by making war more humane, he perpetuated the institution of war (Forsythe, 2005: 22–3).

To those unfamiliar with the history of the Red Cross, its multiple levels of organization can seem especially confusing. In addition to the International Committee of the Red Cross (ICRC), headquartered in Geneva, a number of National Societies were formed, each of which acknowledged the basic humanitarian principles of the Convention. After World War One (1919), another body, the League of Red Cross (and Red Crescent) Societies, was created. This was primarily the initiative of Henry Davison, chairman of the American Red Cross (ARC) War Council. Initially, it was designed to be both a federation of National Red Cross Societies, independent from the ICRC, and, potentially, "a humanitarian version of the newly-established League of Nations in which the ARC would be in the driving seat" (Walker and Maxwell, 2009: 27).

McAllister (1993: 7–8) observes that the relationship between the International Committee of the Red Cross, the League and the National Societies has tended to be particularly complicated and has generated a certain tension. During this initial period, the League "not only challenged the role and authority of the old ICRC, it also implicitly challenged its notion of neutrality, then inextricably linked with the neutrality of the Swiss state" (Walker and Maxwell, 2009: 27). Davison, backed by US President Woodrow Wilson, evidently had ambitious plans to turn the League into a world health organization, but problems with funding, politics, and personal rivalries scuttled this.

Historically, the ICRC has focused on the application of international humanitarian law in war-linked disasters, most notably through carrying out its mandate under the Geneva Convention to visit prisoners and assess whether they are being treated properly. The League, currently known as the International Federation of Red Cross and Red Crescent Societies (IFRC), has focused primarily on natural disasters and capacity-building activities.

Until quite recently, it was difficult to find an historical account of the Red Cross that did not tend toward beatification. This has been especially true for the ICRC, which has always protected its reputation rather vigorously. One of the first attempts to restore some measure of balance was David Forsythe's (2005) book *The Humanitarians: The International Committee of the Red Cross*. While acknowledging the ICRC's many fine achievements, Forsythe presents it as "an organization replete with paradoxes." In his book, Forsythe shows that the ICRC displays liberal goals, putting supreme value on the welfare of individuals, but pursues them through conservative means. It claims to be non-political, he states, but is inherently part of humanitarian politics. It "professes impartiality and neutrality, but it calculates how to advance humanitarian policies that are in competition with other policies based on national and factional advantage" (2005: 2). On this latter point, Forsythe is referring specifically to the ICRC vulnerability to "the siren call of Swiss nationalism," even as it positions itself as a universal movement stressing global humanity. As you will see in the final section of this chapter, these contradictions came to a boil in the 1970s and 1980s, resulting in a schism in the humanitarian relief movement that still endures today.

Humanitarian Relief during World War One and its Aftermath

During World War One, the Commission for Relief in Belgium (CRB), an ad hoc private international organization headed by Herbert Hoover, later President of the United States (1929–33), raised over US$20 million, and delivered an estimated 28 million tonnes of emergency food and medical supplies both in occupied – and then in liberated – Belgium (Walker and Maxwell, 2009: 26). The CRB flew its own flag, issued its own passports, and operated a large fleet of ocean-going vessels and canal boats.

For five years after the war (1919–24), various private and governmental relief initiatives (American Relief Administration (ARA), European Children's Fund, European Relief Council) directed by Herbert Hoover were active in supplying food and other aid to those still struggling to recover from the harsh effects of the conflict. These groups delivered US$5.25 billion in aid to over 10 million people in Europe (Stephens, 1978: 28–9). Most prominent among them was the ARA, which had morphed out of the Commission for Relief to Belgium, with Hoover still at the helm (Walker and Maxwell, 2009: 26). National governments directly and indirectly supported these efforts, but mostly they were preoccupied with delivering assistance to the large number of refugees that had been displaced during the war (Kent, 1987: 35).

"Something New for Humanity"

The one notable effort to establish a more permanent mechanism to deal specifically with disasters was the International Relief Union (IRU). Stephens (1978: 29) calls this "the first and to date only attempt to guarantee relief assistance by treaty." The IRU was the brainchild of Giovanni Ciraolo, an Italian senator and one-time President of the Italian Red Cross. Ciraolo was outraged by the muddled and improvised response to the earthquake and tsunami that flattened the southern Italian towns of Messina (Sicily) and Reggio in December 1908, killing over 100,000 people (including many among his own family and friends) and leaving 200,000 homeless (Walker and Maxwell, 2009: 29). In response, Ciraolo devised a scheme for organized disaster relief in which each country would establish a disaster insurance plan for its own citizens; and, additionally, would participate in an international organization for mutual assistance modeled on the International Red Cross. For Ciraolo, mutual insurance against disaster represented the very embodiment of international solidarity (Hutchison, 2001: 262).

From the outset, Ciraolo's plan was opposed both by the British government, who raised doubts about its feasibility and about the suitability of modeling its structure on the International Red Cross; and by the US government and the American Red Cross, who found its mutualism ideologically repugnant and its Eurocentric focus politically distasteful (Hutchison, 2001: 254). At the British Foreign Office, one principal objection was that "a country such as England, not visited by earthquakes or similar disasters, would have to put into a common fund without the prospect of getting anything in return."[1] Ciraolo's scheme was also criticized by the insurance industry in Europe, notably Dr. Karl Luttenberger, a German insurance executive.

Initially proposed as an adjunct to the Red Cross, the IRU eventually came to life as a separate organization established by statute at the Convention of the International Relief Union in July 1927[2] and adopted by the League of Nations. Its principal task was to assemble funds, resources, and assistance of all kinds and furnish these to "stricken people" where the gravity of the disaster exceeded the powers and resources of the state. Additionally, the IRU was expected, in a general way, to "encourage the study of preventative measures against disaster and to induce all people to render mutual international assistance." It was directed by a small Secretariat and governed by a General Council of member states, who supplied funds.

The saga of the International Relief Union is a cautionary tale with lessons, largely ignored, for a succession of subsequent international disaster agencies. Despite their expressions of humanitarian concern, few of its member states had much serious interest in coughing up much money. Kent (1987: 35–6) quotes Camille Gorgé (1938), one of the few authors to write in English about the work of the IRU, to the effect that the "niggardly financial contributions" of participating governments was consistent with the way the international community gave help in disaster situations. That is, the nations of the world piously expressed sympathy, but then shrewdly and conveniently cited the respect of sovereignty as a valid reason for holding back their generosity. This was as true in 1938, Gorgé lamented, as it had been of the international response to the Japanese earthquake of 1923.[3] On this point, Hutchison (2001:

287) quips, "Duzmans [Charles Duzmans, the Latvian delegate to the IRU preparatory committee] had not grasped that his fellow delegates under instructions from governments wished to create the appearance but not the substance of 'something new for humanity.'"

As early as 1930, the IRU was showing signs of faltering, a victim of the Great Depression and the gathering clouds of war. In the handful of cases where the IRU did step forward, its efforts were mostly spurned. For example, in 1934, the IRU offered assistance to the Indian government for the Orissa earthquake, but this was declined and assistance was channeled through the Red Cross (Walker and Maxwell, 2009: 30). The organization disappeared during World War Two, only to miraculously re-emerge in 1945. However, it was more or less ignored by its member states and turned to encouraging scientific studies for disaster prevention, before being liquidated in 1968, with its assets and responsibilities transferred to the UN.

To have succeeded, Ciraolo's plan would have required several seemingly impossible concessions. It was mandatory that the members of the League of Nations contribute handsomely to a global mutual insurance scheme, from which only the most disaster-prone were likely to derive benefit. Reinsurance companies, banks, and the world of high finance had to be willing to offset losses to the scheme on a potentially gargantuan scale (Hutchison, 2001: 265). Individual nations needed to surrender a measure of sovereignty. All this may yet be possible in a better world. However, if the International Relief Union, in unexpurgated form, had somehow managed to beat the odds, we would have a framework for dealing with disasters that differs markedly from what we have today. There would be no need for the media-driven charity appeals that follow major catastrophes such as the Haiti earthquake and the Indian Ocean tsunami. Nor would there be any space for the thousands of NGOs and charities that currently descend upon disaster-stricken regions. Reflecting Ciraolo's sense of justice and idealism, people around the world who are innocent victims of nature's wrath would have an unchallenged legal right to receive international assistance.

A New Order Rising

With World War Two finally concluded, the Cold War starting to ramp up, and colonial empires crumbling, the international political landscape was in flux. Hope was running high that the United Nations, created in 1945, would succeed where its predecessor, the League of Nations, had not. Encouraged by the perceived success of the Marshall Plan in helping to rebuild war-torn European economies, the extension of foreign aid to other parts of the world seemed like a good idea. It was in this context that international humanitarianism and its stepchild, the international disaster relief network, re-emerged with strengthened resolve and in expanded form.

In contrast to World War One, the lion's share of the post-1945 reconstruction and relief in Europe had been undertaken by intergovernmental organizations rather than ad hoc private initiatives. The most prominent of these were four agencies under the United Nations banner: the United Nations International Children's Emergency Fund (UNICEF); the International Refugee Organization (IRO); the Food and Agriculture Organization (FAO); and the World Health Organization (WHO). Kent (1987: 37) describes this quartet as "the new vanguard of relief: all were experimental in design and function." All four, Kent says, carried more weight politically than NGOs.

Furthermore, national governments assumed a more extensive and direct relief role. Evidence of this can be found in the creation in 1961 by President John F. Kennedy of the United States Agency for International Development (USAID) and the Office of Foreign Disaster Assistance; and in the establishment of CIDA (Canadian International Development Agency) and the Ministry of Overseas Development (UK) (van Niekerk, 2008: 358).

Still, the postwar period witnessed the emergence of a new, more muscular generation of international NGOs. Some of these, notably Save the Children (1919), had been around for decades, while others, such as CARE (1945), Oxfam (1942), and World Vision (1950), were founded during or shortly after World War Two. Oriented largely toward relief and charity and reliant on short-term staff and volunteers, these agencies reworked their original mandates to meet the demands of a changing environment. Each came to be associated with a specific operational niche in emergency humanitarian assistance. CARE established a reputation with major donors in large-scale food delivery and logistics; Oxfam became the chief NGO expert in water and sanitation; Save the Children, as its name spells out, focused on the needs of young people (Stoddard, 2006: 5).

Whereas their wartime activities had been carried out primarily in Europe, these agencies now moved into the newly minted states of the developing world, particularly those that had only recently broken their colonial ties and lacked the infrastructure and resources to deal with disasters. In addition to their operational expertise, they "could move much more quickly than could governmental and intergovernmental organizations and could often go where governments could not" (Cuny, 1983: 18). Furthermore, they generally operated at lower cost than did the bureaucratically bloated United Nations agencies, due to their extensive use of volunteers (Lewis and Kanji, 2009: 16), and carried a minimum of start-up costs when crises struck (Stoddard, 2006: 5). Finally, private relief and development organizations, by dressing in "neutral" clothing, could venture into politically sensitive areas that were out of bounds to governmental agencies, something they did in the Biafran war in the late 1960s; the Southeast Asian refugee crisis of the 1970s; the civil strife in Burundi in 1972; and Afghanistan in the 1980s (van Niekerk, 2008: 361).

Oxfam took on a new role, evolving from a famine relief organization into a development organization with a special expertise in disaster response (Cuny, 1983: 122). Founded in Oxford in 1942 as the Oxford Committee for Famine Relief, Oxfam's first campaign involved challenging an Allied naval blockade during the Greek civil war by sending in a ship full of dried milk from South Africa. Subsequently, the committee raised funds for other countries where civilians were suffering, opening charity shops to collect donations of used clothes and to raise funds (Walker and Maxwell, 2009: 43). By the 1950s, this type of activity was winding down, and Oxfam faced a choice of either shutting down or reformulating its mission.

Choosing the latter option, the committee broadened its mandate from starving civilian victims of war to the relief of suffering in any part of the world where an emergency was occurring, including overseas destinations. In its official history, *A Cause for Our Times: Oxfam the First 50 Years*, author Maggie Black (1992: 27) describes Oxfam as first and foremost "a donor body" whose "ideology held that the giver of money, goods or of time fulfilled a mission as spiritually significant as that of the relief worker." It wasn't long, however, before Oxfam's leadership realized that the real action lay in the development sphere. In addition to being a funding agency working in partnership with the Red Cross and relief agencies, Oxfam quickly established a reputation for excellence in research in disaster-related technology, notably the Oxfam sanitation unit.[4]

Originally founded to facilitate the delivery of food packages to Europeans in the aftermath of World War Two, CARE (Cooperative for American Remittances to Europe) reconfigured itself into a permanent body with a mandate to offer development assistance as well as emergency relief. CARE adopted a distinctive business model wherein it designated sold packages (and later, standardized self-help kits) with guaranteed delivery to the recipient or the donor would be refunded. The profit went to fund ongoing operations. Feldman (2010: 217) notes that the kits both "concretized compassion" and "pointed toward the new kinds of measurements of success[5] that were required in the move to development."

Over the following decades, development became the name of the game. Kent (1987: 39–40) offers three reasons for this. First, the international system had been transformed by the tremendous expansion of the United Nations, especially countries of the South, who now represented over two-thirds of the UN membership. Second, competition between the East and West for the loyalty of non-aligned nations played out in terms of escalating offers of development aid. Third, rising levels of affluence meant that donations from middle-class Westerners with an aching conscience were increasingly directed to those in the Third World who were suffering from poverty and misery.

By the late 1960s, Walker and Maxwell (2009: 45) conclude, "just about the full cast of what we would term the international humanitarian system had gathered on stage – donor states, UN bodies, the Red Cross and Red Crescent, and major international NGOs." While labeling this a "system," nevertheless, they acknowledge that it was a very porous system "more like an eco-system than a purpose built structure." The cast lacked any sense of a common purpose, and frequently had competing aims.

Disaster Relief and the Development Orientation

While the more prominent humanitarian NGOs were able to successfully manage the relief-to-development transition, disaster relief per se was cast as a bit player in all of this, with an occasional turn as best supporting actor. Kent (1987: 40) describes its plight in this way:

> The development orientation, however, pushed disaster considerations even further down the scale of institutional priorities. If development was a growth industry, disaster relief was a no-growth area. Not only were disasters perceived as being the responsibility of affected governments, but, for the development agencies they were an interference in their preoccupations with development. The big money was in the major infrastructural projects – dams, road networks, airports, turnkey industries – which marked governmental and IGO approaches to development in the late 1950s and 1960s. "You can't build a career on disasters" was a statement that summed up the attitude of many.

Conceptually, development theory assigned natural disasters to a purely liminal status. That is, professionals in the field understood disasters to be "interruptions" in the linear process of development, after which "normal," longer-term development work could be resumed (Lewis and Kanji, 2009: 187). Disaster mitigation and preparedness were not included in this model, or were subsumed under the rubric of "rehabilitation," which constituted "a bridge between relief and development work" (Lewis and Kanji, 2009: 187).

The disaster relief sector held only one coveted face card. While the "big money" was in development, dams and airports did not hold much appeal for the public-at-large in Western nations. Then, as now, it was the images of starving children and dazed villagers confronting a bleak future in the aftermath of a cyclone or earthquake that touched a chord of sympathy. NGOs figured out quickly enough that this could be exploited in order to publicly fundraise and, at the same time, raise their level of recognition. As Kent (1987: 41) puts it, the drama of disasters could be turned to their advantage, filling their coffers and providing the resources to continue with their principal objectives, which were development related.

UNDRO

Throughout the late 1960s and early 1970s, a series of high profile natural disasters occurred in the countries of the Southern hemisphere. Within the United Nations community, a mixed view prevailed. On the one hand, there was wide recognition that the existing response system to these occasions was clearly inadequate. Coordination was minimal, information transfer insufficient, and shared knowledge spotty. On the other hand, many nations were reluctant to open the door to disaster czars descending from abroad who might violate their sovereignty.

In 1972, the Office of the United Nations Disaster Relief Coordinator (UNDRO) came into being. Even before it saw the light of day, UNDRO was mired in controversy. Kent (1987: 52) says that "two years of arduous discussion" occurred prior to the decision to move ahead with the creation of a relief coordination office within the UN system. Stephens (1978: 14–15) suggests that the creation of UNDRO was, in many respects, the result of the United States and several other influential member governments imposing a managerial approach that places a high value on coherence, order, efficiency, and coordination on the General Assembly. Evidently, a number of key stakeholders – other UN agencies (e.g. UNICEF), voluntary agencies (the League of Red Cross Societies), and various governments (including the Soviet Union and France) – were deeply split on what its role should be. Some professed considerable discomfort with a brief that would task UNDRO with *directing* relief activities in a stricken country, rather than just mobilizing and coordinating.[6]

According to Stephens (1978), there was a fair bit of political dealing associated with the appointment of UNDRO's first director, a position that carried with it the rank of Under-Secretary-General at the United Nations. The four leading candidates were considered to be: Prince Sadruddin Aga Khan, UN High Commissioner for Refugees; Sir Robert Jackson, a veteran UN administrator who was widely known as the author of a controversial 1969 report on the need to reform the United Nations; Henrik Beer, who was Secretary-General of the League of Red Cross Societies; and Faruk N. Berkol, a Turkish career diplomat who at that time was Ambassador to Belgium. Beer was initially offered the post, but ultimately, the Turkish government successfully pressured several key nations (United States, Canada) to support their man, arguing that Turkey had been an early proponent of the creation of an international disaster agency and therefore deserved some recognition. While Berkol possessed international negotiating credentials and diplomatic experience, he had limited knowledge of and experience with the intricacies of the UN bureaucracy.

As was to be the case for every subsequent United Nations disaster agency, UNDRO was under-financed right from the start. For its first three years of operation, the agency just barely limped by, chronically starved of funds with which to pay for salaries and paperclips. As Stephens (1978: 188) puts it, the "financial sword of Damacles" hung over UNDRO, and this severely hampered its ability to carry out its mandate and "gain the attention and respect of the international relief community." By early 1975, it was clear that something had to be done. Consequently, a special voluntary trust fund was established by a few contributing member states. The following year, the General Assembly decided to cover UNDRO's administrative and staffing expenses from the regular UN budget, while keeping the trust fund for a while longer. Besides limiting what the agency could realistically do, especially in terms of field operations, its heavy and frequently ad hoc financial reliance on contributing governments meant that the Coordinator's office was "particularly susceptible to those same governments' wishes and pressures for changing or modifying UNDRO's structure and activities" (Stephens, 1978: 189). Note, however, that increased funding alone was not a panacea. By 1980, UNDRO staff had grown from six to 50, and the annual budget from US$330,000 to US$3.6 million (Richter, 2005: 291), but this failed to turn things around.

By all accounts, UNDRO's first decade was "a floundering experiment" (Kent, 1983: 699). Cuny (1983: 152) blamed this on UNDRO's abject failure to understand the links between disasters and development. Fundamentally, this was a consequence of the decision to give it autonomous status within the UN system, rather than place it under the auspices of the United Nations Development Programme. Cuny (1983) especially objected to the protocol whereby UNDRO coordinated the receipt and dispersal of funds from foreign donors. It made more sense, he argued, to designate a local group to coordinate the emergency response, insofar as outsiders unfamiliar with local conditions and politics were flying blind. Furthermore, UNDRO's mandate was restricted to coordinating an emergency response, thus ruling out undertaking any longer-term measures that recognized the intertwined nature of disasters and development.

Thomas Stephens, a political scientist who closely studied UNDRO's early years as the topic of his doctoral thesis at the University of Geneva, offered up another explanation. Voluntary agencies and NGOs, particularly the League of the Red Cross, were generally more willing to assist UNDRO than her sister UN bodies; and the standing relief agencies within the UN system, even though they were not overly helpful, still did not attempt to hinder UNDRO's activities. Rather, "the major source of resistance to UNDRO came from UN Headquarters in New York, not from the relief community" (Stephens, 1978: 132). The agency's capability to respond was further handicapped both by its geographic location in Geneva rather than in New York – the power center of the Secretariat – and by the outsider status of its director.

Kent (1983) argued that UNDRO was fatally weakened by the intentional vagueness of its mandate. "Was UNDRO intended to have an operational role, that is, to get involved in the actual running of relief work, or merely a non-operational, coordinating role?" (Kent, 1983: 699). Early on the agency director made a fateful decision that, unfortunately, seemed to definitively answer this question. In 1972, the newly created country of Bangladesh was reeling from the challenges of coping with massive numbers of refugees, disrupted agriculture, armed conflict, the beginning stages of a famine, and the lingering effects of a tropical cyclone and storm surge in 1970 (Cuny, 1983: 54). In mid-March, Secretary-General Kurt Waldheim met with Berkol in Geneva and asked him whether he would be willing to take charge of a major UN relief mobilization and operation. Berkol declined, saying that his office was still finding its sea legs and therefore would not be able to undertake such an enormous task. Furthermore, he was not sure the proposed operation fell within the mandate of his office. Berkol may have been correct on both counts, but this had "critical repercussions" in terms of damaging UNDRO's perceived image at UN headquarters (Stephens, 1978: 133–4). In the event, Waldheim appointed Sir Robert Jackson as Under-Secretary-General in charge of UNROD (United Nations Relief Operation in Dacca), a relief effort that came to be heralded as one of the UN's more notable successes.

In 1980, the Joint Inspection Unit published a scathing report[7] on UNDRO's performance. First of all, it was not delivering very much disaster relief. In 1976, for example, UNDRO had confined its largesse to sending out a few thousand dollars worth of emergency cash in major disaster situations. Sophisticated telecommunications at its headquarters and high-frequency radio sets in the field were seldom used or malfunctioned. Its senior staff were constantly traveling, but mostly to seminars and donor capitals rather than to disaster areas. The inspectors recommended reducing its staff by half, restricting its brief to sudden natural disasters, and handing over disaster coordination in the field to the UNDP (Richter, 2005: 291).

Rather than follow these recommendations, the General Assembly decided to clarify the agency's mandate and strengthen its capabilities. A resolution of the General Assembly in December 1982 named UNDRO, on behalf of the Secretary-General, as the central coordinator with the responsibility to develop concerted relief programs as a basis for united appeals which UNDRO, in turn, would also be responsible for coordinating (Kent, 1983: 699–700). While this dissipated the fog of ambiguity, it did not guarantee that UNDRO would perform effectively as coordinator during the emergency period.

Asked, by British journalist Rosemary Richter in June 1984, what it had done to alert the world to the Ethiopian famine, UNDRO replied that it had sent out three round-robin telexes (Richter, 2005: 291). As had happened in Bangladesh in 1972, and again in 1973–4 during the Sahel famine, another ad hoc unit emerged and took charge, and carried out a successful operation. The Office for Emergency Operations in Africa (OEOA), spearheaded by Bradford Morse, a former US congressman, and Maurice Strong, a Canadian millionaire businessman who most notably organized the Rio Summit on the Environment, marshaled support from major donors and voluntary organizations, built a computerized information base, and engineered a joint airlift among several European nations (Richter, 2005: 291–2).

While it was rarely in the foreground, UNDRO seems to have been an early proponent of disaster risk reduction (DRR) or, at least, its more technical/ scientific version. Stephens (1978: 168) observes that, as early as 1975, UNDRO's Prevention and Planning Division "demonstrated a higher profile, more visible range of programs and activities than its post disaster counter-part" (Relief Co-ordinations Division). Its achievements here included writing scientific and technical reports, preparing surveys of disaster damage, attend-ing conferences and seminars, and arranging advisory missions for pre-disaster planning.

Rather than receive credit for this, however, UNDRO seems to have raised some hackles, especially among donor governments and some NGOs. Stephens' (1978: 168–70) sources within the United Nations in the late 1970s told him that there was a certain amount of disillusionment with the disas-ters preparedness and prevention side of the office. In part this reflected the view that disaster prevention and mitigation activities took resources away from what was considered really important – disaster relief. Additionally, these activities potentially intruded upon other units' territory. Accordingly, the 1980 report of the Joint Inspection Unit warned that if UNDRO were to take on technical specialists to deal with preparedness and prevention meas-ures, these steps might be interpreted as duplicating skills already available within other UN organizations that are larger, better funded, and longer established. The result, the inspectors claimed, would be "frictions" (Joint Inspection Unit, 1980; cited in Kent, 1983: 707).

In an early signal of things to come, critics of UNDRO's disaster prepared-ness and prevention activities looked askance at the highly scientific and technical nature of DRR activities such as the application of satellites for disaster technology. In particular, they targeted several of UNDRO's more "grandiose" schemes, notably a "World Survey of Disaster Damage." Eventually, a compromise solution was worked out, wherein 60 percent of UNDRO's resources were to be earmarked for relief coordination, 30 percent to prepar-edness, and 10 percent to prevention[8] (Stephens, 1978: 173).

UNDRO limped along until 1992, when it was disbanded as part of a reform package by the incoming UN Secretary-General Boutros Boutros-Ghali and absorbed within the newly created Department of Humanitarian Affairs, an office that was given a wider, more political brief covering complex emergen-cies such as famines, as well as natural disasters (Walker and Maxwell, 2009: 42). UNDRO's epitaph, to paraphrase van Niekerk (2008: 359), might well read, "It was always the poor relation to other, larger UN agencies that were directly involved in relief operations."

Humanitarian Battlefields

Walker and Maxwell (2009: 45) argue that, "It was on the humanitarian battle-fields of the 1970s and 1980s that this [international humanitarian] system was to flex its muscles and discover its less pleasant limitations."

The first of these crises occurred in 1968–70 in the erstwhile Republic of Biafra in the oil-rich Niger delta region of Nigeria. In a move reminiscent of the Allied blockade during the Greek civil war in 1942, the Nigerian federal government cut off Biafran supply lines, inducing widespread malnutrition and death. When it was denied access, the International Committee of the Red Cross (ICRC) withdrew, leaving a group called Joint Church Aid as the only source of airlifts to the rebels. Although Church Aid's actions probably prolonged suffering in a civil war that was already lost, the ICRC was vilified, especially by doctors and journalists in France, for not standing up to the Nigerian government. In reaction, a whole new generation of more militant humanitarian workers was spawned and two new humanitarian agencies, Médecins sans Frontières (France) and Concern (Ireland), were born (Walker and Maxwell, 2009: 48). The former was awarded the Nobel Peace Prize in 1999. Confronted by this challenge, established humanitarian agencies responded in various ways. Some tried to modernize their structures and functions, while others, such as Oxfam, adopted more radical ideas about humanitarianism and development (West, 2001: 31).

The second iconic case was the 1984–5 famine in Ethiopia. While the crisis was triggered by a massive famine, it was exacerbated by the actions of the military, which systematically diverted or manipulated food aid. To maintain unfettered access to famine-affected populations, there was evidently a silent agreement between the aid agencies and the army that the agencies would maintain a "hands-off!" policy towards the war (De Waal, 1997; Walker and Maxwell, 2009: 57). In addition, there was the now legendary Band Aid fund-raising and awareness campaign led by rock star Bob Geldof, featuring the global *Live Aid* concert on July 13, 1985. With US$140 million raised, Band Aid changed the face of humanitarian fundraising forever.

The 1984–5 Ethiopian famine was the first widely acknowledged example of what has come to be known as a *complex emergency*. Complex emergencies are protracted political crises that have the ability to erode or destroy the cultural, civil, political, and economic integrity of established societies. As such, they are different from natural disasters and deserve to be understood and responded to as such. Alas, as Duffield (1994) pointed out nearly 20 years ago, the international relief apparatus has consistently failed operationally to distinguish complex emergencies from natural disasters.

While the proliferation of complex emergencies may have represented a serious setback to international development efforts, it was a boon to humanitarianism. Duffield (1994) reported that, by the early 1990s, expenditure on development aid had begun to stagnate and decline, even as relief assistance was increasing. Furthermore, the latter was at the expense of the former; within complex emergencies it was a complete substitution. Furthermore, the incredible success of Band Aid/Live Aid presented humanitarian NGOs with a fail-safe template for fundraising in all manner of emergencies.

Katarina West (2001: 211) notes that throughout the 1980s and 1990s, NGOs slowly lost their inferior status in the international humanitarian system, became more professional, influenced the UN system more, increased their resources, and made more effective use of the media. Contrary to the "realist" view that attributes this growth of humanitarian NGOs to the sudden wealth of opportunities provided by the withdrawal of superpower nations from geopolitically unimportant countries in peripheral regions, West argues that it was more consistent with a trend that had been evolving since the 1960s. Practically speaking, NGOs have the "right qualities" for acting in large-scale relief responses, "They are flexible and speedy; they disregard state borders, are cheaper in relative terms, have links at the grass roots level and are not bureaucratic" (West, 2001: 7). Furthermore, attitudes toward humanitarianism had been changing, with national governments, the United Nations, and the media all becoming more open to recognizing humanitarian norms. Finally, the rise of humanitarianism was linked to the globalization of world politics, insofar as national states admitted that humanitarian crises generate transnational problems that could best be solved by cooperating with NGOs.

By the end of the 1980s, the safety net systems established around the Horn of Africa spread to protracted crises in other parts of Africa, and the position of NGOs as relief implementers became well established (Duffield, 1994). "Permanent emergencies" such as the Ethiopian drought/famine began to replace short-term crises as the main focus of humanitarian relief agencies. One result of this was the increasing professionalization of relief work. However, this did not mean that there was any heightened attention paid to the long-term vulnerabilities of those trapped in these permanent emergencies to recurrent disasters.

Writing in the late 1990s, Pierre Laurent (1999) expressed grave concern that humanitarian assistance had reached a structural impasse that could jeopardize its very existence in the long term. One explanation he gave for this was the increasing assimilation of humanitarian organizations into the international community. Partly, this was said to be the fault of the politicians, rebel leaders, and guerrilla movements in the emergency zone. Lacking an official pipeline to the outside world, they exploited the humanitarian agencies by deputizing them as spokespersons and negotiators. Another explanation is the increasing confusion of humanitarian assistance with intervention in the name of humanity. The former denotes delivering medical care, food, and shelter to all those in need, no matter what their politics are. Intervention in the name of humanity means taking sides in a conflict, even if this requires denying aid to one party in the conflict or using coercive, military means. According to Pieterse (1998: 256), one "sinister interpretation" that emerges here states that humanitarian intervention constitutes "the military corollary of neo-liberal globalization." Whatever the case, as the blurb on the back cover of a recent text on humanitarian intervention reads, "Since the end of the Cold War, humanitarian intervention has been propelled to the top of the international political agenda, sparking a divisive debate which shows no sign of abating" (Hehir, 2010).

Conclusion

Until the rise of disaster risk reduction (DRR) in the 1990s, humanitarianism remained the preferred approach to disaster management. While it can be traced all the way back to the founding of the International Committee of the Red Cross in the 1860s, the large-scale provision of aid to disaster victims by private humanitarian organizations first took hold during and immediately after World War One. The International Relief Union (IRU), an early experiment in multilateralism under the auspices of the League of Nations, was ahead of its time in proposing a global mutual insurance scheme, but foundered on the shoals of national sovereignty.

After World War Two, a new humanitarian order arose, with a quartet of United Nations agencies (UNICEF, IRO, FAO, WHO) at its epicenter. Also active in an emerging international disaster relief network were a number of NGOs (CARE, Oxfam, Save the Children, World Vision). As the Cold War developed, these NGOs assumed a higher profile. Partly, this reflected their operational expertise in sanitation, food delivery, logistics, and other activities, especially in the newly created nations of the South. Governments also found them useful, insomuch as they could move more quickly and at lower cost than IGOs in disaster situations, and often go where governments could not. By the early 1970s, the UN community began to worry that coordination was minimal, information transfer insufficient, and shared knowledge spotty in high profile natural disasters. Their answer was to create a relief coordination office, UNDRO (Office of United Nations Disaster Relief Coordinator). Operating under a vague mandate, and chronically underfunded, UNDRO floundered, limping along until 1992 when it was absorbed within the newly created UN Department of Humanitarian Affairs.

After several decades of escalating success, the humanitarian NGOs encountered some rough seas in a series of civil wars and other emergencies in Africa in the 1970s and 1980s. In particular, they encountered difficulties securing entry to the field, unless it was under a set of restrictive conditions set by governments or rebel armies. Their reluctance to carry out aid operations under these conditions led to the emergence of a whole new generation of more militant humanitarian agencies, most notably Médecins sans Frontières. As we will see in the next chapter, by the late 1980s the discursive winds were also changing, with a rising chorus of demands that disaster prevention be given equal footing with disaster assistance.

Further Reading

M. Barnett and T.G. Weiss (eds.) (2008) *Humanitarianism in Question: Politics, Power, Ethics*. Cornell University Press, Ithaca, NY.

D.P. Forsythe (2005) *The Humanitarians: The International Committee of the Red Cross*. Cambridge University Press, Cambridge.

P. Walker and D. Maxwell (2009) *Shaping the Humanitarian World*. Routledge, London and New York.

CHAPTER FOUR

A Safer World?

In the 1980s and early 1990s, a swell of international scholarly interest and response rose among "natural hazards" researchers in the geophysical, meteorological, and engineering sciences around the perceived threat posed by disasters. There are two possible explanations for this previously unparalleled burst of activity.

First of all, scientific concern is said to have grown in direct proportion to a corresponding increase in the severity of, and damage caused by, natural disasters. Looking back on this era, almost every article, paper, and report in the disasters-related literature begins with a litany of recent natural disasters around the globe, followed by the claim that the fatalities, property damage, and disruption resulting from such events were on the rise. For example, in 1994, G.O.P. Obasi, Secretary-General of the World Meteorological Organization (WMO) from 1984 to 2003, published a piece in the *Bulletin of the American Meteorological Society*. Obasi enumerates a string of recent natural disasters and their human and financial toll: Hurricane Gilbert (1988) – more than 300 deaths and damages in excess of US$5 billion in Jamaica and Mexico; Typhoon Mike (1990) – 500 lives and losses of over US$350 million in the Philippines; Cyclone Bob (1991) – 138,000 people killed in Bangladesh; flooding on the Yangtze River in China (1991) – four million dwellings destroyed. Obasi buttresses these examples with an analysis of natural disasters compiled for the period 1967 to 1991, classified by type of event: weather events, weather-related events, and geological events. These data, he reports, indicate a rising trend in the number of people affected by natural disasters. In particular, he highlights the impact of extreme meteorological and hydrological events,[1] which killed 3.5 million people and touched the lives of 2.8 billion (Obasi, 1994: 1657). Obasi urged measures to enhance international collaboration on disasters by the scientific community, most notably environmentalists, atmospheric scientists, hydrologists, computer and space scientists, and engineers. "It is becoming increasingly clear," he observes, "that the world community should address the need to invest in low-cost measures of disaster preparedness that reduce the vulnerability of people in disaster-affected communities and not just in high-cost disaster relief operations" (Obasi, 1994: 1660).

Was Obasi correct in his assessment? Were the traditional disaster agents (hurricanes, typhoons, earthquakes, volcanoes) suddenly and unexpectedly proliferating in nature? In a 1999 review published in the journal *Science*, the Board on Natural Disasters (BOND) of the (US) National Research Council expressed considerable doubt:

> Most of this increase [in annual natural disaster losses in the United States] cannot be attributed to increased occurrence of hazards. Although some types of events, for example, heavy rains, have increased in frequency since the 1950s, others such as hurricane landfalls in the eastern United States have declined. Thus, it is difficult to attribute U.S. disaster loss increases in any significant measure to this factor.

If not the increased occurrence of natural hazards, then what *was* the cause? Demographic change was one frequently cited factor. Housner (1989: 45) claims there had been a quadrupling of the world's population, with the consequence that disasters were becoming more frequent and greater. Specifically, growing populations do not disperse broadly, but rather concentrate in high-risk urban areas such as seismic regions, mountains and hillsides, coasts, and flood plains. The members of BOND elaborate further. First of all, they point to a steady migration in the United States since the 1950s to both the earthquake-prone Pacific Coast and the hurricane-prone Atlantic and Gulf coasts. Furthermore, they detect an increasing concentration of population in large cities. The metropolis requires complex infrastructures – roads, bridges, sewer, and water systems; these are rapidly aging and are vulnerable to breakdowns that can be triggered by even relatively minor disaster events. For example, they point to the failure of a single span of the Bay Bridge that disrupted traffic for several months in the San Francisco area after the Loma Prieta earthquake in 1989 (Board on Natural Disasters, 1999: 1944).

Recently gathered statistics from that era paint another picture. Testifying before the UK Select Committee on International Development in February 2002, Jonathan Walter, editor of the *World Disasters Report*, stated that the number of deaths per reported disaster had been steadily tumbling since the 1970s, but that more people overall were being affected – 256 million in the year 2000 versus about 73 million people each year on average in the 1970s. Furthermore, for the 1990s compared to the 1970s, there had been a five-fold increase in economic losses.[2]

Another explanation points to the global expansion of communication channels and networks within science and government in the late twentieth century as the key factor that encouraged and facilitated the emergence of a cooperative international program to reduce and prevent natural disasters. In this view, the formation of a critical mass of hazards researchers is situated within a broader *zeitgeist* in science and global governance. When natural hazards researchers came together in the 1980s, they had the advantage of a firmly established and quite well understood architecture of informational/ infrastructural globalism to guide them. Many of them were already embedded in networks of applied science that emerged from the Cold War era.

Clark Miller (2001: 170) has taken this a step further, identifying "a political culture of international governance that explicitly linked science, technology and politics in a liberal vision of postwar order." Focusing specifically on the early postwar period (1947–58), he argues that United States foreign policy articulated three modes of scientific and political cooperation: (i) intergovernmental harmonization (expert organizations where international technical cooperation could help rationalize policy choices), (ii) technical assistance, and (iii) international coordination of scientific research – the model for this was the 1957–8 International Geophysical Year (IGY). With the advent of the IGY, governments added other important new components to international science by establishing and coordinating joint scientific research agendas and funding global data collection.

In his history of the evolution of the WMO, Paul Edwards (2006) argues that the WMO illustrates a profoundly important transition from a voluntarist internationalism, based on shared interests, to a "quasi-obligatory globalism" based on a more permanent shared *infrastructure* (2006: 230). Edwards notes that the weather data network, along with its cousins in the other geophysical sciences, especially seismology and oceanography, are the oldest of all systems for producing globalist information. The International Meteorological Association (IMA), founded in 1873, was tasked with coordinating international standards, a task made next to impossible by its complete dependence on voluntary compliance. Some national weather services used British units, while others favored the metric system. Standard observing hours and methods of sea surface temperature measurement varied from nation to nation. National weather service directors, who saw their primary identity as scientists, remained sharply divided over the desirability of conferring intergovernmental status on the IMA, a move that some saw as leading to control of meteorology by politicians.

In 1950, the IMA was replaced by a new agency, the World Meteorological Organization (WMO). To conform to its obligations as a United Nations "specialized agency," membership in the WMO was restricted to "sovereign states" as defined by the UN, thereby excluding units such as the Republic of China (Taiwan). Although it lacked policing powers, the WMO found ways to rationalize and align technical standards. These "institutional powers" were manifested through setting WMO standards for new instruments (weather balloons, automated weather stations) and technological systems; via peer pressure exerted through meetings and official publications; and by means of the WMO technical assistance program. Edwards cites Clark Miller's (2001) argument that these seemingly "technical" activities, in fact, formed part of a "new politics of expertise."

In addition to meteorology, Miller highlights the crucial role played here by the geophysical community:

Geophysicists in particular, especially in the U.S. and Europe where local geophysical research had reached high degrees of sophistication, felt that fundamental questions about global-scale environmental processes would remain unsolved unless opportunities could be created to collect data on a worldwide basis. Such opportunities, they argued, required international collaboration (Miller, 2001: 199).

International Decade for Natural Disaster Reduction (IDNDR)

By the mid-twentieth century, earthquake engineering in the United States was a mature, applied academic field, embarking on a period of growth and influence. In no small part, this reflected the mounting concern generated by a series of high profile seismic events during the 1970s, both domestically and abroad.

In 1971, the San Fernando earthquake (magnitude 6.7 on the Richter scale) rocked the Los Angeles area, in a location just to the east of the subsequent 1994 Northridge quake that resulted in direct losses of a staggering US$44 billion. The earlier San Fernando quake left 65 people dead and caused more than half a billion dollars in property damage. It is said to have served as the chief inspiration for a 1974 Hollywood film, *Earthquake*. Two hospitals, two freeway interchanges, and the Lower Van Norman Dam were destroyed. Only opened a month earlier, the Olive View Medical Center was literally pushed a foot off its foundation, causing the first floor to buckle. The San Fernando earthquake revealed the inadequacies of previous building practices, in particular, un-reinforced concrete structures. It led to more stringent building codes, especially in the design of hospitals, and to major advances in the field of earthquake engineering.

Damage and loss of life was far more extensive four years later in the 1976 earthquake in Guatemala: 23,000 killed, 77,000 injured, 1.1 million left homeless. Worst hit were poor Guatemalans with homes in the landslide-prone ravines and gorges. The extensive damage and loss of life in the capital, Guatemala City, were primarily attributed to the use of adobe as a building material rather than the more resilient concrete block or wood. Adobe huts were further weakened by the absence of corner posts or columns in the walls (Bates and Killian, 1982).

Two senior scholars, both closely linked to the California Institute of Technology (Caltech), enjoyed special status in the earthquake engineering community. In the early 1980s, Frank Press was just beginning the first of his two six-year terms as president of the US National Academy of Science. Press was already professionally eminent and extraordinarily well connected politically, having served as Science Advisor to President Jimmy Carter from 1977 to 1981. He came to Caltech in 1955, and soon became director of a laboratory that still employed Charles Richter and Beno Gutenberg, who together developed the famed Richter scale of earthquake magnitude. In the 1960s, Press was a key figure in designing the worldwide network of seismic stations in connection with the 1963 Nuclear Test Ban Treaty. After a decade in California, Press moved to a new post as head of department at MIT, where he successfully expanded the laboratory into other areas besides seismology, most notably oceanography.

Equally renowned was George Housner, widely known as "the father of earthquake engineering." His innovative techniques were used to strengthen the dozens of dams and aqueducts running through California. Of particular importance was his pioneering method for the seismic analysis of liquid storage tanks, subsequently the primary basis for their design. In 1976, Housner led a scientific delegation to China to investigate the effects of the massive earthquake that destroyed the city of Tangshan, a trip that evidently had a powerful effect on him.

Both Housner and Press had come to fervently believe that fatalities, property damage, and disruption resulting from earthquakes and other natural disasters were sharply on the rise worldwide. Writing in the second volume of the journal, *Natural Hazards*, Housner cited a series of recent disaster events: an earthquake in Soviet Armenia, a flood in Bangladesh, a typhoon in the Philippines, a volcano in the United States, a wildfire in China, a tsunami in Japan, a destructive landslide in Ecuador. Numerically, this translates into more than 2.8 million lives lost in natural disasters over the previous two decades, 820 million people suffering adverse effects, and property damage estimated to be as much as US$100 billion (Housner, 1989: 46). Speaking on behalf of "the scientific and technological world community," Housner warned that natural disasters would become increasingly severe unless a coordinated, international program on hazard reduction and disaster mitigation was initiated as soon as possible.

In a keynote address at the Opening Ceremony of the 8th World Congress on Earthquake Engineering held in San Francisco in 1984, Frank Press called for the establishment of an International Decade for Natural Hazard Reduction (IDNHR), to begin in 1990. As copies of the speech circulated, interest began to build. The International Association of Earthquake Engineering immediately endorsed the proposal to promote the IDNHR in the earthquake engineering community and associated fields. In 1986, an Advisory Committee on the IDNHR was struck under the auspices of the National Research Council, the National Academy of Sciences, and the National Academy of Engineering, with George Housner as chair. The following year, the Committee released a booklet entitled "Confronting Natural Disasters," followed by another official publication in 1989.

Initially, the IDNHR Advisory Committee recommended a model whose objectives – to reduce catastrophic loss of life, property damage, and social disruption from natural hazards – were to be accomplished through cooperative research, demonstration projects, information dissemination, technical assistance, technology transfer, and education and training. Global governance practices such as monitoring, warning, and early intervention were acknowledged as being important, but were assigned to individual countries or regional clusters.

Housner (1989: 57) sums up the case for a new approach to hazard reduction as follows. Most measures now in use to cope with natural hazards (firefighting, search and rescue, emergency medical care, debris clearance, provision of food and temporary shelter, provisions for temporary water supply and waste disposal) are reactive. Major reductions in losses of life and property can only come when the emphasis shifts from reaction to anticipation. Emergency response and post-disaster relief will always be necessary, but will decline in importance as "disaster preparedness, hazard-conscious land management use, hazard-resistant construction, and other anticipatory measures reduce the world's vulnerability to natural hazards."

During this initial period, social vulnerability generally took a back seat to physical vulnerability, as might be expected given the applied science credentials of the IDNHR founders, and, subsequently, the backgrounds of those on the Scientific and Advisory Committee of its successor group, the IDNDR. Consider, for example, a talk given in 1990 by Patrick Sham Pak at the Fourth World Congress on Tall Buildings and Urban Habitat. Sham, Director of the Hong Kong Observatory (1984–95) and founder of the Hong Kong Meteorological Society, observes that "the IDNDR has a strong 'engineering' background" and guesses that "this may perhaps be one of the reasons why the organizers of this Conference have chosen to have a special session on IDNDR" (Sham, 1990). In the body of his remarks, Sham strongly urges meteorologists and hydrologists in Southeast Asia and the Western Pacific to engage in a dialog with structural engineers and building designers to devise plans for structural preventive measures, something which "are either non-existent, not effective, or not effectively implemented" (p. 7).

Nevertheless, there were a handful of disaster experts who argued that it was necessary to address social as well as physical vulnerabilities. During a panel discussion at "Challenges of the IDNDR," a symposium organized by the United Nations Centre for Regional Development (UNCRD) in Japan in April 1989, Carlo Pelanda, an Italian sociologist, raised the question as to whether a country's vulnerability to disasters could ever be improved without a general raising of its development levels. To reduce the scale and number of disasters, Pelanda argued, it is mandatory to change the level of social vulnerability. The final panelist to speak, Tadateru Kanoe, Director of the Japan Red Cross Society, concurred:

> Today a notion is increasing that general levels of development must be raised in order to increase the level of disaster resistance. To this end, the Red Cross has gradually expanded its scope from simple relief activities to embrace the function of a development agency (Challenges of the IDNDR, 1989).

While most historical descriptions of the founding of the International Decade for Natural Hazard Reduction give the impression that momentum for this initiative cascaded widely and uncritically throughout the 1980s, the story actually appears to be somewhat more complicated. The editor of The Society for Earthquake and Civil Engineering Dynamics (SECED) newsletter in the UK notes that efforts to publicize the Decade in *The Daily Telegraph* had been less than successful. In a guest editorial in the same issue of the newsletter, Professor Willy Aspinall, a SECED board member, wrote rather candidly:

> Great enthusiasm for the Decade [International Decade for Natural Disaster Reduction] has been engendered in Earth scientists, but this may not be entirely due to pure altruism. The predictive certainty which attends short-term weather forecasting has not yet been achieved for the other chief killers: earthquakes and volcanoes. Some scientists may view the decade as a vehicle to facilitate prediction research on these topics, success in which would bring acclaim and personal advancement (Aspinall, 1989).

In his presentation to a 1995 symposium in honor of George Housner, organized by the Consortium of Universities for Research in Earthquake Engineering (CUREE), Professor Kenzo Toki of Kyoto University suggests that the Advisory Committee, in fact, undertook very little of a specific nature. In an attempt to get something going, in 1988, Frank Press called 31 specialists from various countries to discuss how to promote the IDNHR worldwide. Within the year, a decision was made to approach the United Nations and request that the Decade be operated under its auspices.

On December 22, 1989, the General Assembly of the United Nations unanimously decided in its Resolution No. 44/236 to make prevention and preparedness against disasters caused by natural extreme events their task and declared the 1990s as the International Decade for Natural Disaster Reduction.[3] The governments of Japan and Morocco were especially active in supporting this resolution at the UN General Assembly. Initially, the Secretary-General created an International Ad Hoc Group of Experts consisting of 25 scientists and technical experts drawn from all over the world and representing a spectrum of disciplines engaged in disaster reduction, with Frank Press as Chair, and Emilio Rosenbleuth, a Mexican earthquake engineer, as Vice-Chair. After a series of five meetings, the group submitted a final report, known as the "Tokyo Declaration," that set out an organizing framework for the IDNDR.

Structurally, the IDNDR consisted of a Special High Level Council that included serving and former presidents and prime ministers, whose duties were to mobilize financial support and serve the UN Secretary-General in an advisory capacity; a Scientific and Technical Committee (STC), composed of 25 international experts, who were asked to develop and evaluate bilateral and multilateral Decade programs; and a Secretariat, based in Geneva, Switzerland, that was expected to provide support for the Council and the STC, serve as a clearinghouse for disaster reduction information, and be responsible for the day-to-day coordination of Decade activities (*A Safer Future*, 1991: 49). Additionally, individual member states were strongly encouraged to set up individual national committees or designate focal points to coordinate national-level activities.

For Frank Press, George Housner, and their fellow earthquake engineers, the decision to approach the international community of nations may well have turned out to be a devil's bargain. To be sure, the UN *imprimatur* provided instant legitimacy, and access to a wealth of interorganizational contacts and resources. But coming under the United Nations banner also paved the way for a significant discursive shift. In the early 1990s, the predominant conversation in UN circles addressed issues of poverty, sustainability, and development. Keep in mind that the UN Conference on Environment and Development (UNCED) in Rio de Janeiro, Brazil, was held in 1992, just two years into the IDNDR. Five years before, the authors of *Our Common Future (The Brundtland Report)*, the "first mainstream expression of a sustainable development approach" (Pelling, 2011: 4), had observed that during the 1970s twice as many people suffered each year from "natural disasters" as during the 1960s, noting specifically that the numbers of victims of cyclones and earthquakes shot up "as growing numbers of poor people built unsafe houses on dangerous ground." In this context, social vulnerability was increasingly starting to be recognized as noteworthy.

As the International Decade for Natural Disaster Reduction progressed, the strong technical orientation that had initially occupied center stage began to attract criticism from multiple and diverse directions. Terry Cannon, a geographer at the University of Greenwich specializing in the politics of development, complained that the focus of the IDNDR "betrays the strength of the old outlook." By this he meant an approach to disasters that focuses on the behavior of nature and encourages technical solutions. Elaborating further, Cannon notes, "The Resolution that established the UN Decade for Natural Disaster makes no mention of vulnerability or even the possible role of social science in preparing for disasters. It is overwhelmingly oriented to scientific and engineering approaches" (Cannon, 1994: n. 10, 29–30).

German earth scientists Erich Plate and Wolfgang Kron (1994) published a piece in the journal *Soil Dynamics and Earthquake Engineering* in which they reported on the activities of the German National Committee of the IDNDR. While these were primarily being carried out within the disciplines of water research, atmospheric sciences, geosciences, oceanography, civil engineering and geophysics, geomorphology, and volcanology, the authors stress that such projects need to be interdisciplinary and involve ethnologists, psychologists, social geographers, and disaster sociologists.[4] Disaster, Plate and Kron observe, is rarely democratic, "Apparently, the most severe events occur in coastal zones and in regions where many of the poorest developing countries are located" (p. 46); and, "The poorer a region, the deeper are the social effects of natural disasters" (p. 45).

Two years later, in an article in the *Humanitarian Exchange Magazine*, published by the Overseas Development Institute,[5] the author (identified as

"RRN") lamented the under-representation of the social sciences in many IDNDR activities, and cited the Decade's emphasis upon scientific and engineering "solutions" "as a reason why the NGO community has not been as closely involved with the IDNDR as it might" (Humanitarian Practice Network, 1994). Additionally, the author claims that drought, the principal natural hazard type in sub-Saharan Africa, "has been largely by-passed by much of the IDNDR activity so far – a fact reflected in the number of countries that have not formed National Committees in the region and the low level of activity among many of those that have been established."

Despite its new United Nations home, some felt that the IDNDR initially did not seem to achieve very much of note. Included in this group was George Housner himself, who seems to have become rather disillusioned. According to his colleague Kenzo Toki,

> Professor Housner had been waiting patiently for something to happen in the developed countries of the world and under the auspices of the United Nations. Nothing happened except the holding of many meetings that produced no active action for reducing natural disasters of the world. Then Prof. Housner suggested that something be done only in the earthquake engineering community. The World Seismic Safety Initiative has been organized and accepted during the 10th World Conference on Earthquake Engineering held in Madrid in 1992. Only WSSI has mounted continuing efforts to promote the IDNDR in the world, particularly in developing countries.

Toki's version probably inflates the WSSI contribution. Nevertheless, it seems to be widely accepted that the early years of the IDNDR left many in both the disaster and humanitarian sectors rather disappointed. With tongue only barely in cheek, Terry Jeggle of the Asian Disaster Preparedness Center in Bangkok entitled his opinion piece in the *Natural Hazards Observer*, written on the eve of the Yokohama Conference, "Is the IDNDR a slow-onset disaster in the making?" (Jeggle, 1994).

Yokohama Conference

From May 23 to May 27, 1994, the World Conference on Natural Disaster Reduction met in Yokohama, Japan. This was the first international conference on disasters to be held under the auspices of the United Nations. Over 3,000 participants[6] came to Yokohama, including representatives from 148 countries.

Sharing their on-site observations with readers of the journal *Disasters*, Ian Davis and Mary Myers (1994) note that the conference embraced three main activities or mini-conferences. The political conferences mainly attracted politicians and civil servants; the technical sessions attracted academics, scientists, and consultants; and the open, non-political sessions appealed to the development community. On a positive note, Davis and Myers report that the latter turned out to be well balanced, with good coverage of both the physical and social aspects, thus taking note of persistent early criticism of the focus of the IDNDR. Nevertheless, according to one estimate, there were fewer than 40 [NGO] agency representatives present, and those that did attend felt that they were marginalized into a second-class role. While they generally accorded the Yokohama Conference positive marks for successfully re-launching the International Decade for Natural Disaster Reduction at its halfway mark, Davis and Myers complain that:

> The NGO voice was sorely missed at the conference, just as it had been for the first four years of the IDNDR. The reality is that most NGOs have largely ignored the Decade. Thus, in this conference there was no radical critique from the NGO community and none from an informed media to challenge the rather comfortable accepted wisdom that was being all too readily endorsed (Davis and Myers, 1994: 371).

John Handmer, a member of the Australian delegation at the Yokohama Conference, rendered a similar verdict in a "Trend Report" published in the *Journal of Contingencies and Crisis Management*. Handmer felt that some key sessions on disaster vulnerability failed because "they covered the issues largely from the perspective of the industrialized countries, and, in addition, had a strong technocratic orientation" (Handmer, 1995: 36). He cites the specific example of a conference session on advance warnings that focused entirely on the largely technical issues of predictions and forecasts rather than dealing with how to motivate people to respond to these warnings. Nonetheless, Handmer reports, there were a few bright spots. Especially notable was a panel discussion on "vulnerable communities" that featured case studies from Bangladesh, Zambia, and Latin America. Presenters here "tackled the hard issues underlying vulnerability, such as poverty, war, environmental degradation, lack of political power, rapid urbanization and economic change" (Handmer, 1995: 36). The International Federation of the Red Cross and Red Crescent Societies and UNICEF jointly organized this session. "Although both are global organizations," Handmer observed, "they are linked to local communities, and their mandates and interests lie with the world's more vulnerable people" (p. 36).

At a plenary session on the final day, the Conference adopted the *Yokohama Strategy and Plan of Action for a Safer World*. In the preamble, the document cites "the rapidly rising world-wide toll on human and economic losses due to natural disasters." It further recognizes that "Sustainable economic growth and sustainable development cannot be achieved in many countries without adequate measures to reduce disaster losses, and that there are close linkages between disaster losses and environmental degradation, as emphasized in Agenda 21 adopted at the United Nations Conference on Environment and Development."

This link between sustainability, disasters, and the environment was re-affirmed in the ten core "Principles." Especially noteworthy was the ninth principle, which stated, "*Environmental protection as a component of sustainable development consistent with poverty alleviation is imperative in the prevention and mitigation of natural disasters.*" Again, in the section of the document entitled "Basis for the Strategy," this theme is featured. After acknowledging that, "*In all countries the poor and socially disadvantaged groups suffer most from natural disasters and are least equipped to cope with them*" (#3), the *Strategy* goes on to assert, "*Some patterns of consumption, production and development have the potential for increasing the vulnerability to natural disasters, particularly of the poor and socially disadvantaged groups*" (#4).

In addition to endorsing measures meant to reduce physical vulnerability (early warning systems, proper design and patterns of development), the document addresses several other issues of rising concern to the disasters/development community. Writing in the *Asian Disaster Management News*, Andrew Maskrey and Sonny Jegillos claim that, by the time of the Yokohama Conference, a broad consensus was emerging in favor of Community Based Disaster Management (CBDM). In contrast to established, top-down programs that "fail to address the specific local needs of vulnerable communities, ignore the potential of local resources and capacities and may in some cases even increase people's vulnerability" (Maskrey and Jegillos, 1997), CBDM emphasizes local knowledge and networks. The *Yokohama Strategy and Plan* officially recognizes this:

> *Vulnerable developing countries should be enabled to revive, apply, and share traditional methods to reduce the impact of natural disasters, supplemented and reinforced by access to modern scientific and technical knowledge. The existing knowledge and know-how should be studied and efforts should be made to ameliorate, develop and better apply them today* (Basis for the Strategy, #5).

The Yokohama document also acknowledges the lack of attention given in the past to droughts and "slow-impact" natural disasters. In addition to small-island developing states and land-locked countries, drought-prone nations are singled out as being especially vulnerable, "*Developing countries affected by desertification, drought and other types of national disasters are also equally vulnerable and insufficiently equipped to mitigate natural disasters*" (Basis for the Strategy, #2).

By 1999, the International Decade for Disaster Reduction was starting to wind down. Opinions differed as to its achievements thus far. On the one hand, an international framework had been put in place that had not existed nine years earlier and a number of UN agencies had expanded or refocused their activities in support of the Decade. Conferences, workshops, technology transfer, and pilot projects were proliferating, especially on a regional basis. Furthermore, the discourse of disaster politics had been broadened to include development issues and the topic of social vulnerability.

Nevertheless, most IDNDR member states declined to make a firm and meaningful commitment to disaster reduction, especially financial. Quite clearly, this severely constrained the agency's activities.[7] At the initiation of the Decade, the United Nations made it absolutely clear that activities related to the IDNDR should be performed on an extra-budgetary basis. Evidently, financial contributions in excess of regular budgets amounted to only a few million dollars per year, with the largest amounts coming from Japan and several European countries. The United States contributed relatively little in funds (Board on Natural Disasters, 1999).

Speaking at an electronic conference of American emergency managers in 1999, Philippe Boullé, Director of the IDNDR Secretariat, addressed the theme of "Disaster Reduction as a Central Element of Government Policy." Boullé castigated national states for marginalizing disaster reduction in their national development plans:

> Environmental disasters are a threat to almost every country, directly or indirectly. But disaster reduction, up until today, has been treated as a technical, sectoral issue by government, not a central policy issue. In fact, when we look at the initial targets of IDNDR, we see that these are technical – hazard assessment; early warning systems; drafting of national disaster mitigation plans. We now have to go many steps further and ensure that disaster reduction becomes a policy matter for governments; an essential policy issue within the country's national planning (Boullé, 1999).

Alas, how to best convince policymakers of the importance of this objective has proven to be a much thornier task. During the question and answer session, Boullé sidestepped specific queries about how the IDNDR (or its successor) intended to shape a strategy for the future directed at making disaster reduction an essential element of government policy, replying generically about the value of community capacity building, public–private partnerships, and global policy research. Clearly, the case for disaster reduction was not selling itself. In a lecture in 2000 to the Executive Council of the World Meteorological Organization, J.C. Rodda, a British hydrologist, expressed his dismay at the failure of the IDNDR to capture the attention it deserved. Switching the emphasis from post-disaster relief to extensive support for pre-disaster preparedness would, at the very least, offer attractive financial savings for governments and funding agencies. Alas, those who control the purse strings don't seem to be able to see this, opting instead to contribute large sums to clearing up in the wake of disaster (Rodda, 2000: 2–3).

Wisner et al. (2004: 21–2) detected another shortcoming. In their view, the chief development during the final three years of the IDNDR was a turn toward cities, as evidenced by the creation of RADIUS (Risk Assessment Tools for Diagnosis of Urban Areas Against Seismic Disasters), an ambitious pilot program for urban earthquake risk assessment and mitigation (1997–2000) that involved a core of nine medium-sized cities in different parts of the world. Why focus on earthquake risk reduction in cities as opposed to floods, storms, or volcanic eruptions? They identify two possible reasons:

> Part of the explanation is found in the origins of the IDNDR. Earthquake engineers were very prominent in its creation and remained influential. Also important was the fact

that two costly earthquakes had recently surprised authorities and experts alike in the USA (Northridge, California in 1994) and Japan (Kobe in 1995) (Wisner et al., 2004: 22).

International Strategy for Disaster Reduction

No matter, the following year (2000), the Economic and Social Council and the General Assembly of the United Nations announced the creation of the International Strategy for Disaster Reduction (ISDR) as the official successor to the Decade. The ISDR was meant to be a system of partnerships involving governments, IGOs and NGOs, international financial institutions, scientific and technical bodies and specialized networks, as well as civil society and the private sector, with the overall objective of generating and supporting a global disaster risk reduction movement (Audit Report, 2010: 1). Its emphasis was to be on reducing vulnerability and building resilient communities. As Wisner et al. (2004: 324) note, no fewer than three of the four "Goals for the International Strategy for Disaster Reduction" were directly concerned with the human dimensions of risk reduction. As part of the rollover from the Decade, all assets of the Trust Fund for the IDNDR were transferred to a newly formed Trust Fund for Disaster Reduction. Structurally, the ISDR had two parts: the Inter-Agency Task Force on Disaster Reduction (IATF/DR) and the Inter-Agency Secretariat.

The former was designated as the political arm of the Strategy. Its stated purpose was "to serve as the main forum within the United Nations for continued and concerted emphasis on natural disaster reduction, in particular for defining strategies for international cooperation at all levels in this field, while ensuring complementarity of action with other agencies." The Inter-agency Task Force was composed of a maximum of 30 members: up to 14 representatives of agencies, organizations, and programs of the United Nations system; up to eight representatives from regional entities, and up to eight representatives of civil society and relevant professional sectors. The Under-Secretary-General for Humanitarian Affairs chaired the Task Force, while the Director of the ISDR Secretariat acted as its secretary. The Secretariat is the ISDR civil service. Reporting to the UN Under-Secretary for Humanitarian Affairs, it is based in Geneva, with regional offices in Bangkok, Dushanbe (Tajikistan), Nairobi, and San José (Costa Rica). Initially it had an annual budget of US$4 million, funded exclusively from the Trust Fund rather than from the regular UN budget, and a staff complement of 20.

As was the case with its predecessor, the IDNDR, the ISDR has periodically encountered a rocky reception, both from within the United Nations, and externally from other participants in the global disaster policy field. In 2004, Jan Egeland, the Under-Secretary-General for Humanitarian Affairs, commissioned an external evaluation of the Secretariat, which was carried out by a three-person team of experts in disaster management and reduction.[8] The evaluation team consulted widely, carrying out 151 in-depth interviews with key stakeholders, as well as an email survey, website and publication analysis, and review of ISDR documents. Their findings were delivered in a June 2005 report, *External Evaluation of the Inter-Agency Secretariat of the International Strategy for Disaster Reduction* (Christoplos et al., 2005).

The 2005 *Evaluation* concluded that, "Despite a large quantity of initiatives, the Secretariat has been uneven in acting as a 'clearinghouse' for a wide spectrum of DRR information and it has not established an appropriate communications strategy for fomenting broad political will and public commitment to DRR" (p. 2). To be fair, the Secretariat was handicapped right from the start by the vagueness and lack of direction of its brief. With little guidance as to priorities, the Secretariat did not seem able to decide on an agenda or to follow through on it. Management unwisely tried to please a diverse array of stakeholders, resulting in a vague profile and weak program continuity. Things were made worse by unstable and unpredictable funding arrangements. On occasion, this led the Secretariat to direct its priorities to follow the money – that is, producing visible and tangible products to convince individual donors that they were receiving good value, even at the cost of not being able to achieve its disaster reduction goals.

The evaluation team took the Secretariat to task for being too insular. As was previously the case with the IDNDR, the Secretariat was unsuccessful or lacked a clear strategy in transcending the tendency to preach to the converted – the UN family and those who were already advocating increased attention to disaster reduction. Specifically, it was judged to be making only limited progress in reaching the sustainable development and humanitarian communities. In the latter instance, the evaluators found that "there is very little contact with humanitarian actors in general, and some Secretariat staff do not see this as a priority" (p. 25). One example of this disconnect pertained to disaster preparedness, where the Early Warning Platform focused primarily on early warning as a technical risk identification tool rather than an issue of community preparedness. The assessment team recommended that "The Secretariat's policy efforts should [also] be critically reviewed by experts in mainstream development and humanitarian policy processes to ensure that appropriate and realistic entry points into political decision making can be found" (p. 12).

World Conference on Disaster Reduction (Hyogo Conference) 2005

Despite its ongoing difficulties, even the ISDR's most persistent critics agreed that the Secretariat did a competent job organizing the follow-up meeting to Yokohama. The UN World Conference on Disaster Reduction was held from January 18 to 22, 2005, in Kobe, Hyogo Prefecture, Japan. As fate would have it, the meeting took place just three weeks after the devastating Indian Ocean tsunami that took the lives of 225,000 people. Some journalists referred to the gathering as the "tsunami conference" and (incorrectly) a "global conference on the tsunami catastrophe." One positive outcome of this was higher than expected attendance by representatives of nation states (168) and the world media (562 journalists). As expected, the tsunami assumed a high profile. There were many emotional presentations, and the sobering images of the incoming waves were broadcast at the outset of the technical session (Bisiaux et al., 2005). The majority of media coverage focused on the negotiations leading up to an agreement to create a tsunami early warning system for the Indian Ocean. While this focus on the tsunami is understandable, some commentators from the disasters and development community expressed concern that it might lead to an exclusive concern with early warning and natural hazards. Thus, David Peppiatt, a veteran humanitarian and development worker who was at the helm of the ProVention Consortium, worried that, in the future, DRR policies would be misguided and skewed by the tsunami: "One issue that has been tsunami-driven is the focus on high-impact, low-frequency events, when in fact the high-frequency, low-impact events cause as much, if not more damage over the long term" (IRIN, 2005).

Despite the temporary sense of shared community in the wake of the tsunami, there was one major conflict that briefly split the national states in attendance. This pertained to the issue of global climate change and disaster vulnerability. Not surprisingly, the United States opposed inclusion in the *Framework* of any reference to a link between disasters and climate change. In an interview with a French newswire, Mark Lagon, a State Department official, said that the United States believed climate change was "a well-known controversy" and that there were other, more appropriate venues in which to discuss it (Agence France Press, 2005). Pressing for official acknowledgment of the role of climate change as a major contributing factor to the increasing number of natural disasters were the EU and small island developing countries. In the end, Marco Ferrari, the Chair of the Main Committee, was able to broker a compromise that acknowledged both climate change and variability across nations (Bisiaux et al., 2005). The agreed-upon wording stipulated that regional and international organizations and other actors agree to

> Promote the integration of risk reduction associated with existing climate variability and future climate change into strategies for the reduction of disaster risk and adaptation to climate change, which would include the clear identification of climate-related disaster risks, the design of specific risk reduction measures and an improved and routine use of climate risk information by planners, engineers and other decision-makers.

Despite the spotlight on the tsunami, the delegates did more or less manage to address the official agenda that had been under preparation for many months. In a nutshell, the message of the conference was that the substantial

> **Box 4.1 Hyogo Framework for Action 2005–2015: Priorities for Action**
>
> 1. Ensure that disaster risk reduction is a national and a local priority with a strong institutional basis for implementation.
> 2. Identify, assess and monitor disaster risks and enhance early warning.
> 3. Use knowledge, innovation and education to build a culture of safety and resilience at all levels.
> 4. Reduce the underlying risk factors.
> 5. Strengthen disaster preparedness for effective response at all levels.

reduction of disaster losses must assume the highest priority. Doing so requires the full commitment of all actors concerned, including governments, regional and international organizations, civil society, the private sector, and the scientific community. In the official declaration, the *Hyogo Framework for Action 2005–2015*, the conference adopted five priorities (see box 4.1). Broadly, the *Framework* stressed the centrality of integrating disaster risk reduction into sustainable development, recommending that "a 'culture of prevention and resilience' must be fostered . . . between disaster reduction, sustainable development and poverty reduction" (*Media Monitoring Report*, 2005: 3).

As had been the case in Yokohama a decade earlier, some delegates, especially those who worked in the civil society sector, went home disappointed. Writing in the *Earth Negotiations Bulletin*, an online reporting service operated by the International Institute for Sustainable Development (IISD), Alice Bisiaux and her team noted, "The main criticism leveled by participants at the negotiated document is the absence of clear donor commitments and time-bound targets. Indeed, even the reference to halving the number of lives lost through water-related disasters by 2015 was relegated to a footnote" (Bisiaux et al., 2005). Jan Egeland, the UN Under-Secretary, was outspoken on the issue of underfunding. Expanding on prior criticism of "stingy nations," Egeland called to account newly wealthy countries including the Gulf States. "The contribution of many relatively well-off countries," he said, was "very, very low" (Pilling, 2005).

More broadly, critics complained that the *Framework* hit all the right notes in terms of general principles, but provided few specifics. While acknowledging that the Kobe conference was a step forward, nonetheless, Peter Walker, Director of the Feinstein International Famine Center at Tufts University in Boston, noted, "The [final] report alludes to the possibility of targets, but does not set them" (IRIN, 2005). In an interview with the Reuters wire service, John Sparrow, an East Asian official at the International Federation of Red Cross and Red Crescent Societies, drove home this point, "Some of the terminology in key passages [of the draft copy of the *Framework*] would appear to be so vague it's difficult to see what it means other than being rhetoric" (Lies, 2005).

Once the political heavyweights returned home, it was once again left up to the International Strategy for Disaster Risk Reduction to implement the recommendations of the *Hyogo Framework*. One organizational reform designed to give the ISDR greater clout was the abolition (in 2008) of the Director position in the Secretariat, and its replacement by an Assistant Secretary-General who is concurrently the Special Representative of the UN Secretary-General for the implementation of the Framework. Another measure designed to broaden stakeholder participation was to convene the Global Platform for Disaster Risk Reduction[9] as a successor to the IATF/DR.

By the end of its first decade, the budget and staff of the Secretariat had both increased substantially. Annual expenditures grew from approximately US$4 million in 2000–1 to US$67.9 million in 2010–11, while staffing rose from 20 in 2000 to around 100 in 2009 (Audit Report, 2010: 5, 12). As impressive as this seems, the Secretariat remains quite small in comparison to other UN units. While the Secretariat continues to be funded exclusively through the Trust Fund for the International Strategy for Disaster Reduction (DXA), it now administers two other ISDR funds for activities relating to contingency planning and an early warning mechanism, the "Sasakawa Disaster Prevention Award Endowment Fund" and the "Trust Fund for Tsunami Disaster Relief."

Despite improved access to resources, the ISDR has continued to draw criticism. In July 2010, the UN Office of Internal Oversight Services released an Audit Report on the governance and structure of the Secretariat. The report is written in the arcane language of the United Nations bureaucracy, but several points stand out. First, disaster risk reduction is an orphan activity, not specifically described in the UN resolution creating the Humanitarian Assistance Programme (#22), although it falls within its purview. Additionally, there is only passing reference to the work of the ISDR Secretariat in contributing to the implementing of sustainable development goals within the United Nations. Second, the ISDR Secretariat has only made limited efforts to establish partnerships with the private sector to coordinate risk reduction efforts and investment (p. 10).

More recently, the UK Department for International Development (DFID) ranked the ISDR next to last among 43 agencies in its 2011 Multilateral Aid Review (MAR) (DFID, 2011), a result deemed so poor that all core funding was withdrawn.[10] DFID pointed to failings in past evaluations that still stubbornly remained by 2010. Under the heading "Contribution to UK Development Objectives," the reviewers declared, "UNISDR has not demonstrated sufficient leadership or ability to coordinate global efforts on DRR, despite a strong mandate for these roles." Under "Organizational Strengths," the Review detected that "the middle is missing." This means that the UNISDR "has no clear line of sight from its mandate to a strategy, to an implementation plan, resulting in a lack of strategic direction." The likelihood of positive change, it judged, was "uncertain."

Writing in *AlertNet*, a humanitarian news website run by Thomson Reuters Foundation, Tom Mitchell (2011) felt that these criticisms were rather unfair, insofar as ISDR is a coordinating body, rather than an agency that directly distributes aid. As such, it is at a distinct disadvantage when it comes to providing hard figures on services provided such as the number of people fed or vaccinations given. Alas, "a coordinating agency is just not sexy enough in an era of 'results,'" and axing ISDR was likely to unleash less political fallout than would occur if funding for larger and better known organizations were to be cut off.

Conclusion

In the 1980s and 1990s, an erstwhile epistemic community formed among natural hazards researchers in the geological, meteorological, and engineering sciences, with the goal of creating "a safer world." In part this reflected a shared perception that the magnitude and severity of damage caused by natural disasters was sharply on the rise. This initiative occurred within the context of the global expansion of international governance, scientific communications channels, and applied research networks during the Cold War and its aftermath. The center of gravity of this community was to be found within the discipline of earthquake engineering, most notably in the United States and Japan. Two policy entrepreneurs, Frank Press and George Housner, were especially influential. Press's call at the World Congress of Earthquake Engineering in 1984 for the establishment of an International Decade of Natural Hazard Reduction (IDNHR) struck a chord within that discipline.

After some initial difficulty getting out of the gate, the United Nations came to the rescue, and in 1989 the General Assembly declared the 1990s to be the International Decade of Natural Disaster Reduction (IDNDR). The involvement of the United Nations was a mixed blessing. On the one hand, it brought instant recognition and a global platform for the dissemination of information. On the other hand, the United Nations disaster operation tended to stand apart from the NGO relief network discussed in the previous chapter. As a result, the IDNDR was regarded by many at the time as being somewhat of a failure in building recognition for disaster risk reduction in practice.

The late twentieth and early twenty-first centuries saw the creation of a rolling cast of UN disaster management agencies and conferences: the Yokohama Conference (1994), the International Strategy for Disaster Reduction (created in 2000), the Hyogo Conference (2005). A growing consensus finally emerged in favor of disaster prevention rather than disaster relief alone. At the same time, there were continuing debates over the essence of disaster vulnerability (physical vs. socioeconomic); and about the nature of the relationship between disaster reduction, sustainable development, and poverty reduction.

Further Reading

I. Christoplos, A. Liljelund, and J. Mitchell (2001) Re-framing risk: the changing context of disaster mitigation and preparedness. *Disasters*, 25, 185–98.

Clark Miller and Paul N. Edwards (eds.) (2001) *Changing the Atmosphere: Expert Knowledge and Environmental Governance*. The MIT Press, Cambridge, MA.

CHAPTER FIVE

Climate of Concern

At the inaugural World Conference on Natural Disaster Reduction in Yokohama, Japan, in 1994, the topic of global climate change barely registered on the collective radar. Indeed, until relatively recently, climate was thought to be predominantly stable, with extreme events being no more than normal variations within the existing climatic spectrum (Oliver, 1977: 3).

Starting in the 1970s, climatologists had begun to warn of a significant and protracted shift in climate, although this was initially predicted to take the form of colder weather. One of the first in the global policy community of natural disasters to pick up on this was Munich Re. In a 1973 brochure entitled *Flood/Inundation*, Munich Re warned that the insurance industry faced the prospect of growing losses due to rising temperatures. Four years later, *Climatic Change*, an interdisciplinary journal that features research on the description, causes, and implications of climate change, was launched, with Stephen Schneider of the (US) National Center for Atmospheric Research as editor. Just short of two decades later, this link between climate change and natural disasters has become both widely attributed and fiercely debated.

Climate change is said to impact disaster risk in two ways (Schipper and Pelling, 2006: 19). In the short run, climate change is accused of triggering an increase in the range and frequency of extreme weather-related events, notably severe flooding and storms, but also possibly cyclones, hurricanes, and heat waves. The evidence for this is by no means ironclad,[1] but it is frequently cited as a powerful set of "grounds" for taking action.

A second way in which climate change is said to affect disaster risk pertains to longer-term variability. For example, by altering global weather patterns, climate change is expected to provoke changes in agriculture and food production, with especially serious consequences for the economies of Southern nations. In the tropics, most agriculture is in rain-fed systems, and crops have a narrow threshold for success. Production is therefore threatened by long-term, slowly changing rates of precipitation, as well as by extreme climate events that occur over a short time span (Lin et al., 2008: 847).

On a policy level, the climate change/disaster risk nexus has grabbed a higher profile in three major "realms of action" – the climate change agenda, international development policy, and disaster risk management (Schipper and Pelling, 2006). At the World Bank, development and climate change are increasingly being treated as "interlinked challenges." In the first part of the fiscal year 2011, more than 80 percent of its country assistance or partnership strategies with developing countries substantially addressed climate change issues. In a news report on its website, the Bank spells out its rationale for going in this direction:

> The jury is in on climate change and it is clear that it is the poorest and most vulnerable countries that will suffer most from its impacts – increased drought and flooding, sea level rise and dysfunctional and unpredictable weather patterns ("Developing countries ratcheting up action on climate change," 2011).

At the World Bank, the main hub and catalyst to promote the integration of disaster risk management, climate adaptation, and its own development efforts is the Global Facility for Disaster Reduction and Recovery (GFDRR). According to the GFDRR, disaster risk reduction is the first line of defense in adapting to climate change. Accordingly, it recommends an integrated approach to disaster risk reduction (DRR) and climate change adaptation (CCA), and urges Bank clients to address these risks in developing countries.

In the humanitarian relief community, climate change is not an everyday priority for workers in the field. Nonetheless, some key agencies have endorsed the convergence of DRR and climate change adaptation. The Red Cross/Red Crescent established a designated Centre on Climate Change and Disaster Preparedness in 2002, and tasked it with integrating climate information into disaster risk management and health programs. Also note the release by Tearfund, an influential UK-based Christian evangelical relief and development agency, of a paper, "Linking Climate Change Adaptation and Disaster Reduction" written by Richard Weaver, senior policy adviser at the charity (see Weaver, 2009).

In the disaster risk reduction community, climate change has regularly surfaced as a high profile topic at conferences, policy forums, and workshops. This is usually grounded by reference to the Hyogo Framework for Action (2005). As we saw in the previous chapter, the final version of the climate change clause was watered down somewhat from the draft version, but nonetheless it specified that DRR strategies should take into account clearly identified climate-related disaster risks and climate risk information supplied by planners, engineers, and other decision-makers.

Constructing the Climate Change/Disaster Risk Nexus as a Global Problem

Building on Best's (1987) approach to the social construction of social problems, I suggest that the discursive shape of environmental issues can be unraveled through focusing on the "rhetoric of claims-making" (Hannigan,

2006). Rhetoric, as it is employed here, involves the deliberate use of language in order to persuade. This does not mean that the putative environmental issue/problem is necessarily phony: both valid claims and invalid claims need to be defined, legitimated, and marketed. Rhetorical statements contain three principal components or categories of statements: grounds, warrants, and conclusions.

Grounds: Disasters by the Numbers

Grounds (data) furnish the basic facts that shape the ensuing policymaking discourse. One frequently employed category of grounds statements depends on the use of *numeric estimates*. By establishing the magnitude of the problem, claims-makers establish its importance, its potential for growth, and its range (Hannigan, 2006: 64).

In validating the importance of the DRR–climate change nexus, the rhetorical use of numeric estimates has been of crucial importance. As we saw in chapter 4, those scientists whose efforts led to the creation of the International Decade for Natural Disaster Reduction routinely cited a score of recently occurring natural disasters around the globe, followed by the claim that the fatalities, property damage, and disruption resulting from such events were steadily on the rise. Today, researchers and policymakers who embrace the convergence of DRR and climate change adaptation insist that global levels of disaster risk have continued to spike, and greenhouse gases are likely to be deeply implicated.

Weather-related events (floods, cyclones, hurricanes) qualify as the most frequent and prominent natural hazards. The prima facie evidence here is the database assembled by CRED (Centre for Research on the Epidemiology of Disasters) at the University of Louvain, Belgium.[2] These figures reveal that weather-related disasters affect the greatest number of people globally, as well as causing the largest amount of property damage.[3] They are not responsible for the greatest loss of human life – seismic events are – but this is largely attributable to a handful of monster earthquakes that kill hundreds of thousands of people. Crucially, weather-related hazards are said to be far more sensitive to global climatic changes associated with greenhouse gas emissions than are geological ones. This narrative has been widely disseminated both within and beyond the disaster community.

Numerical data of this type were deployed a decade ago in a synthesis paper "outlining the issues and latest scientific conclusions about climate change and severe weather events" prepared by Canadian scientists James Bruce[4] and Ian Burton,[5] both strong advocates of the human-induced global warming thesis. Employing the CRED data and statistics supplied by Munich Re and Swiss Re, Bruce and Burton note that climate-related disaster losses were increasing many times more rapidly than were those from earthquakes. After briefly considering and rejecting the possibility that there could well be a greater rate of economic development in areas affected by floods and storms than those affected by earthquakes, the authors conclude that weather-related hazards are decisively outstripping earthquakes in their frequency and severity (Bruce et al., 1999). Bruce et al. do not directly indict climate change as the perpetrator, although this is implied.

Very much the same message infused a 2007 Reuters news item that prominently cites Dame Barbara Stocking, Chief Executive of Oxfam GB:

> This year we have seen floods in South Asia, across the breadth of Africa and Mexico that have affected more than 250 million people. This is no freak year. It follows a pattern of more frequent, more erratic, more unpredictable and more extreme weather events that are affecting more people. The number of people affected by disasters has risen by 68 percent, from an average of 174 million a year between 1985 and 1994 to 254 million a year between 1995 and 2004. Action is needed now to prepare for more disasters otherwise humanitarian assistance will be overwhelmed and recent advances in human development will go into reverse (Sinnott, 2007).

Time's Bitter Flood   Four years later, Oxfam released a research report entitled *Time's Bitter Flood: Trends in the Number of Reported Natural Disasters* (Jennings, 2011) based on research by economists Fabian Barthel and Victoria Johnson and written by Oxfam staffer Steve Jennings. Like Bruce and Burton a dozen years earlier, Jennings and his team rely on data from two key sources: the Emergency Events Database (EM-DAT) at CRED in Belgium, supplemented by the independent Munich Re NatCatSERVICE database, which is based on insurance claims, mostly from developed countries. Neither of these is flawless; however, the researchers explain in some detail the measures that they took in order to minimize bias.

Time's Bitter Flood reports an upward trend in the number of reported disasters,[6] chiefly driven by a steep rise in floods from all regions, and, to a lesser extent, storms in Africa and America. An exception here is geophysical events (earthquakes, volcanoes, landslides) and droughts, which have remained relatively stable over time. Changes in population do not fully explain the rising number of floods, nor do differing methods of recording disasters. While Jennings acknowledges that it was not possible to directly analyze the effect of climate change on disaster trends, he allows that this possibility cannot be excluded.

Keep in mind that, in less than a decade, this practice of using a reported upward trend in storms and floods as grounds for linking natural disasters and climate change has migrated from the science-based hazards research community to the much more extensive charity/development sector. More recently, some environmental activists and journalists have followed suit, but, alas, without following the disciplined methodological caution of Oxfam.

In an article entitled "What should we make of all these natural disasters?" written for the *Washington Post*, and circulated widely in the blogosphere, best-selling environmental author and activist Bill McKibben[7] injects a strong measure of irony to suggest a causal link between climate change and a bevy of recent disasters: a killer tornado in Joplin, Missouri, wildfires in Texas, Oklahoma, and New Mexico, unprecedented mega-floods in Australia, New Zealand, and Pakistan:

> It's very important to stay calm. If you got upset about any of this, you might forget how important it is not to disrupt the record profits of our fossil fuel companies. If worst did ever come to worst, it's reassuring to remember what the U.S. Chamber of Commerce told the Environmental Protection Agency in a recent filing: that there's no need to worry because "populations can acclimatize to warmer climates via a range of behavioral, physiological, and technological adaptations." I'm pretty sure that's what residents are telling themselves in Joplin today (McKibben, 2011).

Three weeks after McKibben's piece appeared, environment editor John Vidal published a similarly themed article in the online version of the British newspaper, *The Guardian*. After enumerating a long list of recent extreme weather events – a spring drought followed by massive storms and flash floods in Germany and France; flooding in Queensland, Australia that has been described as the country's "worst natural disaster;" a "once-in-a-100-years" drought in southern and central regions of China; and, of course, the Joplin, Missouri tornado – Vidal cites the Oxfam report, *Time's Bitter Flood*, and its author Steve Jennings. These environmental disasters now striking the world are signs of "global weirding," American climate scientist and frequent media contributor Katharine Hayhoe says; and, according to William Chameides, an atmospheric scientist at Duke University, they "are consistent with climate change" (Vidal, 2011).

Note, however, that the science is scarcely settled. In a recent article in the journal *Climatic Change*, Fabian Barthel and collaborator Eric Neumayer analyze trends in *normalized insurance damage*. By normalization they mean making an adjustment "for the fact that a disaster of equal strength will typically cause more damage in the current period than in the past because there is typically a greater value of assets at risk in the present compared to the past" (Barthel and Neumayer, 2012: 2). While insured losses are not interchangeable with total economic losses, they can be estimated with greater precision. Indeed, total economic losses are often calculated by multiplying insured loss.

With financial support from the Munich Re program "Evaluating the Economics of Climate Risks & Opportunities in the Insurance Sector" at LSE, Barthel and Neumayer analyzed trends in normalized insured damage at the global level over the period 1990 to 2008, over the period 1980 to 2008 for West Germany, and 1973 to 2008 for the United States. They found *no significant trends at the global level*, but detected some significant upward trends in normalized insured losses in the United States and Germany for non-geophysical disasters and some disaster sub-types (e.g. flash floods, tornadoes, winter storms). In the latter case, Barthel and Neumayer caution that one needs to be careful in attributing such a trend to climate change caused by greenhouse gas emissions caused by human activities, "Our findings reported in this article could be down to natural climate variability that has nothing to do with anthropogenic climate change" (Barthel and Neumayer, 2012: 21).

Natural Disaster "Hotspots" In 2001, the World Bank's Disaster Management Facility (DMF), now rebranded as its Hazard Management Unit (HMU), initiated discussions with the newly established Center for Hazards and Risk Research (CHRR) at Columbia University to consider the possibility of undertaking a global-scale, multi-hazard risk analysis focused on identifying key "hotspots" where the risks of natural disasters are particularly high. In keeping with its mandate, the Bank spelled out that the project "would aim to provide information and methods to inform priorities for reducing disaster risk and making decisions on development investment." Four years later, the project having come together, the HMU released a monograph on this research as part of its "Disaster Risk Management Series" under the title *Natural Disaster Hotspots: A Global Analysis* (Dilley et al., 2005).

By a natural disaster *hotspot*, the authors mean "a specific area or region that may be at relatively high risk of adverse impacts from one or more natural hazard events" (p. 24). The phrase packs a powerful rhetorical punch, insomuch as it evokes images of crisis and dread: predictions of global heating come true; "tropical" nations beset by pandemics and disease where killer viruses and the diseases of the future are percolating (Minkel, 2008). In this it joins the list of terms – "belt of pain," "rim of fire," "typhoon alley" – that are often used by the media and science to define and sensationalize certain regions as faraway places where disasters are commonplace (Bankoff, 2001: 24). In their report, the World Bank researchers assess the risks of two disaster-related outcomes: mortality and economic losses. The prime source of their data is the EM-DAT dataset maintained by CRED in Brussels, which they describe as being "the most comprehensive, publicly available global database on natural hazards and their impacts."

In *Natural Disaster Hotspots*, the World Bank researchers identify three main types of hazards: geophysical (volcanoes, earthquakes), hydro-meteorological (floods, cyclones), and drought-related. They are especially interested in those geographic regions that are exposed to more than one type of hazard. Nearly 800 million people or 13 percent of the world population, they calculate, live in grid cells that have relatively high exposure to two or more hazards (Dilley et al., 2005: 48). Areas subject to *both* geophysical and hydro-meteorologically-driven hazards are situated primarily in East and South Asia, Central America, and western South America. Many of these areas, the authors point out, are also more densely populated and developed than average, leading to a high potential for casualties and economic losses. By their calculations, the most dangerous places to live on the planet are Guatemala (5 hazards, with 40.8%

of the population exposed), Philippines (5, 36.4%), Ecuador (5, 23.9%), Taiwan (4, 73.1%), Chile (4, 54.0%), Costa Rica (4, 41.1%), and Japan (4, 15.3%).

Furthermore, these areas are especially vulnerable to the interactions between different hazards, for example, landslides triggered by cyclones and flooding; or earthquakes that damage dams and reservoirs needed for drought and flood protection (Dilley et al., 2005: 2). Of course, the most dramatic recent example of this is the monster tsunami that not only caused unprecedented destruction along the northern coast of Japan, but also provoked a disaster at a nuclear plant. This provides a powerful rationale for concern over global climate change, insomuch as extreme weather events are said to pack a kind of "double whammy," not only causing destruction on their own, but also triggering secondary disaster events.

Warrants: Is Climate Change a Development Emergency or a Social Justice Issue?

By establishing "grounds," we set the boundaries or domain of the problem/issue and give it an orientation; that is, a guide as to how to interpret it (Hannigan, 2006). However, it is further necessary to explain why it is vital and necessary that we take action. This is the task of warrants. In making the case for engaging in climate change adaptation/disaster risk reduction, there are several types of warrants. These are not mutually exclusive, but the emphasis and related course of action differ significantly.

In the first warrant package, climate change and its kit bag of nasty tricks are indicted first and foremost for undermining global efforts towards achieving sustainable development and poverty eradication. This theme was quite prominent at the 2008 Oslo Policy Forum on "Changing the Way We Develop: Dealing with Disasters and Climate Change." In his opening remarks, Jonas Gahr, Norway's Minister of Foreign Affairs, declared that climate change is leading to a "development emergency." Next on the program was the keynote address by Jeffrey Sachs, a decidedly high profile speaker. Sachs directed the UN Millennium Project, an independent advisory body created to advise Secretary-General Kofi Annan on the progress since 2000 in achieving the Millennium Development Goals (MDGs). In his Oslo talk, Sachs notes that climate change lies at the core of the global economy. Unless climate change mitigation and economic development are combined, existing financial commitments made by Northern countries to those in the South will falter, and the MDGs will not be achieved. Conflict and security are also part of the equation. If large regions of the planet become uninhabitable, mass migration will be triggered and development chaos will ensue.

In the first discussion session at Oslo, several of the panelists reported a widespread perception in the South that climate change "is being used as an argument to renege on commitments to the MDGs and divert resources that have been committed to poverty alleviation" (Christoplos, 2008: 7). Disaster risk reduction, they noted, suffers from a perception that it is primarily a humanitarian aid issue dressed in a different set of clothes. However, they allowed that the language of risk reduction could be highly relevant if it were to be employed as a bridge between climate change and development concerns.

In a second bundle of warrants, climate change is depicted as magnifying the already uneven global distribution of risk. In particular, poor communities that are currently especially vulnerable to damage and loss of life from flooding and certain types of tropical storms will become even more so under conditions of global warming. It then becomes primarily a matter of social justice and environmental equity. This holds true for both rural and urban settlements. In the former case, changes in climate may lead to greater water stress and lower agricultural productivity, as well as widespread disease; while, in cities such as Dhaka, Mumbai, and Shanghai that lie only 1–5 meters above sea level, informal settlements housing squatters and other poor inhabitants will be deluged (*Risk and Poverty in a Changing Climate*, 2009: 16).

Unlike with the first set of warrants, climate change adaptation/disaster risk reduction is more than just a strategic bridge between climate change and development. Rather, it has the potential to really make a practical difference at a grassroots level. For natural scientists and civil engineers, this translates into coming up with improved climate monitoring and early warning systems, as well as undertaking structural measures such as flood embankments, community shelters, and more resistant buildings and infrastructure (Thomalla et al., 2006: 41, 44). For DRR advocates who stress the central importance of reducing socioeconomic vulnerabilities, it means understanding the complex mix of factors that shape the vulnerability of a community and then designing policies that might reduce vulnerability and facilitate adaptation. A classic example of this is Kelly and Adger's (2000) field research in coastal Vietnam (box 5.1). Put succinctly, the "imperative for urgent action" (*Risk and Poverty in a Changing Climate*, 2009: 18) refers to the opportunity to counter disaster impacts and poverty outcomes through practical and sustainable intervention.

Conclusions: Risk Reduction, Climate Adaptation, or Both Combined?

Conclusions, the third component of rhetorical construction, spell out the specific action that is needed to alleviate or eradicate an environmental problem (Hannigan, 2006). In the case of climate change and disaster, these actions aren't entirely hypothetical, insomuch as numerous initiatives are currently up and running, primarily at a local level.

Climate Change Adaptation   According to the Intergovernmental Panel on Climate Change (IPCC), climate change adaptation is defined as, "*an adjust-*

Box 5.1 Miraculous mangroves

Traditionally, mangrove forests have played an important role in coastal Vietnam. First and foremost, they provide storm protection in a region susceptible to being battered by frequent tropical cyclones or typhoons. As the world learned after the 2004 Indian Ocean tsunami, mangrove swamps provide a buffer zone for storm surges that would otherwise roll directly onto settled areas. Additionally, they protect against wave action by creating a physical barrier and stabilizing the sea floor. Less well known are some of the other benefits of the mangrove ecosystem: staple food plants, fertile grazing land, protected nurseries for coastal and offshore fisheries, breeding grounds for numerous birds, fuel from peat (Kelly and Adger, 2000: 342).

In recent years the mangrove forests have come under threat in some districts along coastal northern Vietnam. What is provoking this is *doi moi* (new change or renovation), a process of economic growth that has involved the privatization of state-owned businesses and changes in property rights in the agricultural sector. In Quang Ninh Province, wetlands with a significant proportion of mangroves are being converted for use in agriculture and aquaculture. Ownership, previously invested in state-managed cooperatives or under common property rights, is being systematically privatized.

Kelly and Adger (2000), who carried out three case studies in the Red River Delta in the mid and late 1990s, found that these changes were shifting patterns of both physical and social vulnerability. Not only was coastal vulnerability to cyclones magnified, it was the poorer sections of the community that stood to suffer most. For example, the resources available for sea dyke maintenance have been diverted to other projects such as road building; and certain meteorological forecasts, previously provided for free, are being invoiced. Poorer households, who rely more on the mangrove for their livelihood, suffer disproportionately from the enclosure and conversion to other agricultural uses of mangrove forests.

Kelly and Adger's field research in coastal Vietnam holds some wider implications for disaster risk reduction. On one level, it sends a signal that the underlying causes of social vulnerability must be included when looking at the longer-term threat of global climate change, as well as in short-term events such as tropical cyclones. Furthermore, it provides a cogent illustration of the blind spot of national or regional economic development schemes. While *doi moi* may well increase the overall wealth of a district, this is unlikely to trickle down to individual families and homes. This buttresses Kates' observation that "The interests of the poor are not always the same as the interests of poor countries, since in the interest of 'development,' the poor may grow poorer" (Kates, 2000: 16).

ment in natural or human systems in response to actual or expected climate stimuli or their effects, which moderates harm or exploits benefit opportunities" (IPCC, 2007). It is one of the five pillars of the "Bali Action Plan," the framework worked out in advance of the 2009 Copenhagen Conference.

Within the UNFCCC, those who promote the importance of adaptation have struggled to keep it from being overshadowed by mitigation, which in the climate change context means the reduction of greenhouse gas emissions. Schipper (2006, 2009) describes this as constituting a "dual policy path," wherein adaptation has been relegated to a secondary role. Roger Pielke, Jr. (1998) offers four reasons why the climate change community has discouraged consideration of adaptation responses. First, there is a widespread perception that engaging in a discussion of adaptation could create the impression of being soft on mitigation, and perhaps even being "anti-environmental." Related to this is the perception that embracing adaptation is paramount to throwing in the towel when it comes to mitigation. In other words, it constitutes passive acceptance or fatalism. Third, there is the difficulty of incorporating adaptation measures into the international negotiation process. Mitigation measures, by contrast, are numerically expressed, thus permitting compromises and trade-offs. A final reason is the perception that it is impossible to rationally plan adaptation responses if you do not know with any degree of confidence what future climate impacts will be. This is especially so because global circulation and integrated assessment models do not have the capacity to accurately predict climate impacts at regional or local scales (Pielke, Jr., 1998: 167).

Note, however, that Pielke's article was written in the late 1990s when prospects for an international-level agreement on mitigation initiatives seemed brighter than they do today. In the aftermath of the collapse of negotiations at the 2009 (Copenhagen) UNFCCC climate conference designed to renew or replace the Kyoto Protocol (and the adoption of a vague and toothless compromise two years later at Durban), adaptation has suddenly become a more politically attractive option.

The Hartwell Paper   One indicator of this is the generally positive reception given to the "Hartwell Paper." In February 2010, 14 prominent natural and social scientists from Asia, Europe, and North America met at Hartwell House, a country house in Buckinghamshire, not too far from Oxford, to discuss the perceived failure of existing approaches to climate change. Professors Steve Rayner of the University of Oxford, and Gwyn Prins from the London School of Economics and Political Science, both policy insiders in the UK, convened the meeting and co-authored the subsequent discussion paper. Among the 12 "wise men and women" gathered there were geographer Mike Hulme of the University of East Anglia, author of the widely reviewed book *Why We Disagree about Climate Change*, and Roger Pielke, Jr. himself. The "Hartwellites," as *The Economist* branded them, express grave doubt that top-down regulated carbon reduction schemes such as those considered in Copenhagen can ever be made compelling. Instead, they recommend an alternative approach that treats decarbonization as a clean energy issue, the centerpiece of which is public subsidies for the development of new energy technologies.

Furthermore, the authors stress the importance of making sure that the capacity to adapt to climate change is treated as seriously as the need to avoid it in the first place, rather than as some sort of admission of defeat ("Oblique strategies," *The Economist*, May 11, 2010). As the Hartwell scholars explain it:

> Adaptation and mitigation are not trade-offs, but complementary strategies. The category of the risks best managed by adaptation is certainly much larger than that assumed under the "Kyoto" approach, which (falsely) presented adaptation as a cost of failed mitigation, and thus something to be avoided. Since the Kyoto road effectively ended in Copenhagen, it is time to activate adaptation strategies with much greater vigour. Adaptation is significantly a development challenge (Prins et al., 2010: 15).

Nature of Climate Change Adaptation   Pelling (2011: 13, 20–1) characterizes adaptation as rather a "slippery" concept, deceptively simple at a theoretical level, but quite complex empirically where it necessarily must take into account the interactions among individuals, communities, economic sectors, and nations. For some, it is a narrowly defined technical term, for others, it represents an entire field, similar in content to sustainable development. One recurrent blind spot here involves matters of scale. For example, a family in Barbados may benefit from living in a hurricane-proof house (Pelling labels this "low micro-vulnerability") but, nevertheless, will be paralyzed financially by the flight of tourist dollars in the wake of a devastating tropical storm. This can be especially problematic because the Barbadian economy is not very diverse (low macro-adaptive capacity). Vulnerability and adaptive capacity at one scale "can have profound and sometimes hidden implications for other scales" (Pelling, 2011: 21).

As an intellectual construct, adaptation cannot be directly observed, especially when it is treated as a forward-looking attribute whose impacts have not yet happened. This is not well understood by international and national policymakers. As Pelling observes, they prefer to seek a clear measurement of the impacts and adaptation associated with climate change. In addition, policymakers are normally reluctant to recognize that climate change must be contextualized with a host of other social, political, and economic factors. For example, an economic analysis of the farming sector of a country, an approach compatible with climate modeling, would likely exclude any consideration of the social processes driving and limiting adaptive decision making such as markets and regulatory regimes (Pelling, 2011: 14).

David Etkin and his colleagues at York University (Canada) argue that CCA and DRR frame risk reduction in very different ways. Risk management (RM) discourse is currently the dominant approach in DRR studies. RM is "a systematic approach to managing risk based upon rational decision-making; it includes identifying and analyzing hazard, exposure and consequences, and determines which combinations of management strategies yield optimal outcomes" (Etkin et al., 2011: 4). By contrast, CCA favors a precautionary principle (PP) discourse, which states that the "burden of proof lies with those whose actions may cause severe harm, in the absence of a scientific consensus that the harm would not occur." While Etkin and his team concede that each approach has its relative merits, they foresee that PP discourse could clash with current DRR measures and institutions, if climate change adaptation and disaster risk management were to converge. For example, in the context of urban flooding, an RM approach might favor the economic development of new areas where the current risk is low, whereas PP would likely recommend creating parkland on the assumption that the land faces the threat of severe flooding decades down the road.

One underappreciated, but really important, issue pertaining to adaptation and disasters has to do with climate variability. Long before the IPCC Assessment Reports declared that the Earth could face catastrophic collapse brought on by a significant rise in our planet's surface temperature, and driven by greenhouse gas emissions, extreme weather events were known and expected. Partly this is attributable to single events, for example volcanic eruptions, partly to anomalies. Nevertheless, the mandate of the UNFCCC includes only incremental, anthropogenic (human created) climate change, not natural climate variability (Schipper and Pelling, 2006: 29). It may even be the case that the impact of human-induced climate change on natural resources in some cases might not be as significant as that of natural climate variability (Hulme et al., 1999; cited in Schipper and Pelling, 2006: 29). This being so, then the obvious question is whether it makes any sense to distinguish between adaptation/disaster reduction undertaken for flooding and storms attributable to natural variability, as against those attributable exclusively to climate change, if indeed this is even possible. After all, villagers on the brink of being rendered homeless by torrential rains really don't care much what the proportion of blame might be. This assumes, of course, that disasters provoked by climate change will not demand extraordinary adaptive measures, as compared to those required by "normal" disasters.

Is Convergence Possible?

In a recent article in the *Journal of International Development*, Jessica Mercer (2010) sums up the current prospects for closer collaboration between climate change adaptation and disaster risk reduction:

> A number of researchers, policy makers and practitioners have recently discussed and critiqued similarities and differences between DRR and CCA. Some advocate for increased convergence, whilst recognizing existing differences between the DRR and CCA agendas . . . Others outline the need to embed CCA within DRR, making it one factor amongst many, which should be considered in reducing community vulnerability (Mercer, 2010: 249).

Some of those who have commented on this issue have recommended constructing a bridge between climate change adaptation and disaster risk reduction. For example, Frank Thomalla and his colleagues at the Stockholm Environmental Institute detect quite a bit of common ground. Both policy research networks employ a kit of analytical tools and methodologies based on risk management approaches. For both, poverty reduction is an essential component of reducing vulnerability to natural hazards and climate change. Finally, each appears committed to remedying its prime deficiency: the disaster risk management network is increasingly adopting a more anticipatory and forward-looking approach, while climate change adaptation is more focused on working to improve governance and participation at the local level (Thomalla et al., 2006). While noting that a number of recent key studies have observed a lack of coordination and communication between the adaptation and disaster risk communities, nevertheless, Tearfund concludes that both have similar aims and mutual benefits and "there is a very strong rationale for adopting a more integrated approach to these issues" (Weaver, 2009: 4).

At the Stockholm Forum for Integrating Disaster Relief and Recovery in October 2007, the delegates adopted a systematic plan of action for integrating risk and climate change impacts in poverty reduction. The Stockholm plan calls for action in five priority areas:

1. enhanced institutional and policy coordination at the level of individual countries, regions, and global institutions on disaster risk reduction and climate change;
2. identification and measurement of risks due to disasters and climate change;
3. integration of disaster and climate change into national planning processes, including the poverty reduction strategy process in each country;
4. factoring disaster risk reduction and climate change adaptation in key sectors (agriculture, energy, health, urban resources, urban development, forestry, environment); and
5. capacity building at local, national, regional, and global levels (Stockholm Plan of Action, 2007).

According to the Global Facility for Disaster Reduction and Recovery (GFDRR), there have been many identifiable points of progress in addressing these priorities, at least as far as their own efforts are concerned.

Yet, many problems still remain. Schipper detects sharp differences between the two communities of scientists and practitioners: "In actuality the two communities are supported by entirely different sets of institutions, individuals, methodologies and policy frameworks" (Schipper, 2009: 17). This has been highlighted, she points out, by the fact that climate change adaptation "has come onto the scene quite unrelated to much of the ongoing work on disaster risk reduction" (Schipper, 2009: 17). While most of those in the DRR community generally acknowledge climate change as an important challenge, there is also a feeling that it is abstract and difficult to conceptualize, as compared to disasters that are seen as "real" (Schipper, 2009: 24).

Somewhat surprisingly perhaps, O'Brien et al. (2006: 69) argue that climate change adaptation is much closer in nature to humanitarian intervention than it is to disaster risk reduction: "The irony is that planning for climate change impacts to date resembles far more the 'needs assessment and delivery' approach that has evolved in the planning toolbox of humanitarian assistance in conflict and post-conflict situations." In particular, CCA tends toward "top-down" service delivery, while DRR puts more emphasis on "the self-protection efforts made by households and communities themselves, actions based on local knowledge and the activities of the civil society that work on natural and technological hazards from the 'bottom up'" (O'Brien et al., 2006: 67).

One rationale cited by CCA practitioners for shying away from bottom-up methods is that the types and scales of risk posed by global warming render traditional/indigenous knowledge at the local level insufficient for (re)establishing community resilience (Mitchell and van Aalst, 2008: 5). By contrast, scientific knowledge is said to possess greater potential. For its part, DRR is by no means opposed to research; indeed, its networks include quite a few natural and social scientists. However, some DRR specialists are uneasy about the prospect that CCA experts will focus exclusively on longer-term scenarios as suggested by GCM (global climate change) modeling, while failing to acknowledge the social factors behind vulnerability (Mitchell and van Aalst, 2008: 16).

Future Prospects

Perhaps the most detailed and realistic assessment of the prospects for convergence of CCA and DRR is a 2008 review commissioned by the DFID (Department for International Development) in the United Kingdom, primarily for the benefit of its staff members. The authors, Tom Mitchell and Maarten van Aalst, develop a score of detailed recommendations of how DFID can promote convergence of adaptation and DRR. However, a close reading of this document reveals more about the obstacles to convergence than the prospects of its occurring any time soon.

Financing

While disaster risk reduction is broadly acknowledged as being important, insomuch as it represents the first line of defense against climate change, nevertheless, it suffers from serious problems of financing, especially in comparison to climate change adaptation.[8] As discussed in the previous chapter, DRR has been, and continues to be, seriously underfunded since first entering into the UN tent in 1990 in the form of the International Decade for Natural Disaster Reduction. This has carried over to the UN International Strategy for Disaster Reduction.

Compared to adaptation, considerably less money is available for DRR, especially for undertaking field projects. Mitchell and van Aalst (2008: 8) note that many DRR programs are funded from humanitarian budgets and coordinated by humanitarian aid departments. This brings with it a legion of disadvantages. For one thing, it ghettoizes disaster reduction, cutting it off from regular development operations. Some NGO actors consulted in the course of researching the DFID report "expressed concern that the persistence of the close relationship between humanitarian assistance and DRR in terms of its organizational structures is damaging the profile of DRR as a developing issue and is inhibiting the ability of DRR people to communicate effectively with key development and climate change counterparts" (Mitchell and van Aalst, 2008: 13). Furthermore, this sort of financing means that it is more difficult to undertake long-term initiatives, insofar as humanitarian funding is inherently time-restricted. The same holds true for the emergency recovery loans (ERLs) that have been heavily favored by the World Bank. These must be prepared quickly and have limited three-year life spans. By specifying a three-year lending period, ERLs discourage borrowers from undertaking the types of activities that can have the greatest impact on reducing vulnerability[9] such as building code development or revision and the development of insurance mechanisms (IEG-World Bank, 2006: xxi–xxii).

Given its financial difficulties, then, DRR could benefit considerably from easier access to the much greater pool of money available under the climate change adaptation umbrella. Accordingly, O'Brien et al. (2006: 75) suggest that the UNFCCC, which "has greater resources," could share these with the UN/ISDR, especially "resources and mechanisms made available through the Special Climate Change Fund."

Alas, there are some hurdles that must be cleared before this can happen. First and foremost, there is the climate variability issue discussed earlier in this chapter. Donors are not always eager to see money that they wish to be directed to fighting global climate change go towards coping with disasters. Pressure is thus exerted on DRR-oriented actors to manifestly demonstrate *additionality*. On the one hand, DRR actors need to show donors that floods and other extreme hazard events are demonstrably the result of climate change, not just regular climate variation – something that is not always easy to do. At the same time, they feel compelled to segregate a certain portion of the funding to use exclusively for developing and implementing adaptation measures related to changes in climate. As Mitchell and van Aalst (2008: 13) point out, "DRR actors perceive these requirements as ineffective, forcing attention on climate change rather than [on] the most urgent disaster risk."

Not everyone in recipient nations is thrilled about receiving climate loans or about where these loans are being directed. For example, in June 2011, civil society groups in a number of countries[10] that have been chosen as recipients of loans from the World Bank's Pilot Program for Climate Resilience (PPCR) wrote to Andrew Mitchell, UK Secretary of State for International

Development, and Chris Huhne, Secretary of State for Energy and Climate Change, asking that the UK stop providing climate loans for adaptation, and stop pushing for the World Bank to have a role in climate finance. These were not specifically related to disaster reduction. However, given the signatories' demand that the UK pay reparations for "causing" climate change instead of supporting loans, it is unlikely that disaster reduction loans pegged to climate change adaptation would be any more positively received. In one early assessment of how the PPCR funds were allocated in Tajikistan, a landlocked country in Central Asia that has recently been hit with unseasonal rains, rising temperatures, and climate extremes, Oxfam International reported that some of those most vulnerable – smallholder farmers and households headed by women – were not given any say about where the money was to be distributed (Oxfam International, 2011).

Political Resources and Governance

At first glance, DRR seems to be better situated politically than CCA. Under the UNFCCC, disasters are only mentioned within a narrow context – Article 8 says that countries that are most prone to climate change include those in disaster-prone areas (Schipper and Pelling, 2006: 32–3). By contrast, disaster risk reduction is formally guided by an international protocol (Hyogo Agreement) with its own administrative infrastructure (International Strategy for Disaster Reduction), reporting directly to the UN Secretary-General (through the Special Assistant). It has the advantage of being broader in its mandate and not restricted by a legal framework, as is CCA. But appearances can be deceiving. Schipper (2009: 22) points out that the Global Platform on Disaster Risk Reduction "does not carry the same legal weight as the UNFCCC secretariat nor any administrative or technical body of the Kyoto Protocol, and is not associated with the same level of political controversy, media frenzy and global awareness – although this is not a consequence or reflection of its relative importance."

In their review for the DFID, Mitchell and van Aalst (2008: 6) concur. While both agendas (climate change adaptation and disaster risk reduction) lack the political influence to "raise the profile of risk management in mainstream development planning and practice," adaptation is better positioned to do so, since it "now has significantly more political attention and human capacity in the UK than DRR." Additionally, those in the climate change adaptation community are better versed in the language and methods of international negotiation than their DRR counterparts.

Resilience, Transition, and Transformation

Not everyone in the disaster risk reduction community is entirely enthusiastic about the prospects of convergence. This is especially evident among some

DRR academics. While they regularly attend interdisciplinary workshops and conferences, co-author articles and reports with colleagues in environmental and climate change institutes, and even contribute to the IPCC Assessment Reports, nonetheless, they regard climate adaptation, at least that version indigenous to the CCA community, as something of a cop-out. Partly this is because CCA is thought to privilege technologically based solutions (e.g. early warning systems) and humanitarian-style needs assessment. But there is more to it than that. Like humanitarian disaster relief, climate change adaptation, they say, does not demand the deep-seated social and political change that is necessary to combat vulnerability.

In his book, *Adaptation to Climate Change*, Pelling argues that adaptive actions potentially deny the deeper political and cultural roots that call for significant change in social and political relations. He distinguishes among three types of adaptation: resilience, transition, and transformation. Adaptation to build resilience acts at the most contained level. It seeks to restore "normality" through changes in technology, management practice, and organization. Resilience does not question underlying assumptions of power or its unequal distribution in society. Transformation, on the other hand, is the deepest form of adaptation. It aims to change the overarching political-economy regime, reconfigure the structures of development, and introduce new political discourses that refine relationships among climate change, human security, and disaster risk. Transition is an intermediate level that focuses on bringing about changes in the practices of governance. Pelling sees disasters as being potential "tipping points" for transition, and, in extraordinary circumstances, transformation, insofar as they temporarily open up a window of opportunity for fundamental political change (see chapter 6 of this book).

How does climate change adaptation fit into Pelling's typology? The difference between resilience and transformation, he says, is akin to the distinction between treating the symptoms and causes of illness:

> The extent to which adaptation to climate change can embrace transformation will depend on the framing of the climate change problem. Where vulnerability is attributed to proximate causes of unsafe buildings, inappropriate land use and fragile demographics adaptation will be framed as a local concern. This is more amenable to resilience and transitional forms of adaptation. However, if vulnerability is framed as an outcome of wider social processes shaping how people see themselves and others, their relationship with the environment and role in political processes, then adaptation becomes a much broader problem. It is here that transformation becomes relevant (Pelling, 2011: 97).

Pelling's underlying message is that conventional approaches to climate change adaptation and disaster risk reduction are proving to be too conservative. This being so, then another, more radical direction may be desirable. Pelling does not specify what this might be, but the implication is that transformation may only be possible through grassroots collective action.

Conclusion

Until recently, climate was thought to be predominantly stable, with extreme events being no more than normal variations within the normal climate spectrum. Starting in the 1970s, this view began to change, as climate modelers began to warn of a significant warming trend. Climate change is said to impact disasters in two ways: it triggers a spike in the range and frequency of severe floods, storms, and other weather-related events; and it provokes radical changes in the economies of Southern nations, especially in the agriculture and food sectors.

The climate change/disaster synapse has become a major site of both cooperation and contestation within the global policy field of natural disasters. At the World Bank, development, climate change, and disaster risk management are increasingly discussed in the same breath. To facilitate an integrated approach, the Bank created the Global Facility for Disaster Reduction and Recovery (GFDRR). Most of the major players in the humanitarian relief and development sectors have embraced the climate change issue. Thus, the Red Cross/Red Crescent established a Centre on Climate Change and Disaster Preparedness and the Christian charity, Tearfund, released a paper, *Linking Climate Change Adaptation and Disaster Reduction.*

In highlighting the importance of the DRR–climate change synapse, the rhetorical use of numerical data highlighting a significant surge in extreme weather events has been crucial. Most famously, Oxfam released a research report entitled *Time's Bitter Flood: Trends in the Number of Reported Natural Disasters* that charts an upward trend in the number of reported disasters, notably storms and floods. Another strategy here has been to identify those nations and regions that are at maximum risk due to their vulnerability to multiple natural hazards. This is the topic of a 2005 monograph published by the Hazards Management Unit of the World Bank entitled *Natural Disaster Hotspots: A Global Analysis.*

Within the disaster risk reduction community, there has been a lively discussion of whether or not to join forces with colleagues from within the much larger and more powerful climate change community. Historically, the latter has privileged mitigation policies such as carbon emissions trading over adaptation measures. However, as international negotiations over carbon reduction have stalled, climate change adaptation (CCA) has begun to look more politically attractive. DRR proponents recognize that CCA is more generously funded and is able to more widely tap into public discussions. The downside of convergence is that the two communities are supported by different sets of institutions, individuals, methodologies, and policy frameworks. While CCA generally leans toward longer-term scenarios, top-down planning, and technologically based solutions, DRR is more attuned to developing grassroots adaptive measures directed toward mitigating the effects of recurrent hazards, notably cyclones and floods, that result from regular climate variation. Furthermore, the risk management discourse that characterizes DRR potentially conflicts with the precautionary principle discourse that is central to CCA.

On a broader canvas, climate change adaptation raises the hackles of various analysts, practitioners, and stakeholders in the international development sector in a way that DRR does not. Southern nations fear that CCA is being used as an argument to sidestep multilateral commitments to poverty alleviation. Civil society groups in countries designated for World Bank climate change resilience loans have mounted global protests on the grounds that Northern nations should be paying reparations rather than giving loans. Some commentators argue that climate change adaptation is nothing more than humanitarian intervention clad in a different set of clothes.

Further Reading

Steve Jennings (2011) *Time's Bitter Flood: Trends in the Number of Reported Natural Disasters*. Oxfam Research Report, Oxfam GB, May 27.

P.M. Kelly and W.N. Adger (2000) Theory and practice in assessing vulnerability to climate change and facilitating adaptation. *Climatic Change*, 47, 325–52.

Jessica Mercer (2010) Disaster risk reduction or climate change adaptation: Are we reinventing the wheel? *Journal of International Development*, 22, 247–64.

Lisa Schipper and Mark Pelling (2006) Disaster risk, climate change and international development: scope for, and challenges to, integration. *Disasters*, 30, 19–38.

CHAPTER SIX

Disaster Politics as Game Playing

Reflecting on relief efforts in Haiti after the 2010 earthquake, a lead editorial in the prestigious British medical journal *The Lancet*[1] comments, "Domestic and international point-scoring during times of crisis and disaster is a common game played by many governments and politicians" (*The Lancet*, 2010). This game-playing metaphor is consistent with a *realist* perspective on international relations, an approach that dominated the field from the 1940s through the 1960s (Dougherty and Pfaltzgraff, 1981: 84) and still remains influential today.[2]

In classical realist theory, politics is all about the pursuit of military and political goals. Decisions are directed by foreign policy, where "ideas are ruled by power relations, interests and manipulated strategies" (Nishikawa, 2005: 27). Consider, for example, the current political situation surrounding North Korea, as a new leadership coalesces in the wake of the death of Kim Jong Il. Despite continuing reports that many North Koreans remain on the brink of starvation, the country's immediate neighbors (China, South Korea, Japan) all have a vested interest in preserving the political status quo. For China, North Korea represents an important buffer zone against American intervention in the Asia-Pacific region, as well as a potential partner in mining rich deposits of coal, iron, and copper. Japan and South Korea may be unnerved by the intermittent saber rattling of the North Korean military, but it is considered preferable to the prospect of millions of North Korean refugees streaming across their borders, should the current regime collapse.

Realists assume that there is no natural harmony of interests among nations. Efforts to shape and transform global politics can never succeed through moral suasion alone. Rather, the aggressive tendencies of nations can only be kept at bay by a system of checks and balances. For realists, then, nothing but states and economic organizations really matter (Boli and Thomas, 1997: 171). Realist political theory, especially that which intersects with game theory, finds that national states are both inherently self-absorbed and competitive. When it collaborates with other nations, a state prefers that the jointly produced gains that may result should not advantage its partners. In fact, this concern about relative gains may constrain a state's willingness to cooperate in the first place (Grieco, 1988; Jervis, 1988).

In this realist tradition, humanitarian intervention is not sanctioned unless it is tightly constrained and properly regulated (Mason and Wheeler, 1996: 94). While realists can hardly deny the spread of international law, institutions, and organizations since World War Two, they discount its efficacy, arguing that international regime building is mostly cosmetic. Indeed, national states can be expected to contravene international treaties and institutions when they no longer perceive benefits to continued participation (Parks and Roberts, 2010: 138). At the same time, generals and cabinet ministers do not hesitate to co-opt utopian language and institutions, if this can enhance their strategic maneuvering. This is evidenced by the recent rise of "militant humanitarianism."

In this chapter, I will examine the realist or "international relations" interpretation of disaster politics under five headings: political considerations in allocating and providing disaster assistance, political considerations in accepting or rejecting disaster assistance, disaster diplomacy, disaster as a crisis of political legitimacy, and disaster as a catalyst of political and social change. I conclude the chapter by briefly introducing a recent, muscular intrusion of international politics into the delivery of disaster assistance known as "militant humanitarianism."

Political Considerations in Allocating and Providing Disaster Assistance

In keeping with this realist paradigm, one predominant and enduring view of disaster assistance features the impact of interest politics upon the relief process. Kent (1987: 119) cites Morris Davis' (1975) observation in *Civil Wars and the Politics of International Relief*, "real or potential donor nations habitually put their perceived national interests over humanitarian concerns." Similarly, Nelson (2008: 34) concludes that "disaster aid is a political process and is not the neutral and apolitical refuge that supporters and critics sometimes assume." In its 2007 Report for Congress on International Crises and Disasters, the Congressional Research Service makes this quite explicit:

> Political considerations play a role in the way assistance is given and to whom. Humanitarian assistance often means doing something to avert a crisis, to provide support to allies and to maintain a presence in the region. How it is used and whether it becomes more of a strategic policy tool depends on the situation, what other governments are doing, and the degree to which the United States has further interest in the region (Margesson, 2007: 17).

Not that this is entirely of recent vintage. In the aftermath of Lisbon's 1755 earthquake, tsunami, and fire, events that destroyed 75 percent of Europe's fourth largest city, the English sent disaster aid.[3] This decision was undertaken not just out of charitable feelings, but also for strategic advantage, insofar as both England and Portugal were mutual enemies of Spain (Dynes, 2005; McNeil, 2010).

Within the American political science literature, there is a critical mass of research studies that takes as its problematic the question: what factors influence the allocation and provision of aid to communities and countries impacted by natural disasters? Most conclude that, in such situations, governments make decisions about how much assistance to approve and where it should be directed not on the basis of the interests of victims but rather in light of perceived political imperatives (Green, 1977: 12; Mandel, 2002: 124).

This is consistent with a large body of literature which points to the dominant political motivation in the provision of international development aid (Hayter, 1971; Kent, 1983: 708). Commenting on South Africa's recent decision to create its own official development agency whose mandate is to funnel aid to other poorer nations in the region, Glennie (2011: 44) observes:

> While one reason the South Africans are setting up an aid agency is to improve their contribution to peace and development on the continent, it would be foolish to see the effort as purely altruistic. The rise of southern aid agencies holds a useful mirror to the motives of those who give aid. Somehow, the strategic interests of other countries are always more obvious than those of your own.

In a study published in 2003, Garrett and Sobel found that nearly half of all disaster relief dispensed by FEMA (Federal Emergency Management Agency) in the United States was motivated politically rather than strictly by need. They looked at FEMA disaster expenditures for all 50 states over the period 1991 to 1999. After a disaster strikes, the state governor makes a request to the President of the United States for assistance. To be eligible, the stricken community must be declared a disaster area. The President has unilateral authority to do this without being bound by any established set of criteria. Garrett and Sobel found that states that were politically important to the President had a higher rate of disaster declaration. As soon as the President officially declares a disaster, FEMA, which operates directly under Congressional oversight, decides the appropriate funding amount. The researchers found that states that had representation on the Congressional committees that oversaw FEMA received more funding. Garrett and Sobel (2003) conclude that altruism is trumped by political calculation in the case of FEMA assistance and question the relative effectiveness of government versus private disaster relief.

Analyzing US foreign disaster assistance data from 1964 through 1995, Drury et al. (2005: 455) show that American domestic and foreign policy influences two sets of disaster decisions: (1) the initial yes/no decision to grant any assistance at all, and (2) if affirmative, the "how much to allocate" decision. At the allocative stage, it clearly helps to be a friend of the United States: even in average-sized disasters, close allies receive humanitarian relief. This was particularly true during the Cold War. What does not seem to matter significantly is whether the ally is a democratic regime or not. The Office of US Foreign Disaster Assistance (OFDA) takes its cues from Congress, cutting back on its aid allocations in years when the federal deficits balloon. Drury and his colleagues found that these "political" considerations are generally more important than the severity of the disaster event, as measured by number of deaths and number of citizens rendered homeless. At the "how much" stage, manifest political considerations play a lesser role, but still operate. While the OFDA is given more leeway here, the agency mandarins are generally sensitive to the foreign and domestic preferences of their political masters.

Tavares (2008) analyzes more recent OFDA statistics, in this case from 1993 to 2004. In addition, she uses data from the United Nations Office for the Coordination of Humanitarian Affairs (OCHA) ReliefWeb Financial Tracking Service (FTS), a database providing all reported international humanitarian aid donated through NGOs, bilateral assistance, in-kind assistance, and private donations.[4] Tavares specifically tests the relationship between perceptions of corruption and the provision of disaster relief. The results suggest that a higher risk of corruption lowers the likelihood of the United States government providing disaster relief. In the case of international humanitarian aid, however, corruption and levels of democracy do not seem to make much difference.

In a 2008 Harvard Business School working paper, Charles Cohen and Eric Werker (2008) introduce and test a formal model of disaster mitigation that incorporates a decidedly instrumental, if not cynical, view of politics. As Garrett and Sobel reported for FEMA expenditures in the United States, governments were found to use natural disasters to redistribute power through a political effect, favoring disaster spending in regions that are politically aligned with the donor nation. The authors propose three other "effects" related to humanitarian aid. According to the *bailout effect*, governments in calamity-prone areas of the world underinvest in disaster prevention when they know that they will be bailed out in the event of disaster.[5] With the *racket effect*, governments, especially those without other sources of external income, deliberately neglect a population so as to attract – and steal – humanitarian aid in the event of a disaster. Finally, Cohen and Werker identify a *desperation effect*. In the case of major disasters that decimate local populations, governments increase their level of theft, something reluctantly tolerated by international organizations since there is an urgent need to deliver aid.

Political Considerations in Accepting or Rejecting Disaster Assistance

For recipient governments, too, considerations relating to political interest can play an important role. In the extreme case, a government may even reject foreign offers of assistance.

After the 2004 Indian Ocean earthquake and tsunami, the reclusive military junta that rules Myanmar (Burma) initially refused assistance.[6] Again in May 2008, the junta allegedly refused 15 separate attempts by the US Navy to help survivors of Cyclone Nargis, as well as forbidding the use of military helicopters from Thailand and Singapore to deliver supplies to isolated populations. Furthermore, it was reported that the ruling generals delayed visas for United Nations aid workers and seized two planeloads of food intended for survivors (Kurlantzick, 2008). According to the Associated Press, state media in Myanmar reported that the country feared an invasion by US forces interested in seizing its oil deposits ("Unable to help Myanmar relief efforts," 2008).

Thirteen years earlier, the government of Japanese Prime Minister Tomiichi Muryama had been similarly intransigent, initially discouraging offers of international aid in the Great Hanshin Earthquake of 1995.[7] This reluctance stemmed from three sources (Fukushima, 1995: 1). First, a strong sense of national pride and self-sufficiency predisposed some Japanese authorities to reject such aid, especially from nations that they considered less developed than Japan. Second, bureaucratic gridlock prevented quick processing of offers of aid from countries around the world. Third, risk-averse Japanese officials were unwilling to relax the rules governing the entry of medicines, animals, and humans from abroad into their country. For example, France/ Switzerland offered to supply rescue teams with dogs that could sniff out people trapped in rubble. But bureaucrats refused to allow this without first subjecting the dogs to the requirements of animal quarantine measures.

There may have been another reason. In an incident reported at the time by the *Los Angeles Times*, at a press briefing Kazutoshi Ito, director of the National Land Agency's disaster prevention coordination division, angrily defended his nation's decision not to immediately accept aid offers from 55 nations. Ito justified this on the grounds that the central government was compelled to respect the wishes of local authorities: "In a situation of an emergency like this one, if you are referring to the central government having the power to suppress and suffocate the will on the part of the local municipalities, it reminds me of the rebirth of Japanese militarism" (Watanabe, 1995).

In one of the few systematic explorations of this topic, Travis Nelson of the University of Vermont analyzed aid refusals in major disasters occurring between 1982 and 2006. This happened about 25 percent of the time. Nelson (2008) concludes that disaster aid can be both an opportunity and a danger for recipient regimes. It is an opportunity in that it permits a faster and more efficient recovery with reduced human suffering. On the other hand, it can be politically dangerous insofar as it generates a popular perception that it is external actors who are responding to the disaster instead of the political elite within the state. Nelson stresses that a national government must take charge of the disaster response. Passive disaster aid acceptance sends a signal

Box 6.1 A "Foreign Aid Twist"

To be sure, the United States is just about the last place on earth that one would think of as a recipient nation in times of disaster. And, prior to 2005, this perception would have been more or less spot-on. According to a report from the United States Government Accountability Office (2006), "Unlike many other countries, the U.S. government has previously never[8] asked for nor accepted disaster assistance directly from foreign countries, choosing instead to direct offers of assistance to nongovernmental organizations such as the Red Cross." Hurricane Katrina changed all this – sort of.

Incredibly, a total of 151 nations and international organizations offered aid in various forms after Katrina (Townsend, 2006). Most of this was unsolicited, an exception being the European Union (EU), which fulfilled an official American request for emergency assistance in the form of first-aid kits, blankets, water trucks, and prepared meals. Some of these offers came from unexpected places: India offered US$5 million plus medicine, a medical team, and water purification systems; while China indicated that it too was willing to send US$5 million as well as rescue workers, including medical experts. While some of these offers were accepted, most were repelled.

There were several major reasons for this rejection (van der Linde, 2008). First of all, significant amounts of humanitarian aid fell through the cracks because of "bureaucratic failure." A self-assessment carried out in 2006 by the General Accountability Office pointed to various administrative failings: confusion over which agency, DOS (Department of State) or FEMA, was legally empowered to formally accept foreign military assistance; inadequate inter-agency information sharing, leading to the United States Department of Agriculture (USDA) and the Food and Drug Administration (FDA) blocking the distribution of food and medical items. Other foreign aid offers, however, were rejected for more pointed political and economic reasons.

Three "hostile" nations – Venezuela, Cuba, and Iran – extended offers of help, but their motives were considered suspect. Venezuela offered to send food, oil, water, and aid workers, plus soldiers to help tackle looting in New Orleans. Insomuch as Venezuelan president Hugo Chavez had offered cheap gas to poor Americans and free eye surgery for Americans without health care access just prior to Hurricane Katrina, this aid package seemed designed primarily to embarrass America. Cuba offered more than 1,000 doctors and over 26 tonnes of medical supplies, followed soon after by a resolution in the Cuban parliament attacking President Bush and the American government. Through third-party channels, Iran offered to provide 20 million barrels of crude oil. However, Iran's offer was conditional on the United States agreeing to lift economic sanctions and was not accepted. As van der Linde (2008: 10) notes, "While seemingly demonstrating humanitarianism, the purpose can be seen to be achieving long-term political gains."

Third, some foreign aid offers were offered and rejected for economic reasons (see van der Linde, 2008: 14–16). In the aftermath of Hurricane Katrina, the Dutch government announced that it would send a naval frigate to provide humanitarian assistance, most notably 2,500 gallons of clean drinking water, water pumps, and five experts to help operate these pumps. However, it soon became evident that the Dutch saw this as an opportunity for private entrepreneurs to promote their expertise in water management, including dredging, without having to navigate protectionist procedures for bidding on government contracts. On their part, the Greeks offered to send two cruise ships free of charge to house those left homeless by the hurricane. However, the Greek offer was refused. Instead, under pressure from Florida Governor Jeb Bush, FEMA awarded a US$236 million no-bid contract to Carnival Cruise Lines, a Florida-based company with links to the Republican Party (King, 2006).

of weakness, and a weak regime is a regime that has lost a portion of its basic legitimacy. Aid refusal, then, is "at least partially about maintaining domestic legitimacy and protecting the political livelihood of the existing regime" (Nelson, 2008: 34).

Disaster Diplomacy

Combining an international relations perspective with a "critical" approach to natural disasters, Ilan Kelman of CICERO (Center for International Climate and Environmental Research) in Oslo has pioneered an approach to the topic of disasters as catalysts of political change that he calls *disaster diplomacy*.

Do natural disasters induce international cooperation amongst countries that have traditionally been enemies? In his recent book, *Disaster Diplomacy: How Disasters Affect Peace and Conflict*, Kelman (2011) reviews a number of case studies from around the globe in a variety of political and disaster circumstances. No evidence is found, he concludes, to suggest that disaster diplomacy is a prominent factor in conflict resolution. Put succinctly, "Disaster can act as a catalyst, but not a creator of diplomacy" (Kelman, 2003: 116). Disaster-related influences can sometimes make a difference in the short term, provided that a firm foundation has already been established. Over the long term, however, disaster-related influences fade and the forces that contribute to bilateral conflict – competition over scarce resources, historical grievances, claims concerning sovereignty – reappear. This recalls the model of community cooperation and conflict that was once thought to be typical of local disasters in the United States and Canada (Hannigan, 1976).

In theory, the expectation that natural disasters will create opportunities for feuding countries to come together seems to make sense. As Kelman and Koukis (2000: 214) observe, "The cooperative spirit generated from common efforts to deal with disasters – through either perceived necessity or choice from the humanitarian imperative – possibly overrides pre-existing prejudices, breaking down barriers which then may never be rebuilt." The key word here is "possibly."

The claim that natural disasters bring nations together and dampen conflicts has several variations. First of all, there is the hypothesis that the goodwill generated by working together on disaster relief will carry over into the post-disaster period. It is expected that the bonds between donor and recipient countries may be strengthened as recipients feel grateful toward donors and donors feel compassionate toward recipients (Mandel, 2002). McNeil (2010) calls this a "geopolitical valentine." Citing comments by Andrew Natsios, USAID director under George W. Bush, he notes that every federal emergency aid package sent by the United States now bears the label "From the American People" accompanied by a logo: a blue, clasped-hands logo for USAID; an eagle for State Department aid; a red ribbon for the President's Emergency Plan for AIDS relief.[9]

Second, it is proposed that networks established during the disaster, be they technical, scientific, or humanitarian, will persist and flower after the emergency has ended. Third, disasters may have "a multiplying and legitimizing effect on diplomatic rapprochement" (Ker-Lindsay, 2000). This appears to have been the outcome of suggestions by Chinese Premier Wen Jiabao to the Japanese government at a high-level meeting on relief efforts for tsunami-ravaged Indonesia in early 2005 that China and Japan should step up cooperation on disaster prevention and reduction in the region (Liu, 2008).

Kelman and Warnaar (2004) have proposed a typology of disaster diplomacy. This sets out four dimensions on which the potential for rapprochement between countries is likely to be encouraged or discouraged. First, there is propinquity. States that share a land border or are near one another might be expected to perceive a common threat, as against those that are not physically near one another. Second, states in conflict that engage in mutual aid or combined aid to a third state are more likely to cultivate a lasting relationship, versus those in a donor–recipient relationship. Third, there are three levels at which disaster diplomacy is conducted: government-led, organization-led, and people-led (i.e. the grassroots directs the efforts). Ideally, all three levels will overlap and reinforce each other (Kelman, 2007). Finally, the reasons why the parties conduct disaster diplomacy matter. There are five possibilities here: survival of oneself, mutual benefit, long-term, global gains, re-affirmation of old prejudices and enmity, and to prove humanitarianism.

Disaster as a Crisis of Political Legitimacy

When a major disaster occurs, the political situation ramps up dramatically. As nonprofit development consultant and blogger Steve Klingaman (2010) has aptly phrased it, the reactive nature of representative government dictates, "It is impossible to build sufficient urgency to overcome political inertia until there is blood on the floor or oil on the beach." Suddenly, political reputations are fragile and a crisis of legitimacy can occur. As noted above, this is especially the case where foreign aid and aid workers take up the slack.

Duncan Green, Head of Research for Oxfam GB, recalls a conversation that took place among civil servants and academics in the course of a meeting about disasters and climate change held in the Treasury Room at the British policy think tank, Chatham House:

> But perhaps the main contrast was how much more aware of politics this group was than many in the development community. Gordon Brown was seen to have had a "good flood" in the summer of 2007, whereas the French government had a disastrous heat wave in 2003, when tens of thousands of people died in their homes. One speaker portrayed it as the beginning of the end for President Chirac (Green, 2008).

It is a political cliché that presidents and prime ministers are expected to immediately rush to the scene of a catastrophe or risk being painted by the media as being callous and uncaring. The chief executive who declines to interrupt a family vacation or an overseas diplomatic visit to fly home to the disaster site is asking for trouble at the next election. No matter that there is little that politicians can actually do short of comforting victims and boosting the morale of emergency workers, they must be seen by the public as exercising leadership.

Despite his dubious foreign policy adventures in Iraq and Afghanistan, George W. Bush absorbed a more punishing hit to his credibility from his stumbles in handling disaster communications during Hurricanes Katrina and Rita. President Bush was slow in acknowledging the unprecedented magnitude of the storm damage, and did not visit the Gulf States immediately. He continued to insist that the federal government had matters under control, even though it was evident that this was not the case. At a press conference at the Mobile, Alabama Regional Airport, Bush praised FEMA director Mike Brown ("Brownie, you're doing a heck of a job"), a declaration that famously came back to haunt him when the media exposed Brown as both unqualified (prior to his FEMA posting he had been director of the International Arabian Horse Association) and largely ineffective.[10]

Pakistan's president, Asif Ali Zardari, provoked a hornet's nest of critical comments when he opted to go ahead with his official visit to the UK rather than return home to lead the country's response to floods in the northwest and central regions of the country that killed 1,600 people and impacted more than 13 million. In addition to pressure to return from opposition political leaders in his country, Zardari encountered an angry reception in Britain. When he arrived at his hotel in central London, he was met by protesters who accused him of wasting money on the visit that might better be spent in assisting flood victims. Two Muslim politicians, MP Khalid Mahmood and Labour peer, Lord Ahmed, canceled meetings with Zardari. Mahmood told the press, "The issue is the huge environmental catastrophe that's going on – a lot of people are dying there. No matter what he can or can't do, he should be there to try to support the people, not swanning around in the UK and France." In response, Zardari addressed a rally at the Birmingham Convention Centre, where he assured his supporters that he was doing more to help by raising funds overseas than by rushing back to the disaster site.[11] A week into the flood emergency, newspapers around the world were predicting Zardari's political demise, with headlines such as "Flood Water May Wash Away Pakistani President's Career" and "Zardari Faces Own Katrina." Things could have been worse for Zardari. Visiting her flood-hit constituency in the Muzaffargarh district of Punjab province, junior economic affairs minister Hina Rabbani Khan's convoy was stoned by local residents who were angry that a nearby canal had been breached (Toosi, 2010).

Whereas Zardari was slow in visiting the site of the flooding, President José Sarney of Brazil was downright reluctant to go anywhere near the scene of the major flood disaster that impacted Rio de Janeiro and its environs in

February 1988. As is so often the case, those most impacted by the flooding and landslides were the communities of the poor, especially the *favelados* or shantytown dwellers. Sarney, who was already unpopular in Rio's low-income settlements for his draconian economic measures to control rampant inflation, initially refused to undertake an on-site inspection. He cited a traumatic experience during a previous, private visit, when angry demonstrators stoned his bus. Only after the intervention of a wealthy media magnate, Roberto Marinho, did Sarney reluctantly agree to change his mind. Even then, he chose to do a quick flyover of the devastated area in a helicopter, avoiding any direct contact with the people (Allen, 1994: 104). By contrast, the current President, Dilma Rousseff, not only did a helicopter flyover, but visited some of the communities in southeastern Brazil devastated by flooding and mudslides in January 2011, "vowing to cut bureaucracy that could hinder prompt delivery of federal funding and aid for overwhelmed state and local officials" (Fick and Prada, 2011).

Russian political strongman Vladimir Putin instinctively understands the political optics and opportunities of natural disasters. During the wildfire crisis in summer 2010, Putin slipped into the co-pilot's seat of a water bomber. In a video clip broadcast across the nation, Putin inquires if a drop of 12 tonnes of water on two fires was a hit. A voice replies, "A direct hit." This may be a stunt, *The Economist* comments, but it will likely help Putin retake the presidency in 2012, even if it will do nothing to make Russia safer and better governed ("Into the Inferno," 2010: 39).

Box 6.2 "Hope Floats"

If there was an award for the best performance during a disaster, one strong contender might be Newark, New Jersey Mayor, Cory Booker. Even as Hurricane Irene bore down on his city, Booker spent Saturday, August 29, 2011, going door to door in evacuation zones urging residents to get out. In between visits, Booker continuously tweeted to his constituents. One tweet read, "Thanks to so many residents who were on the ball and positive in this storm. I discovered beyond a shadow of a doubt that: Hope Floats."

Booker is a skilled practitioner of the "Everyman" style of political positioning. So too is New Jersey's Governor, Chris Christie, albeit with a louder, more direct tone than Booker. Previously criticized for being absent during a monster blizzard in 2010, Christie was everywhere during Irene, telling tourists to the Jersey Shore "Get the hell back on the beach;" upbraiding officials of an electricity company, Jersey Central Power & Light, saying that he had called its parent company about returning power to about 30,000 of its customers (Gershman et al., 2011: A17). New York Governor Andrew Cuomo, an experienced hand in both state politics and, as a former Federal Housing Secretary, in "the swirling logistics of disaster relief" in Washington, assumed the role of the "seasoned general." As the floodwaters advanced, he soared over the swelling river valleys upstate in a Blackhawk helicopter and plowed through flooded main streets snapping photos of what he witnessed with his Blackberry and posting them on Twitter (Gershman et al., 2011: A19). His main messages were that New Yorkers were resilient, and "government worked."

Occasionally, a political regime may fall based on its poor performance record in a natural disaster. An oft-cited example of this is the 1972 Managua, Nicaragua, earthquake that ultimately led to the Sandinista Revolution and the toppling of the Somoza dictatorship seven years later. Note, however, that the opposite result is possible. If the ruling regime performs effectively in coping with a disaster, its hold on power may be strengthened. Fuentes (2009: 103) cites two examples of this from Latin America. Juan Perón's seemingly compassionate role and involvement in the 1944 San Juan earthquake helped him rise in popularity and gain political control of Argentina. Three decades later, in 1974, the corrupt military regime in Honduras solidified and extended its control of the country by engaging in a massive agrarian reform and land redistribution scheme in the aftermath of Hurricane Fifi.

Disaster as a Catalyst for Political and Social Change

Fuentes (2009: 100) observes that natural disasters sometimes challenge political structures and pose an opportunity for change. Rather than a reflexive action, this is more a matter of disasters acting as a catalyst of processes already under way. Duncan Green (2008) describes this using a geological metaphor, "Just as earthquakes release the accumulated tensions in tectonic plates beneath the earth's crust, disasters unleash the underlying social and political tensions that have built up over the decades, and expose the effectiveness of states, whether democratic or authoritarian, to the harshest of scrutiny."

Seven Hypotheses for Disaster and Political Change

In a briefing paper presented to Chatham House, and the following year in an essay in an online development magazine (Pelling and Dill, 2007), Mark Pelling and Kathleen Dill (2006) elaborate on this characterization of disasters as catalysts of political action and change. In their view, the failure of the state to respond adequately to a disaster can create a temporary power vacuum. This opens a window of opportunity for contending forces ranging from current power holders seeking to entrench their position to civil society actors working for systemic change. Consistent with the comments by Fuentes (2009) and Green (2008) cited above, Pelling and Dill observe, "Disasters triggered by environmental phenomena do not cause political change, rather they act as catalysts that put into motion potentially provocative social processes at multiple social levels" (2006: 2). In some cases, this can reify the hold on office of authoritarian political leaders; in others, it can open political systems up to democratic scrutiny. Pelling and Dill propose seven working hypotheses concerning the relationship between disasters and social change.

First, *disasters often hit potentially peripheral regions hardest, catalyzing regional political tension*. To illustrate this, they cite the February 23, 2004, Moroccan earthquake which led to a series of protests by angry citizens in an area of north-eastern Morocco who saw the incompetent response by the regional governor as further evidence of long-standing grievances relating to social inequality and political favoritism.

Second, *disasters are a product of development policies and can open to scrutiny dominant political and institutional systems.* The considerable attention given by the American media to aspects of racial discrimination and bureaucratic bungling in New Orleans following Hurricane Katrina, combined with the federal government's inadequate response, demonstrates this.

Third, *existing inequalities can be exacerbated by post-disaster governmental manipulation.* In particular, unscrupulous developers and speculators, sometimes in cahoots with government agents, attempt to claim rights over low-income settlement space, citing as justification that the land is too dangerous for further habitation. For example, following the Indian Ocean tsunami, coastal land was transferred from village to commercial use.

Fourth, *the way in which the state and other sectors act in response and recovery is largely predicated on the kind of political relationships that existed between sectors before the crisis.* Pelling and Dill cite the case of Cuba, whose excellent track record of efficient disaster evacuation overrides its reputation as an authoritarian regime.

Fifth, *regimes are likely to interpret spontaneous collective actions by nongovernmental sectors in the aftermath of a disaster as a threat and respond with repression.* An example is the actions of the military dictatorship following the 1976 earthquake in Guatemala when emerging local Maya leaders were perceived as a political threat and violently repressed.

Sixth, *in the aftermath of a disaster, political leaders may regain or even enhance their popular legitimacy.* This occurred after the 1976 Tangshan earthquake in China, where Mao Zedong's successor, Hua Guofeng, consolidated his power and dismantled the opposing power base controlled by the "Gang of Four" by appropriating the disaster as a symbolic event from whence great change would flow.

Finally, *the repositioning of political actors in the aftermath of a disaster unfolds at multiple scales.* Sometimes this may even create new political spaces. For example, in the aftermath of Hurricane Mitch in 1988, local NGOs assumed a wider influence (at least temporarily) and regional alliances across Central America were strengthened.

Disasters as Tipping Points for Change

In their most recent paper on this subject, Pelling and Dill (2010) consider the process of post-disaster change by developing an analytic framework organized around moments of transition that act as *tipping points*. These tipping points are capable of opening up or constraining technical, political, and policy change. To illustrate their framework, Pelling and Dill present a case history of the 1999 Marmara (Turkey) earthquake.[12]

The first potential tipping point or post-disaster moment is driven from the bottom up by civil society. It focuses attention on the unequal social and spatial distribution of risk. For example, in Managua, Nicaragua, an estimated 200 poor communities and neighborhoods with more than 300,000 residents are situated on seismic fault lines. According to one recent study, an earthquake registering 6.9 on the Richter scale would leave 30,000 people dead and over 300,000 homeless in the city (Silva, 2010). Furthermore, Pelling and Dill note that the areas hit hardest by disaster are often those that are *politically* peripheral; this can include both remote rural regions and informal squatter settlements situated close to the national political core. Disasters can thus "highlight regional/ethnic/class inequality and feed into nascent or ongoing political struggles along these lines" (2010: 24); or alternatively, be used by powerful elites to further marginalize these groups.

The second potential tipping point is the top-down product of international diplomacy. In certain circumstances, disaster reconstruction funded by governments, international financial institutions, and NGOs from abroad can circumvent the state and inspire initiatives at the local level that open up the processes of political and social change. Alternatively, local political elites can co-opt funds supplied by external actors and use these to strengthen their grip on power.

Neo-liberal Politics and Militant Humanitarianism

Some disaster analysts claim to have detected a new species of neo-liberal politics wherein military-led relief operations have increasingly replaced humanitarian missions formerly led by the United Nations and the Red Cross. According to Chandler (2001: 678), "The new international discourse of human rights activism no longer separates the spheres of strategic state and international aid from humanitarianism, but attempts to integrate the two under the rubric of 'ethical' or 'moral' foreign policy. As the humanitarian NGOs have been integrated into policymaking forums, the policymakers have increasingly claimed to be guided by humanitarian principles." Bello (2006) says that this new *militant humanitarianism* takes the form of a "relief and reconstruction complex" consisting of the Pentagon, the World Bank, corporate contractors, and certain NGOs. The dynamics that are put in play here reflect the intersection of strategic interest, ideologically motivated economics, and muscular humanitarianism.

Militant humanitarianism is a second cousin of the *military humanitarianism* that first surfaced after the Gulf War in the early 1990s. Military humanitarianism or "humanitarian war" (Roberts, 1993) denotes the principle of using military personnel to protect UN-mandated relief operations, especially during complex emergencies. In an IDS (Institute of Development Studies) report written in the mid 1990s, Duffield (1994) downplays the importance of military protection for humanitarian programs, claiming that it is the exception rather than the rule and "has already begun to wane." A trend of greater importance and concern, he argues, *is mandated negotiated access*, whereby NGOs formally agree to take a neutral stance, and follow a fixed aid distribution schedule worked out in advance by the UN and the warring parties, in conflict zones such as Angola, Bosnia, and South Sudan.

In the past, the dangers of blurring the lines between humanitarianism and military involvement have not gone unnoticed. At the outset of the conflict in Iraq in 2003, members of the private voluntary organization (PVO) community in the United States were sharply critical of the practice of military personnel carrying out relief operations in conflict zones. Blurring the line between combatant and relief worker was objectionable, they said, both because it put their field staff at risk, and because it discounted the experience and expertise of relief workers, who had been doing it far longer (McCleary, 2009: 155).

These objections failed to register at the Department of Defense (DoD) where humanitarianism is treated as "soft weaponry," just another tool in its reconstruction and "democracy-building" operations. This is clearly evident in the Biennial Budget Estimates of the (US) Overseas Humanitarian, Disaster, and Civic Aid, which are coordinated with the Department of State, and approved by the Office of the Secretary of Defense (OSD). The DoD community, the document states, has "unmatched capabilities in logistics, transportation, command, control, and communications" in an emergency situation: it transported 13 million pounds of relief supplies to Central America during the first few weeks following Hurricane Mitch in 1998. These "unique rapid response abilities" allow DoD to "assist in the containment of crises" and "limit threats to regional stability" (OHDACA, 2000/2001). With the US military increasingly entering areas of social and political development outside its traditional mandate, and pressure building for humanitarian agencies to integrate into the policy bureaucracy, the time has come, McCleary (2009: 156) says, for PVOs to "reclaim the terrain of humanitarian aid and development."

Apparently, the disaster relief sector has not been spared from this government initiative. The immediate and extensive engagement of the US military after the 2004 Indian Ocean tsunami does not appear to have been undertaken just for altruistic reasons. Thus, Bello (2006: 281–2) cites the case of Indonesia, where the tsunami response was used as a platform to achieve security objectives. Specifically, direct cooperation between the Pentagon and the Indonesian army was treated as an opportunity to roll back a ban on arms sales and to provide military training, restrictions forced on the Americans during the 1990s as a result of a successful campaign by human rights groups. Citing the objective of strengthening the Indonesian military's capability for "disaster relief," in January 2005, Washington allowed commercial sales of "non-lethal" defense items such as spare parts for military planes, followed a

Box 6.3 The Road to Meulaboh

In the aftermath of the 2004 Indian Ocean tsunami, the Bush administration in the United States wanted to underwrite a high profile disaster recovery project in Indonesia. After considering and rejecting the idea of rebuilding a significant portion of the provincial capital, Banda Aceh, into a kind of "signature city," it was decided that the Americans would finance and oversee construction of a modern highway from the capital to Meulaboh, the southernmost coastal town, a distance of 150 miles. Much of the existing infrastructure along the coast had been devastated by the tsunami, including stretches of the existing roadway. This seemed to be a "win-win" situation for the American government. Not only would it be a showcase for Western engineering, it would also enhance the nation's image in a conservative Muslim area that had been isolated by the civil war. The United States Agency for International Development (USAID) was tasked with overseeing the project and was given a budget of US$250 million. According to Walter North, the mission director for USAID, in the future, the road would open up economic rebirth and even a vibrant tourism industry along Aceh's west coast.

Alas, all didn't go according to plan. Land acquisition proved to be a particular problem. With over 3,000 parcels of residential and farmland to be acquired, construction was delayed due to unanticipated legal difficulties. Land titles were lost in the tsunami or never existed. The owners of many properties who did have legal title were killed in the tsunami, and their heirs quarreled over who would inherit. Many villagers along the proposed highway were initially hostile. The road was routed through several hundred graves of mystical and religious significance, including one where a white tiger is believed to stand guard. Furthermore, the Western-style blacktop was incompatible with local life. Along the old meandering road, villagers were able to sell snacks and tea from stalls. The new highway, with its wide shoulder on either side, whisked motorists quickly and efficiently to their destination, making refreshment stops unnecessary. Some local residents insisted on higher compensation. To express their displeasure, villagers demonstrated outside the Indonesian reconstruction agency and erected blockades of barbed wire and boulders to obstruct construction.

To move things along Americans variously threatened to withdraw funding and shift it to Lebanon, and (unsuccessfully) urged the governor of Banda Aceh to employ the tool of eminent domain to take control of disputed land parcels. Five years on, the Acehnese provincial government began to help expedite the project by sending in the police to mediate disputes and take down barricades. As 2011 draws to a close, the road is still only partially finished, although the land acquisition is virtually complete. (Sources: Perlez, 2006; Gelling, 2009.)

month later by the revoking of the ban on military training. Given that the post-tsunami ceasefire with the Acehnese independence fighters was tenuous at best, the Indonesian military no doubt welcomed these initiatives.

As is illustrated in box 6.3, a new, more aggressive and politicized form of disaster management is visible here. *New York Times* journalist Jane Perlez (2006) reported, "The Indonesians say the Americans are imposing first world standards of efficiency on a poor region that was pounded by civil war and then swamped by the tsunami, which killed more than 100,000 Indonesians."

Australia too had foreign policy, if not military, reasons for expanding aid to Indonesia in the aftermath of the tsunami. The country's position as an influential regional player had been strained for some time due to various issues, including East Timor's transition to independence and Australia's restrictive regional refugee policy. A little over a week after the tsunami, the Australian government announced an unexpected and greatly expanded combination of loans and grants to be delivered over a five-year period. While it appears that most of this fresh infusion of funds was targeted to areas outside the tsunami disaster zone, nevertheless, the Australian media treated this initiative as a foreign policy masterstroke (Jayasuriya and McCawley, 2010: 235).

Fidler (2005) concludes that examples such as the Indonesian case discussed above "indicate that the political nature of natural disasters is being significantly reframed so that policy for such disasters connects directly to systemic interests states have in international relations." Rather than continuing to treat natural disasters as largely peripheral, self-interested states are currently engaged in an ongoing process of rational calculation, wherein disasters are treated both as an opportunity to extend their power and as the source of new challenges and opportunities connected to security.

Conclusion

In the field of international relations, "realism" has arguably been the leading approach for much of the past half century. There are multiple versions of realist theory, but all stipulate that national states are exclusively guided by self-interest rather than by moral considerations. Insofar as nations are inherently competitive, collaboration is difficult to achieve and only sticks as long as all parties perceive that they are benefitting equally. In this chapter, I have discussed disaster politics from a realist perspective under five headings: political considerations in allocating and providing disaster assistance, political considerations in accepting or rejecting disaster assistance, disaster diplomacy, disaster as a crisis of political legitimacy, and disaster as a catalyst of political and social change.

Disaster aid is first and foremost a political process wherein national interest routinely trumps moral concern. This was true as long ago as the catastrophic Lisbon earthquake of 1755, when England sent aid to Portugal not just for altruistic reasons, but also to gain strategic advantage in its conflict with Spain. In the contemporary era, researchers have repeatedly found that governments make decisions about how much disaster assistance to approve, and where it should be directed, not primarily in sympathy with the interests of victims, but rather to serve the broader imperatives of statecraft. At the same time, potential recipients of disaster aid also engage in political game playing. In extreme cases, a government may even refuse all assistance; this is what occurred in Myanmar (Burma) immediately after the 2004 Indian Ocean tsunami when the ruling military junta refused all foreign disaster aid.

Combining an international relations perspective with a "critical" view of natural disasters, Ilan Kelman and colleagues have pioneered an approach known as "disaster diplomacy." By this they mean that natural disasters may serve to dampen hostility and bring nations together by breaking down existing prejudices, generating goodwill, and forging new networks of cooperation. Thus far, however, they have concluded that disaster diplomacy alone cannot bring about peace and positive political change. At best, under the right conditions, disasters may act as a catalyst to ongoing efforts toward conflict resolution, at least in the short term. This is what occurred in Sri Lanka and Indonesia after the 2004 tsunami.

In the context of a major disaster, political reputations are enhanced or destroyed. At the very least, presidents and prime ministers are required to rush to the disaster scene and be seen by the media to be in charge, even if this is not actually the case. In the case of major disaster events that attract international aid and media coverage, political leaders must walk a fine line between welcoming the expertise and resources offered by foreign governments and humanitarian agencies, while at the same time communicating to the electorate that they have not effectively given up control to outsiders.

Natural disasters sometimes spark a challenge to entrenched political structures and offer an opportunity for radical change. Pelling and Dill (2010) label these moments of transition "tipping points." Disasters do this by opening a window of opportunity for contending forces and putting into motion potentially provocative social forces. This is what occurred in the aftermath of Hurricane Mitch in 1988. On occasion, reconstruction efforts funded by foreign governments, IFIs, and NGOs can circumvent the state and inspire initiatives at the local level that open up new political spaces. Yet, alternatively, strategically nimble political regimes can sometimes successfully manipulate a disaster situation in order to enhance their political legitimacy and solidify their control over the nation and its people. One way to do this is to co-opt funds and resources supplied from abroad.

In the concluding section, I discuss the rising tide of "militant humanitarianism." Militant humanitarianism aims to integrate strategic foreign aid initiatives with humanitarian relief under the rubric of "ethical" or "moral" foreign policy. You could say that it is a realist politics disguised as normative discourse. In the final chapter of the book, I re-introduce the topic of militant humanitarianism as part of the SCPQ (securitization, catastrophic modeling and scenario building, privatization, and quantification) configuration that is gaining momentum in the global politics of natural disasters.

Further Reading

Ilan Kelman (2011) *Disaster Diplomacy: How Disasters Affect Peace and Conflict*. Routledge, London and New York.

T. Nelson (2010) Rejecting the gift horse: international politics of disaster and refusal. *Conflict, Security & Development*, 10, 379–402.

Mark Pelling and Kathleen Dill (2010) Disaster politics: tipping points for change in the adaptation of sociopolitical regimes. *Progress in Human Geography*, 34, 21–37.

CHAPTER SEVEN

Mass Media and the Politics of Disaster

As Bankoff (2001: 19) observed a decade ago, the mass media are central to the heightened awareness about disasters that is emblematic of the contemporary era:

> Natural disasters seem increasingly to have caught the attention of the Western media in the late twentieth century, carrying reports and images of drought, flood, famine, earthquake, volcanic eruption, typhoon, tsunami and the like into suburban homes on an almost daily basis. Pinatubo, Kobe, Mitch, Izmit, Orissa and countless other hazards have become household names overnight as the glare of Western public attention momentarily illuminates some less well-known corner of the globe.

Nowhere is this more evident than on CNN, the Atlanta-based cable news network with a global reach. Even as it has been steadily losing market share to cable television rivals Fox News Channel and MSNBC on the everyday battleground of political talk shows, CNN remains the industry leader in the United States for its ongoing reportage and analysis of domestic and overseas natural disasters. Evening anchor Anderson Cooper has become a media celebrity in America for his intense coverage of Hurricane Katrina, the earthquake in Haiti, the BP oil spill in the Gulf of Mexico,[1] and the tornado-devastated town of Joplin, Kansas. To his credit, "AC" made multiple site visits to post-hurricane New Orleans and Mississippi long after other reporters moved on. Cooper has been credited with provoking the media to (sometimes) take a more adversarial and social justice oriented stand on disaster issues, quite remarkable given that he is the scion of one of America's wealthiest families.

Coverage of natural disasters is the most common form of environmental reporting. One reason for this is that disasters can easily be presented as dramatic happenings in specific places and times featuring a familiar cast of heroes and villains, leaders and victims (Hannigan, 2006: 84; Young and Dugas, 2011: 4). Furthermore, editors and producers (not entirely correctly) regard natural disaster coverage as one of the "safer" political topic areas to cover, possessing much less ideology, political language, and propaganda than other environmental topics such as global climate change (Shah, 2005).

As with so much media content, the operative phrase here may be *caveat emptor* (buyer beware). Tyler Brûlé is a Canadian journalist and design guru who founded the British fashionable-living bible *Wallpaper* and currently is editor-in-chief of *Monocle*. Brûlé travels frequently to Japan and writes about it in his column in the weekend *Financial Times*. He was in Japan when the tsunami struck and returned a month later. While beyond the seriously devastated disaster zone, Japan experienced lingering economic effects, nevertheless, Brûlé believes that the world media painted a dire and false picture; and that this frightened away foreign visitors:

> While most international news organizations have called into question Japan's poor PR skills and general mishandling of its messages, the Japanese have been outraged at the irresponsible and inaccurate reporting of events, facts and the overall state of the nation. As late as last week, British and US television channels would have had most of us believing that the Japanese weren't out enjoying the cherry blossoms, but it only took a quick spin in a cab in Kagoshima and later Tokyo to see parks and boulevards packed with families enjoying the delicate fluttering petals (Brûlé, 2011: Life & Arts 20).

Whatever their theoretical perspective, academic researchers generally share Brûlé's view that the media seem to get it wrong when it comes to disasters, both domestic and international. Political scientists and economists have most often opted to study this topic by charting the frequency and magnitude of media coverage of "foreign" disasters, correlating this with disaster severity (usually measured by number of deaths and/or economic loss), geographic and cultural proximity, and extent of disaster assistance (notably from the United States via the Office of Foreign Disaster Assistance). In keeping with a "discursive turn" in the social sciences, geographers and sociologists have been more inclined to engage in frame and content analysis.

Volume and Breadth of Coverage

Researchers have found considerable variation in the attention paid by the media to natural disasters, especially those occurring outside North America. Some events, notably the 2010 Haitian earthquake, and 2011 Japanese earthquake/tsunami and nuclear emergency, garner front-page coverage for months, while others (2005 earthquake and 2010 floods in Pakistan) fade quickly as a news story.

A quarter-century ago, William Adams (1986) tested the hypothesis that the amount of attention that US television devotes to a natural disaster directly reflects the relative magnitude of the event. As his primary measure, he chose number of deaths. Adams' data covered the period from January 1972 through June 1985. According to the *World Almanac, 1986*, there were 35 major disasters over this period, including 17 major earthquakes and 11 major tidal waves and floods. Included here is the 1976 Tangshan (China) quake, which caused the greatest loss of life (800,000) of any natural disaster of the twentieth century.

The results of Adams' analysis were mixed. Generally, the amount of attention paid by US television news showed no significant relationship to disaster severity. Specifically, the loss of life (initial estimate) statistically explained only 3 percent of the variation in the amount of coverage disasters were given in nightly network newscasts. On the other hand, geography seemed to play a more prominent role. When Adams calculated the ratio of TV minutes per estimated 1,000 deaths, the ranking was as follows: Western Europe (9.20), Eastern Europe (3.60), Latin America (1.02), Middle East (0.87), Asia (0.76). Asian countries got the least attention, with the Philippines, China, and Indonesia accorded limited coverage. Even though the disaster in the Philippines caused eight times as many deaths as the one in Italy, it received less than half as much coverage. Curiously, the Tangshan quake failed to register at all, although this may have reflected China's near embargo on news.

Using multiple regression analysis, Adams attempted to measure the effect of factors other than disaster magnitude on the volume of coverage. What emerged as most significant was a nation's degree of popularity with American tourists. This accounted for a third of the variation in news coverage. It may be the case, Adams concludes, that television producers, reporters, and story editors feel a greater sense of cultural proximity with countries such as Italy which they had previously enjoyed visiting on holiday, or perhaps they think that audience members feel this way.

If the latter is true, the media may have miscalculated. According to a 2008 survey conducted by the Pew Research Center for the People & the Press, major media outlets lagged far behind ordinary Americans in following the earthquake in Sichuan province, China. Whereas 22 percent of survey respondents said they followed the earthquake more closely than any other story during the week of May 12–18, 2008, the event attracted only 13 percent of news coverage for that week. The Pew study singles out cable news for ignoring the earthquake – only 4 percent of news coverage was devoted to it, while the ongoing presidential campaign received 74 percent ("Cable disaster coverage gets low marks," 2008).

Fourteen years after Adams' study, Douglas Van Belle (2000) revisited the topic, looking at coverage of "foreign" disasters by the *New York Times* and American network television news over the period 1964–96. While geographic proximity (as measured by distance from Washington, DC) and social distance (gauged by volume of American tourists) both correlated positively with the amount of coverage, the relationship was most robust in the case of major disasters (those resulting in more than 300 deaths).

More recently, Jeong and Lee (2010) looked at the coverage of 137 international disasters[2] over a 14-year period (1996–2009) in 11 representative US news outlets spanning five media types (national newspaper, news magazine, broadcast television network, cable television network, radio network). Six different types of emergency events were identified: meteorological disasters (droughts, heat waves), hydrological disasters (floods), geophysical disasters (earthquakes, tsunamis, volcanic eruptions, avalanches), climatological disasters (cyclones, hurricanes, typhoons), biological disasters (cholera outbreaks), and human-induced disasters (building collapses, chemical spills).

In contrast to the earlier findings of Adams (1986), the researchers found that the magnitude of disaster damage was consistently a significant predictor of volume of coverage at all time periods (i.e. weeks one through four). This held true for both measures of damage – death toll and economic loss – and was not consistently linked to the political, socioeconomic, or geographical condition of a nation or its ties to the United States. Jeong and Lee (2010) found that as the initial impact faded in time, the average number of news stories decreased greatly. Furthermore, from the third week onwards, the size of a country's economy as represented by gross domestic product (GDP) was positively related to the amount of media coverage. Geographic distance (proximity between the US and a country with a disaster) was negatively correlated with degree of media coverage during the second week, the opposite of what was predicted based on previous studies.

Depth and Accuracy of Coverage

Disaster researchers have long noted the tendency of the mass media to construct images of disaster that are both superficial and inaccurate. While Western journalists are considered the main culprits, media in other parts of the world do likewise. In an essay adapted from his monthly column in *Tokyo Business Today*, Glen Fukushima (1995) detects an evident bias by the Japanese media in their reporting of the Great Hanshin Earthquake. Their focus on positive stories of cooperation, discipline, and perseverance by the victims, as well as the orderly and effective manner of their rescue, relocation, and care, is at odds with eyewitness accounts unfiltered by the Japanese media of "arguments, fistfights, looting, price-gouging, hoarding of merchandise, and other conflicts one would expect in societies struck by such massive destruction and temporary loss of legal order." Japanese journalists, Fukushima observes, were "engaged in considerable wishful thinking."

Broadening the definition of disaster, Susan Moeller (1999) comments on the tendency of the media to report in a shallow and simplistic fashion on famine, treating it as if it were a natural disaster, beyond the control of people. Rather than seriously explaining and assessing the factors that created the situation, the media distill a famine's multiple causes into monolithic problems such as drought or general chaos. What follows from this are recommendations for simplistic solutions, such as the giving of money, that "tend to exaggerate the agency of Western aid and to minimize the involvement and efficacy of indigenous efforts" (Moeller, 1999: 105). Moeller (1999: 104), who worked as a journalist and photographer at national magazines and newspapers before becoming a journalism professor at Brandeis

University, notes the stubborn persistence of stereotyped images, stock phrases, and common abstractions that reinforce an established way of interpreting the news and reify a standard formula or template for famine reporting.

One particular difficulty here is that key interpretive frames, constructed by news-workers during mega-disasters, are subsequently applied across the board:

> The problem with this is that our common knowledge regarding the role of the news media in the humanitarian response to crises, and to a lesser extent the provision of development aid, is defined by events like the [2004 Indian Ocean] tsunami. We imagine the norm in terms of the most extreme of the rarest and most unusual events. Over 14,000 disasters have been catalogued since 1965, yet our general understanding of how the media covers them and how that influences the global response is defined by four or five of the most dramatic cases (Van Belle, 2009: 85).

Media Coverage, Politics, and Disaster Aid

In a 2007 article in *The Quarterly Journal of Economics*, Swedish researchers Thomas Eisensee and David Strömberg found that the US government's response to natural disasters abroad varies according to the magnitude of news coverage. They analyzed 5,212 disasters occurring worldwide between 1968 and 2002.[3] Using data provided by the Vanderbilt News Archives, they estimated that about a tenth of these disaster events were covered in the evening news broadcasts of the major American television networks (ABC, CBS, NBC, CNN). Twice this number (about 20 percent) received aid from USAID's Office of Foreign Disaster Assistance. Most notably, Eisensee and Strömberg discovered that natural disasters are most likely to receive relief if they occur when there is a low level of competition from other news stories. By contrast, where news pressure is high (e.g. during the Olympics), the provision of disaster assistance is lower. Statistically, to have the same chance of receiving relief, the natural disaster occurring during the highest period of news pressure must have six times as many casualties as the disaster occurring when news pressure registers at its lowest point.

In the working paper version of their article, the researchers admit, "While we find news coverage to affect disaster relief, we do not uncover the exact mechanism through which this happens" (p. 3). They suggest four possibilities. First, information about the disaster can spur citizens' lobbying of political representatives to provide relief (*public action*). Second, providing disaster relief generates favorable publicity, thus making it worthwhile for politicians to act swiftly (*publicity management*). Third, as Drury et al. (2005) have noted, salience drives disaster relief and media coverage is a measure of salience. A television news story is a signal to the policymaker that the disaster matters to the American public and thus deserves relief (*salience cue*). Finally, the news broadcast itself could increase the importance accorded the disaster by the public, and thus by bureaucrats and politicians (*agenda setting*).

The continuing academic debate over the power of media influence to shape government policy in natural disasters and humanitarian crises has swirled in particular around the credibility of what has been called the "CNN effect" (see box 7.1).

Box 7.1 "At the Whim of Electrons"

Initial awareness of the "CNN effect" is often traced to Somalia in 1992–3, events that are said to have resulted in the media becoming a prime driver of American foreign policy. At that time, there were a series of humanitarian crises going on across Africa, including famines in the southern Sudan and in Somalia. The Bush administration appeared to be paying little attention until CNN correspondents started filing graphic visual reports of starving children in Somalia. When Bush subsequently ordered 25,000 US troops into the country to support a relief effort, it was assumed that this was in direct response to pressure from a public horrified by what they were watching daily on cable television. A year later, American television viewers were shocked to witness Somalis dragging the body of a dead American soldier through the streets of Mogadishu, the capital. Soon after, President Bill Clinton announced that he was withdrawing all US soldiers from the zone. As Stephen Hess describes the situation, "So it's often said that we got into Somalia because of horrible pictures; we left Somalia because of horrible television pictures" (Brookings Institution, 2002).

In the aftermath of Somalia, the media were increasingly perceived as becoming an important power broker in international politics. Former UN Secretary-General Boutros Boutros-Ghali was not pleased, "CNN is the sixteenth member of the Security Council" (Minear et al., 1996: 4). Warren Strobel (1996), a former White House correspondent (who is rather skeptical about all this), describes the CNN effect as "the nexus of media power and foreign policy, where television's instantly transmitted images fire public opinion, demanding instant responses from government officials, shaping and reshaping public policy at the whim of electrons." Gilboa (2005: 38) summarizes the argument in this way:

> Most studies of the CNN effect assume a particular model of policymaking. They link media influence on policy to the impact of coverage on public opinion and to subsequent public pressure on leaders to adopt the policy advocated by the media. The media cover a terrible event; the public sees the pictures, whether starvation in Africa or refugees from Kurdistan, and demands that something be done.

Alas, this account now appears to have been seriously overstated. As Strobel (1996) phrases it, "The CNN Effect is narrower and far more complex than the conventional wisdom holds." Indeed, there are a number of cases (notably, the Rwandan genocide in 1994) where governments declined to intervene despite massive television coverage. Gilboa (2005: 38) distinguishes between "control" and "pressure." Rather than forcing policymakers to adopt a particular course of action, it makes more sense to treat the media as one of several factors competing to pressure governments to do so. Where policymakers appear to cave in to media pressure, it may be that a decision has already been made, and media coverage is sought as a source of legitimation.

Continued

Box 7.1 *Continued*

In the case of Somalia, there is plenty of evidence that, at least initially, policymakers were manipulating the media rather than the reverse. While recognizing that "there's no question that television made a big difference," Lawrence Eagleburger, Secretary of State in the Bush cabinet in 1992, recalls that the decision to go into Somalia was seen as a way for the administration to be seen as doing something right at the same time as taking some of the pressure off not doing anything in the Bosnian civil war, where reports of "ethnic cleansing" were already surfacing (Brookings Institution, 2002). Using "the realist approach to international relations" (Gilboa, 2005: 35), Gibbs (2000) argues that US policymakers employed humanitarian justifications, but they were actually more concerned with American strategic and economic interests, specifically those designed to protect shipping routes and oil exploration projects in the Red Sea region. Finally, a clutch of international NGOs, US government relief agencies, and members of Congress interested in Africa were actively campaigning in 1992 to generate media attention and action by the Bush administration on Somalia (Strobel, 1996). As for the sudden withdrawal of troops in 1993, the televised image of a dead soldier being dragged through the streets no doubt forced a sudden response. But evidently the Clinton administration was already making plans to step down – just days before the video started running on CNN, Secretary of State Warren Christopher had told Boutros-Ghali that Washington had decided to pull out (Strobel, 1996).

In his most recent report on media influence and disaster aid, Van Belle (2009) provides what he terms "the first comprehensive outline of the dynamics of the relationship [between media coverage and disaster aid] and what they mean for future policy and action." Building on his earlier (see Van Belle et al., 2004) study of *New York Times* coverage of US development aid between 1985 and 1995, Van Belle adds data on US foreign disaster assistance and extends the disaster database to include the years between 1994 and 2006.

In the earlier study, Van Belle and his colleagues found that media coverage was the most robust and most consistent influence upon foreign aid commitment. However, in this case, something unexpected emerged. In or near 1990, the influence of the media disappeared from disaster aid allocation, exactly the opposite of what might be expected. The researchers identified a similar disruption in the influence of the media on the allocation of foreign disaster aid in Japan (Potter and Van Belle, 2007). This is puzzling because it occurred at about the very same point as when the CNN effect appeared to be at its zenith.

Delving into the political science literature, Van Belle notes that the news media had their strongest effect on disaster assistance during the Cold War period, when every *New York Times* story covering a foreign disaster led to a corresponding increase in aid of roughly US$1.76 million. The Cold War was a time when policy certainty was high and the decision-making rules for allocating disaster relief were bureaucratically entrenched (in the case of US international disaster aid, in the Office of Foreign Disaster Assistance). In this environment, journalists understood the rules well and tailored their stories to the "realist" demands imposed by the political situation. In return, bureau-cratic officials were extremely responsive to coverage, acting on the basis of as little as a single *New York Times* story. With the end of the Cold War, this overarching realist structure vanished and was replaced by an ad hoc policy environment in international politics. This constituted a kind of free for all where political leaders frequently bypassed their bureaucracies and commit-ted relief funds directly, sometimes in response to massive media coverage, sometimes not. What presidents and prime ministers are less likely to do, Van Belle says, is to step in and engage with a disaster that had a low media profile or minimal political payoff.

Mass Media and Discursive Representations of Disasters

"A Reluctant Venice"

In January 1910, Paris experienced its worst flooding since 1658. After weeks of constant rainfall and rising rivers, the Seine peaked at 20 feet above its regular level. Its waters pushed upwards from the saturated soil, overflowing sewers and subway tunnels, and seeping into the basement of thousands of private homes, commercial businesses, and public institutions in central Paris. The platforms at the Gare d'Orsay railroad station sat under several feet of water, while priceless art treasures in the Louvre remained under threat as the floodwaters rose in its basement. Roadways collapsed, making travel by boat the only viable way of getting around. Virtually overnight, Paris became a "reluctant Venice" (McNicoll, 2010).

While the events of the Great Flood of Paris were widely reported in the daily press, it was in the visual media that the saga was conveyed most memo-rably. Hundreds of photographers fanned out across the city, taking thou-sands of pictures of the flooded city and its inhabitants. Those photographs were reproduced in many formats – in books, newspapers, and magazines, on postcards, sheet music, and pamphlets to raise funds for flood victims (Jackson, 2011: 178). American historian Jeffrey Jackson uncovered multiple narratives embedded within these photos, many of which are still archived in Paris's Galerie des Bibliothèques. Jackson explains,

> But images of the flood did not speak to the experience with the same voice. As they were being produced, visual artifacts of the flood created several narratives, each telling a different powerful story. Those narratives offered Parisians multiple ways in which to understand and construe the significance of the flood and provided interpretive frameworks by which to make sense of, respond to, and ultimately decide, the meaning of this event (2011: 178).

Two of these interlocking visual narratives focused on the urban environ-ment of Paris. The first presented Paris as a *ruined city*. These photographs show roadways being ripped up, buildings demolished or sunken underwater, and personal effects scattered about, creating an overwhelming impression of chaos, disorder, and filth. This stood in stark contrast to the officially sanctioned view that Paris was rapidly becoming a modern, technological city of progress, as symbolized by its sewage system, universally regarded as an engineering marvel. A second visual narrative depicted an ethereal and other-worldly *city of beauty*. Downplaying the widespread damage, professional photographers cast Paris as a mysterious, dead place, frozen in time. This played off a cultural fascination in *fin de siècle* France with decadence, decay, and the "pleasure of ruins."

The third narrative, one of *fraternité*, reinterpreted the flood, not as a tragedy but as a heroic moment in Parisian history, featuring the indomitable spirit of local residents. In terms reminiscent of the "altruistic community" (see chapter 1), this narrative presented a story in which ordinary Parisians selflessly pulled together in their hour of need. Their actions ranged from heroic rescues and constructing protective levees and barriers, to stoically carrying on with the everyday commerce of delivering mail, selling bread and food in the shops, and even fishing off the side of bridges. In the concluding section of his article, Jackson (2011: 201) notes:

> This is not to say that Parisians weren't at their best during January and February 1910. Indeed, the stories of hope and rescue are true. But they are only a part of the story, that the images have preselected for us to see and remember today, and they demonstrate the successful reframing of the story as one of triumph and modernity over despair and political failure.

Just as Parisian photographers framed the Great Flood of 1910 in ways that were simultaneously complementary and conflicting, the media today routinely represent international disasters in a manner that only conveys part of the story. This point is paramount in a report published in the 1990s entitled "Media, Disaster Relief and Images of the Developing World." This was the summation of a project sponsored by the Annenberg Washington Program examining the effects of media coverage on disaster relief. Participants in the project included senior officials from the American Red Cross, BBC, CARE, CNN, the International Broadcasting Trust, the International Federation of the Red Cross and Red Crescent Societies, UK Overseas Development Administration, National Public Radio, Save the Children, and other leading media and relief organizations. The same point was repeated the following year by participants at a Roundtable on the Media, Scientific Information and Disasters held under the auspices of the IDNDR. In "Media, Disaster Relief and Images of the Developing World," Annenberg Senior Fellow Fred Cate, the lead author, wrote:

> Much of the public throughout the industrialized world shares an image of developing countries that is incomplete and inaccurate. The efforts of the media to alert the public and report the news accurately and promptly, and of relief organizations to motivate public and governmental support and save human lives, inadvertently contribute to this

image. Because western audiences often lack knowledge of developing countries, reports of exceptional events, such as famines and floods, may foster misrepresentations of the developing world (Cate, 1994).

"Them" versus "Us"

Mass media researchers have long noted the social distance between journalists and those in the population who are less affluent. In *Deciding What's News*, his classic study of four major American television and magazine newsrooms, Herbert Gans (1980) reports that most of the national journalists that he encountered grew up in middle-class or upper-middle-class homes and tended to be upwardly mobile. Relatively few came from working-class homes, and those that did had lost touch with their origins long ago (p. 210). In and of itself, this did not explain the shape of the news. However, it did lead to a cloistered perspective.

This lack of social proximity is especially evident when it comes to recruiting potential news sources. Gans discovered that reporters find it easiest to make contact with sources similar to them in class position, as well as race and age. They encounter communication barriers when dealing with those beneath them in the stratification ladder, especially where the story requires contact with ordinary people. Furthermore, those who don't speak in standard (national middle-class) English dialect that most of the audience is thought to understand are normally avoided as news sources, especially on television (p. 131).

Where these class differences really manifest themselves is in the differential value put on the social order and, by implication, on the values of upper-class and upper-middle-class sectors of society. The media tend to distinguish between two types of news stories. Those that privilege the existing social order deal with the activities of public officials, business leaders, and professionals. By contrast, "disorder news" reports on the threats to various kinds of order (social, moral) and the measures taken to restore order. While journalists do not hesitate to identify politicians and public officials who violate the law or established ethical codes as misbehaving, "moral disorder news involves, by and large, ordinary people, many of them poor, black, and/or young" (Gans, 1980: 60). This leads to a type of journalistic triage between "us" (middle-class upholders of the social order) and "them" (lower-class violators).

This gap in perception based on class differences is equally evident in the international news coverage, where Southern nations assume the role of "them." In a study of television network news from the early 1980s, the researchers argue that television depicts the Third World as "the other," marked by social disorder, flawed development, and primitivism. By contrast, "we" define ourselves as the peaceful, ordered, stable, ethical, humanitarian, capitalistic, industrialized, and civilized West (Dahlgren and Chakrapani, 1982).

Covering the Tsunami

This polarity between "them" and "us" arises time and again in the international media coverage of the 2004 Indian Ocean tsunami and its aftermath. Tracey Skelton, an English social geographer who has spent time in both the Caribbean and Singapore, analyzed articles about the Indian Ocean tsunami that appeared in the British left of center newspaper, the *Guardian*, from December 2004 through February 2005 (total n = 300) (Skelton, 2006). Skelton's research paper offers up evidence pointing to the predominance of the "them versus us" perspective.

Skelton begins her paper by referring to a critical commentary by the anthropologist Greg Bankoff originally published in the journal *Disasters* (Bankoff, 2001). Bankoff detects a discursive continuity that extends from the seventeenth century through the 1990s. This discursive framework revolves around the contrast between the technologically advanced nations of the West and the more "backward" nations of the South that are seen as being "dangerous." In the seventeenth and eighteenth centuries, the dangers to human health were attributed to disease and decay associated with heat and humidity. Western medicine could "cure" these ills. Bankoff labels this a *discourse of tropicality.*

After World War Two, a new discursive framework developed built on the notion of tropicality. *Development discourse* contrasted Western democracies, with their rapid rates of industrialization and urbanization, educated populace, and improved living standards, with the "Third World," which was poverty-stricken and "underdeveloped." According to this development discourse, Western intervention could help through modernizing these Third World nations and giving them "aid." From the 1990s onwards, a *vulnerability discourse* has emerged. This depicts the nations of the South as prone to natural disasters. Western nations have a moral responsibility to intervene and once again "save" vulnerable peoples, this time through "relief, rescue, scientific and technological expertise" (Bankoff, 2001: 27). Bankoff (2001: 24) refers specifically to this "them" vs. "us" dichotomy, "Whatever the term, however, there is an implicit understanding that the place in question is somewhere else, somewhere where 'they' as opposed to 'we' live, and denotes a land and climate that have been endowed with dangerous and life-threatening qualities."

In her research paper, Skelton identifies "three significant tropes within the *Guardian*'s coverage which demonstrate predominant discourses around natural hazards and disasters and which illustrate Bankoff's critical engagement as well" (2006: 13). First, there is the *trope of the early warning system,* which connects to the technocratic and vulnerability discourse. This trope blames Third World governments for their lax emergency preparedness, notably the absence of an effective Pacific tsunami early warning system. Second, the *trope of Western aid, relief, and expertise* connects to the vulnerability and development discourses. This trope contrasts external aid and relief agencies, who are by and large competent and active, with the tsunami-affected countries, who are "in receipt, accepting and passive" (p. 20). Finally, the *tropes of decay, heat, and disease* relate to discourses of vulnerability and tropicality. These tropes repeatedly focus on dead bodies as a potential source of disease (a myth according to public health experts), contaminated water supplies, and the danger of epidemics. Western expertise is said to come to the fore here, especially in the provision of safe water and the disposal of bodies. These tropes, Skelton says, divide the world into *we* and *them*, where "we represent the scientific, knowledgeable and structured part of the world who try in vain to warn and encourage other parts of the world" (p. 18), while the Indian Ocean countries are represented as "chaotic, foolish, and as recipients and victims" (p. 25).

In a cross-national study of newspaper coverage of the Indian Ocean tsunami, Lyn Letukas and her co-researchers report data that are consistent with Skelton's findings. The Letukas team content-analyzed 594 articles that appeared in the eight days following the initial impact, a time period that includes the immediate post-impact and the short-term rescue and recovery phase. Of these, 224 were taken from the *New York Times* and the *Washington Post*, while 370 came from two leading Swedish dailies (*Dagens Nyheter* and *Svenska Dagbladet*). The researchers found that both the Swedish and the American media used "strategies of simplification and personalization to create an intensively narrow and nativist frame" (Letukas et al., 2009: 7). This was most pronounced in the latter case, where the Swedish media concentrated on Swedish tourists trapped by the disaster in Thailand. Typically, stories were crowned with headlines such as "*A Paradise Smashed to Pieces*" and "*The Tourists' Paradise Island Wiped Out*." Echoing Skelton's concern, Letukas criticizes the American newspapers for their consistent use of a "South Asia frame." In adopting this frame, which they describe as "a simple and familiar one for the American audience," the *New York Times* and the *Washington Post* ignore the complex religious, cultural, and ethnic differences between Indonesians, Sri Lankans, and Thais, while sharpening the contrast between them and us (white Americans).

In a framing analysis of US media coverage of Hurricane Katrina and the Indian Ocean tsunami, three graduate students in the College of Communications at Pennsylvania State University (Worawongs et al., 2007) found "logical similarities and problematic differences." The researchers sampled 146 news stories dedicated to the tsunami disaster and 311 to Hurricane Katrina from the evening news programs on three major US broadcast networks: ABC, CBS, and NBC. Common frames frequently utilized in reporting on both disasters were those of *damage* (to infrastructure or nature), *search and rescue*, and *alterations of living conditions* (displacement, separation of families, loss of loved ones, basic physical needs such as drinking water and food).

At the same time, there were some interesting differences. Victimizing frames were much more prevalent in the portrayals of international disaster, especially *mortality* and *injuries and health issues*. Furthermore, the tsunami was presented in a more emotionally magnified manner than was Hurricane Katrina. This was particularly the case for the death of children, who were said to be the most victimized because of their inability to outrun and withstand the massive waves. By contrast, the US media were more prone to use Government, Prevention Management and Reconstruction frames. For example, the prospects of future development and positive change for the victims were more evident in the reporting of Hurricane Katrina.

In keeping with the findings of Skelton and others, the Pennsylvania State University researchers conclude that geographic and cultural proximity constitute major determinants of international coverage: "For a country that is far away from their scope, the identity of the 'other' will make the coverage more sensational, unsystematic and episodic" (Worawongs et al., 2007: 23). This situation is problematic, they say, since "ideologically manipulated international coverage prevents people from becoming well-informed citizens on international issues" (Worawongs et al., 2007: 23).

This final point is amplified in an essay on CNN's tsunami coverage of Sri Lanka (Silva, 2010). Kumarini Silva, an assistant professor at Northeastern University, Boston, went back to Sri Lanka, her homeland, in the summer of 2005 to visit family and to help on a documentary film project on post-tsunami relief. While there, she conversed with survivors of the tsunami and other locals, as well as collecting a number of written documents from the websites of news organizations and the national news media in Sri Lanka. She argues that the foreign media, and in particular CNN, "constructed updated versions of the native/colonizer polarity by focusing on tourists who were vacationing in Phuket, Thailand, or along the coastal areas of Sri Lanka, including several of their own correspondents." These stories were usually contextualized within the frame of the unsuspecting tourist, vacationing with his/her family or friends, whose normal life was destroyed. At the same time, these news reports left out crucial information about the ongoing war and the unstable political situation in Sri Lanka. In contrast to the human interest stories on Western tourists, stories of Sri Lankan nationals "were amalgamated into nameless, faceless figures – long lines of individuals standing in camps – that evoked and reiterated First World expectations of the Other" (2010: 141).

Perhaps all of this should not surprise us too much. As West (2001: 22) points out in relation to the media reporting of humanitarian conflicts, "Because of the shortage of writing time, editorial pressures on broadcast time or article size, and lack of knowledge about the language, history and politics of the conflict region, journalists routinely simplify and categorize issues into an easily digestible form." Furthermore, it is a journalistic convention that foreign news be refracted through a national lens. For example, if a cruise ship sinks in the Caribbean, the first thing a Toronto news editor wants to know is how many victims are Canadian. Even though they are institutionalized, these norms and routines of "news-work" can powerfully shape our perception of natural disasters.

Conclusion

Unlike donors and humanitarian agencies, the media are not major policy architects within the international politics of disaster. Nonetheless, journalists can be quite influential. The influence wielded by the media derives primarily from their role as a fundraising channel during mega-disasters such as the 2010 Haiti earthquake and the 2004 Indian Ocean tsunami, where televised appeals can attract huge sums of money in donations and pledges. This provides international NGOs with an independent source of operating funds so they do not have to depend entirely on donor nations and IFIs such as the World Bank.

The media are often imagined to be a prime driver of foreign policy in humanitarian crises and natural disasters. This can be traced to the Somalian famine during the early 1990s when the phrase "CNN effect" was first coined. According to this model of policymaking, the media undertake saturation coverage of a crisis; a horrified public demands that something be done; and governments have no choice but to respond accordingly. However, two decades of research have indicated that the CNN effect is largely overstated. Rather than dance to the tune of media coverage, policymakers manipulate the media, employing humanitarian justifications to support strategic and economic interests. One researcher, Douglas Van Belle, compared foreign disaster aid allocation and disaster coverage in the *New York Times* over time, concluding that the news media had their strongest effect on disaster assistance during the Cold War, when bureaucrats rather than politicians made key decisions about aid.

If journalists do not reliably shape foreign policy related to disaster aid, they do contribute mightily to shaping disaster discourse. Media coverage, especially television, dwells almost exclusively on the search and rescue period, with dramatic images of survivors being pulled from the rubble, even as hope seems to have been lost. The efforts of international humanitarian groups are often featured, notably those providing urgently needed medical and surgical help to victims. Only rarely (Haiti, New Orleans) is the situation cast within a wider narrative involving class, inequality, and politics. Social science researchers have consistently pointed to the tendency of the media to frame foreign disasters within a "them vs. us" dichotomy. This has been especially evident in international media coverage of the 2004 Indian Ocean tsunami. Finally, journalists have paid scant attention to disaster vulnerability and risk reduction strategies, except in the context of early warning systems for earthquakes, volcanoes, and tsunamis. In the future, this may change as environmental activists play up the alleged links between global climate change and the escalating frequency and magnitude of disaster events (see chapter 5).

Further Reading

E. Gilboa (2005) The CNN effect: the search for a communication theory of international relations. *Political Communication*, 22, 27–44.

T. Skelton (2006) A Case Study of British Media Discourses of the Indian Ocean Tsunami: the December 2004 Coverage. Asian Meta Centre Research Paper Series No. 21, National University of Singapore, June. Accessed from http://www. populationasia.org/Publications/Research_Papers.htm.

D.A. Van Belle (2009) Media agenda-setting and donor aid. In P. Norris (ed.) *Public Sentinel: News Media & Governance Reform*. The World Bank, Washington, DC.

CHAPTER EIGHT

Disaster Politics: A Discursive Approach

As we saw in chapter 6, scholars who study politics and disaster tend to prioritize issues of material interest, security, and political advantage. Recall, for example, the research of Cooper Drury and his colleagues who conclude that international disaster assistance is most often funneled to American allies, regardless of the magnitude of damage and loss of life. In short, disaster politics is a game where moral considerations take a back seat to strategic ones.

Nonetheless, it is next to impossible to adequately understand the international politics of disasters by exclusively and uncritically settling for this realist perspective. Pinpointing a core weakness of realist theory, Keck and Sikkink (1998: 213) observe, "The problem with much of the theory of international relations is that it does not have a motor of change, or that the motor of change – such as state self-interest, or changing power capabilities – is impoverished." Referring specifically to the case of environmental politics, O'Neill (2009: 2) complains, "The state-centric focus of much international relations theory has traditionally omitted the roles and activities of non-state actors – of environmental movements, corporations, even scientists – in influencing existing, and even creating their own, governance institutions." In the same key, Calhoun (2004: 374–5) insists that we cannot understand "the apparent compulsion to intervene [in disasters]" simply by realist reference to state interests; rather, this is "a new cultural construction."

It is essential then that we take seriously ideas about the nature of disaster, its causes and consequences, and how best to cope with it, although this cannot be surgically separated from the hurly burly of power politics. As Hall (1993: 292) notes, "it is not necessary to deny that politics involves a struggle for power and advantage in order to recognize that the movement of ideas plays a role, with some impact of their own in the process of policymaking." Recall, for example, Katarina West's explanation for the upsurge in humanitarian NGOs in the 1980s and 1990s (see chapter 3). Humanitarianism developed from a marginal societal movement to a major international concern, she argues, "because non-state actors have actively campaigned on its behalf and persuaded states to accept the new norm" (2001: 4–5).

At the same time, more traditional political considerations still need to be taken into account. Focusing on relations between Canada and the United States after Hurricane Katrina, Rhinard and Sundelius (2010) observe that shared cognitive and normative networks can certainly help to explain inter-national cooperation, but conflicting mind-sets can also be an obstacle to working together. In this case, they found that foreign policy imperatives tended to intrude in decisions on whether or how to accept aid. As Kent (1987: 118) cautions, the allocation of aid in international disasters should be treated as a dynamic process, wherein conflicting values and resources play a central role, but these must be pursued within the arena of interest politics with its repertoire of strategies, tactics, trade-offs, and linkages.

Discourses of Disaster

Discourses are broad systems of communication that link concepts together in a web of relationships through an underlying logic (Ferree and Merrill, 2000: 455). A more versatile and overarching concept than ideas, discourse simul-taneously refers to a set of ideas and the interactive processes by which these ideas are conveyed (Schmidt, 2008: 309).

In this book, I argue that, in the early twenty-first century, a discourse of *disaster risk reduction (DRR)* has come to occupy center stage in the global policy field of disaster management (chapter 2). Rather than being self-contained, DRR is situated within a wider "discursive field." Drawing on Schipper and Pelling's (2006) three interrelated "realms of action" or "spheres of influence" that potentially contribute to integrated policy formation on climate change and disaster risk, I depict this using a Venn diagram (see figure 8.1). Disaster risk reduction inhabits the common space created by four overlapping circles, each of which represents a more encompassing discursive realm: hazard, risk, and safety; humanitarian aid; international development; and environmen-talism and climate change.

I have revised and expanded Schipper and Pelling's scheme in several ways. Whereas they describe these realms of action/spheres of influence as consti-tuting "communities of practice," I treat them as "discursive realms." Each of these discursive realms is anchored by an identifiable set of "institutional structures and tools," as Schipper and Pelling put it; and these do, as they suggest, have a tendency to remain somewhat segregated. Conceptually, however, it is easier to depict these differences discursively rather than organ-izationally. One advantage of doing it this way is avoiding having to account for NGOs such as the Red Cross that concurrently deliver humanitarian aid, engage in international development, and embrace climate change adapta-tion measures. Furthermore, rather than a stand-alone realm, as is the case in Schipper and Pelling's model, I depict the paradigm of disaster risk reduc-tion as being both shaped and constrained by the mutual engagement of four other discursive realms. As Christoplos et al. (2001: 193) point out, disaster mitigation and preparedness (DMP), an earlier version of disaster risk reduc-tion, is not a "sector;" rather, it "should be addressed as a continuous and integrated process involving a broad spectrum of actors."

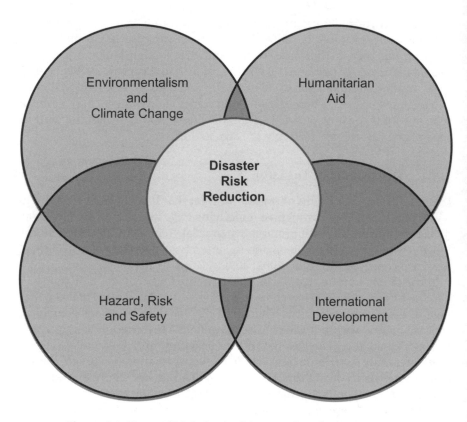

Figure 8.1 *Disaster Risk Reduction Discourse: Contributing Discursive Realms*

In so doing, I am not by any means claiming that discourse can "act" in a sociological sense – only people can do that. As powerful as they are, ideas are not self-propelling. As Schmidt (2008: 19) observes, it's naïve to assume that the power of ideas will somehow magically overcome opposition from those in powerful positions. Ideas motivate, but they do not provide opportunity. Doing that is the role of those institutions that structure political openings for the mobilization and articulation of interests. Morrill and Owen-Smith (2002: 93) make this same point with reference to collective action frames. Frames, they note, do not emerge from thin air, nor do they develop by themselves from organic, mystical processes. Rather, "they require real people in interaction and conflict to formulate, contest, modify, and deploy them." In this spirit, Kingdon (1984) describes the formulation and successful construction of public policy problems, alternatives, and decisions as constituting an interactive process among policy entrepreneurs, experts, bureaucrats, politicians, and the media (see Barzelay and Gallego, 2006: 539).

Four Discursive Realms Contributing to DRR

Hazard, risk, and safety discourse originated within the scientific and technical community. Initially, it was the sole province of "experts and specialists in the natural sciences," who undertook studies regarding "geodynamic, hydrometeorological and technological phenomena such as earthquakes, volcanic eruptions, mudslides, flooding and industrial accidents" (Cardona, 2004: 39). Their central focus here was the physical hazard itself: how to accurately predict its occurrence, and how to optimally reduce the magnitude of structural damage it caused. Typically, earthquake engineers sought to mitigate the widespread destruction experienced in Central American shantytowns by designing residential structures that were more resilient. While this analysis was not explicitly undertaken from a social perspective, such studies often concluded that the space/locations which poor people inhabited and the houses and built environment they lived in were particularly vulnerable to natural hazards (Juneja, 2008).

By the 1980s, this was beginning to change. The social aspects of the risk discourse were becoming more pronounced and it was increasingly recognized that social processes generate unequal exposure to risk by making some people more prone to disaster than others. Cardona (2004: 43) notes that, in addition to physical aspects of hazards, social factors were attracting considerable attention. In Latin American countries, for example, broad risk factors included: "the fragility of the family and the collective economy; the absence of basic social utilities; lack of access to property and credit; the presence of ethnic and political discrimination; polluted air and water resources; high rates of illiteracy; and the absence of educational opportunities."

During the International Decade for Natural Disaster Reduction (1990–9), hazard, risk and safety discourse was paramount, and technocratic solutions were privileged. Bankoff (2001: 25) observes, "A glance at the resolution adopted by the UN declaring the 1990s the International Decade for Natural Disaster Reduction clearly reveals such assumptions with four of its five goals concerned with mitigation through the dissemination of technical information and the transfer of scientific and engineering knowledge."

As I discuss in chapter 3, **humanitarian aid discourse** has its roots in the relief efforts undertaken during and after the two World Wars, but did not really rise to prominence until the early 1990s.[1] Rather than being grounded in warrants that framed disaster management exclusively in terms of risk and safety, humanitarianism emphasized the *moral* duty of those in the developed world to rush to the rescue of those in overseas countries who are left hungry and homeless in major emergencies. Rescue here implied meeting short-term needs rather than addressing the longer-term problems of poverty and chronic exposure to risk. Some versions of humanitarian discourse even implicitly drew on a type of cybernetic or systems approach, affirming that the end goal of international relief efforts was to return the community to the way it was before the disaster struck. In this, it echoed the technocratic paradigm within the hazard, risk, and safety discourse, where disasters were represented as "a departure from a state of normalcy to which a society returns on recovery" (Bankoff, 2001: 24).

A third discursive realm that contributes to DRR is **international development**. As Pieterse (2010: 14) has pointed out, one promising methodology for studying different approaches to development is to employ discourse analysis as an analytic instrument. By doing so, we are able to take a step beyond treating development as purely ideology, or interest articulation. In one popular version of this, development discourse is treated as a narrative or story. While he is not attracted to versions of discourse analysis that are overtly anti-Western, anti-modernist, or that purport to unmask the development narrative as nothing more than a "fairy tale," Pieterse does accept that the meanings of development have changed over time, and these changes reflect general trends both in global society and in social science. From the 1950s onwards, there have been seven distinct perspectives on, or meanings of, development theory: modernization theory (1950s), dependency theory (1960s), alternative development paradigm (1970s), human development (inspired by Amartya Sen's (1985) *capabilities* approach) (1980s), neoliberalism (1980s), post-development (1990s), and the Millennium Development Goals (2000+).

International development as a disaster discourse realm has more or less proceeded in lock step with these discursive shifts. In the 1950s and 1960s, growth was seen in quite narrow economic terms and measured by standard quantitative indicators such as the gross national product (GNP); the terms growth and development were used as if they were interchangeable; and capital-intensive infrastructure projects such as large roads and airports and university campuses were built in what were labeled as the less developed countries (McAllister, 1993: 12–14).

Just over a decade ago, Bankoff (2001: 19) predicted that "Disasters seem destined to be major issues of academic enquiry in the new century if for no other reason than they are inseparably linked to questions of environmental conservation, resource depletion and migration patterns in an increasingly globalised world." Bankoff's prediction has turned out to be partially correct, although he failed to include global climate change on his list of pressing environmental concerns.

Until quite recently, sociological research on natural disasters failed to recognize the logical connection between disasters and the environment (Hannigan, 2010). By contrast, natural hazards researchers, situated as many were within the discipline of geography, were more readily attuned to issues of environmental risk. However, it was in the area of political ecology that this link between disasters and the environment was most vigorously pursued. Eakin and Luers (2006: 370) point out that political ecology, and earlier on, political economy approaches to vulnerability "have evolved from and often in response to risk-hazard assessments of climate impacts and disasters." A good illustration of this can be found in Diana Liverman's oft-cited (1990) article on agriculture and drought in Mexico. Liverman, who had been a Masters student and research assistant in the late 1970s at Ian Burton's Institute of Environmental Studies at the University of Toronto, argued that crop failures in the Mexican states of Sonora and Puebla during drought periods could not be explained purely through precipitation patterns. Rather, these were associated with differences in land tenure and access to resources, sources of inequity that are both social and political.

In the global policy field of natural disasters, the discourse of **environmentalism and climate change** first came to the fore as a result of the Rio conference. Writing in the early 1990s, McAllister (1993: 16) reports that the Red Cross and Red Crescent movement was represented at the Rio "Earth Summit" and more and more national societies are becoming involved in environmental issues. McAllister continues:

> Those most vulnerable to environmental breakdowns are the poorest and most vulnerable – the same groups that represent the major "target groups for Red Cross humanitarian concerns." "Relief" and "development" is becoming a more routinely accepted phrase within the Red Cross: "relief," "development" and the "environment" now require greater recognition as interconnected components (1993: 16).

By the dawn of the twenty-first century, discursive threads from each of these four realms – hazard, risk, and safety; humanitarian aid; international development; and environmentalism and climate change – had knit together sufficiently so that it was possible to speak of a distinct discourse of disaster risk reduction. It is important to keep in mind, however, that this DRR discourse has not replaced its four discursive donors, each of which has continued to exist independently. Analyzing international development approaches from 1950 to 1990, Chabbott (1999: 238) observed that new discursive themes do not entirely replace older ones, but rather merge to create increasingly complex definitions of development and more diffuse responsibilities for nation states and development organizations. Chabbott's insight applies equally well to disaster discourse.

Disaster Risk Reduction Paradigm: Diffusion and Barriers to Adoption

In an ideal world, a new policy discourse would be widely and immediately recognized as sensible and worthwhile, and it would be instantly embraced. The real world, of course, operates differently and new ways of thinking and acting are normally contested, or even ignored. The discourse of disaster risk reduction is no different. Since it first emerged in the 1980s, DRR has moved onto center stage in the global field of disaster management, but it is not universally accepted. A particular problem has been how to mainstream DRR in the international development sector. Furthermore, disaster risk reduction only faintly resonates with the general public, who continue to view "foreign" disasters primarily through the lens of the mass media during major emergencies.

In this section, I intend to trace the diffusion of DRR across the disaster management field; identify the barriers that continue to limit its further progress; and assess the strategic advantages and drawbacks of casting its fate into the cauldron of climate change policy. To introduce this discussion, I will first review several key perspectives from the fields of political science and sociology on paradigm change and the transnational diffusion of new ideas, norms, and institutions.

In his seminal book *The Structure of Scientific Revolutions*, Thomas Kuhn (1996 [1962]) treats paradigm change as the outcome of a conflict between an established and a challenging theory, wherein a "crisis" of understanding and proof has ensued. Crises unleash short bouts of intense ideational contestation that can and do result in one policy paradigm replacing another (Blyth, 2002; Hay, 2004: 207). In Kuhn's model of scientific revolutions (he says this applies equally to political life), as the paradigmatic crisis deepens, we witness the division "into competing camps or parties, one seeking to defend the old institutional constellation, the other seeking to institute some new one." Kuhn characterizes paradigm change as radical and abrupt. However, some political researchers prefer a more gradual model that views paradigm change as "an evolutionary process, the result of cumulative reforms that may take a decade or more and whose outcome is not necessarily a decisive rupture with the past" (Skogstad and Schmidt, 2012: 8).

Transnational Diffusion of New Ideas, Norms, and Institutions

In the 1990s, two perspectives arose which sought to explain patterns of global diffusion of new ideas, norms, and institutions in political life and the mechanisms that facilitate this process. While the dynamics differ, both explanations centrally address the problem of how transnational political actors "force governments to act, that is, translate moral into political imperatives" (Laqueur, 2009: 36).

World Polity Institutionalism

Proponents of *world polity institutionalism*, which has thrived primarily within the area of political sociology, detects a seismic shift wherein cooperative voluntarism, democratic decision making, acceptance of consensually agreed-upon rules, and reasoned settlement of disputes are recognized as basic world-cultural principles. In this view, a set of common global norms and values suffuses more and more states in a world institutional structure, thus subsuming the traditional, international political world (Parks and Roberts,

2010: 138). Contrary to the claims of neo-realists, national states are not the leaders in provoking political and social change. Rather, international non-governmental organizations (INGOs) lobby, criticize, and convince states to act on world-cultural principles (Boli and Thomas, 1997: 187). Changes in world polity (international organization) follow from changes in culture. This process occurs in three stages (Boli and Thomas, 1999; Frank, 2002: 46–51; Meyer et al., 1997).

In the first stage, which occurs more or less concurrently with world-cultural changes, INGOs emerge. INGOs represent the primary arena in which world-cultural conceptions of values, principles, standards, and norms are developed, codified, modified, and propagated (Boli et al., 1999: 73). This leads to a proliferation of intergovernmental transactions, initially in the form of conferences, followed by conventions, agreements, and treaties.

According to the world polity model, more permanent intergovernmental organizations appear, usually as a direct outcome of the second stage. In the international politics of disasters, this has transpired, but only weakly. As we have seen, political and financial support for the International Strategy for Disaster Reduction (ISDR) has been tepid, both from donors and from the family of nations. The package of administrative reforms in 2008 was designed to buttress its support by creating the position of an Assistant Secretary-General who is concurrently the Special Representative of the UN Secretary-General for the implementation of the Framework. Nevertheless, the ISDR continues to be eclipsed by more powerful voices within the disaster policy network, notably DFID, the World Bank, and several of the larger NGOs (Oxfam, Red Cross/Red Crescent, World Vision).

World polity institutionalism has been criticized on the grounds that it fails to specifically address the political and sociological processes through which new norms and culture diffuse, take hold transnationally, and are adopted by specific nation states. Keck and Sikkink (1998: 211) argue that world polity theorists skip over the earlier stages of creating and institutionalizing new norms, focusing primarily on the second part of the process of change when norms acquire a taken-for-granted quality. Any discussion of power, contestation, and conflict is virtually absent. Buttel (2000: 119) complains that the transmission of new cultural directives, for example environmental rationality, from global society to the nation state is portrayed in conflict-free terms, with no mention of coercion or contestation. While they acknowledge the contribution of international organizations and international nongovernmental organizations, world polity theorists treat them "as conveyor belts carrying Western liberal norms elsewhere" (Buttel, 2000). In his study of the genesis and history of long-distance advocacy networks engaged in action against the slave trade in the eighteenth and nineteenth centuries, Stamatov (2010) argues that this notion of the formation of a world culture as a progressive diffusion of core principles is too simplistic. Instead, he asserts that his account "suggests that global cultural transformations are better understood as a contested and contingent process, not a process of the progressive spread of relatively well formed, basic ideas" (2010: 622).

Normative Socialization Theory

In contrast to the world polity model, *normative socialization theory* stresses the central importance of human agency and contestation (Finnemore, 1999: 163). Whereas world polity theory arose within political sociology, normative socialization theory has thrived within the field of international relations. Its proponents draw on an eclectic toolkit of sources that includes network analysis, legal theory, and the sociology of social movements.

One influential version of normative socialization theory privileges the contribution of *transnational advocacy networks*. Keck and Sikkink introduced this perspective in their award-winning book *Activists Beyond Borders: Advocacy Networks in International Politics* (1998). In addition to national states continually engaged in self-interested, strategic game playing, the authors maintain that the international system is composed of advocacy networks of activists organized to promote causes, principled ideas, and norms. Keck and Sikkink take pains to distinguish these from both transnational social movements and global civil society.[2] An important focal point in the activities of advocacy networks is the international *campaign*, which they treat as a process of issue construction, where activists identify a problem, specify a cause, and propose a solution (1998: 8). Throughout their book, the authors remind us that transnational advocacy networks proactively seek to influence public policy, primarily through persuasion and socialization. They also stress that such efforts frequently encounter sharp resistance, suggesting that international campaigns be thought of as an *arena of struggle*.

To explain how transnational advocacy networks work, Keck and Sikkink (1998: 17) point to the construction of cognitive frames as an essential component of political strategizing. In his book on the "new transnational activism," Tarrow (2005: 60) puts a premium on *global framing*, which he defines as "the use of external symbols to orient local or national claims." Ideally, this can broaden and invigorate claims that might otherwise remain narrow and parochial. For example, a "global justice frame" can help to make sense of and unify a variety of local grievances from plant closings to genetically modified crops.[3]

In 1998, Kathryn Sikkink, the co-author of *Beyond Borders*, together with Martha Finnemore, published a model of global "norm dynamics" in the journal *International Organization*. Finnemore and Sikkink (1998) depict norm influence in international politics as a three-stage process: norm emergence, norm cascade (broad and rapid norm acceptance), and internalization. A threshold, or "tipping point," divides these two stages; it is here that a critical mass of state actors adopts the norm (Sikkink, 1998: 518).

In the initial stage, "norm entrepreneurs" attempt to convince a critical mass of national states to embrace new norms, primarily through the vehicle of persuasion. Variously described as "transnational moral entrepreneurs" (Nadelmann, 1990) and "meaning managers" or "meaning architects" (Lessig, 1995), norm entrepreneurs "are critical for norm emergence because they call attention to issues or even 'create' issues by using language that names, interprets, and dramatizes them" (Finnemore and Sikkink, 1998: 896). Henry Dunant of the International Committee of the Red Cross (ICRC) was a proto-typical norm entrepreneur (see chapter 3) or, as Forsythe (2005: 15) puts it, "idea entrepreneur." Buchanan-Smith (2003) describes Peter Walker (of IFRC) and Nick Stockton (of Oxfam) as "policy entrepreneurs" who played catalytic roles in Sphere's birth and in its infancy (see chapter 2).

An essential component in this political strategizing is the construction of cognitive frames that resonate with broader public understandings. Finnemore and Sikkink make two important and interrelated points here. First, new norms "never enter a normative vacuum, but instead emerge in a highly contested normative space where they must compete with other norms and perceptions of interest" (1998: 896). This addresses a weakness in world polity theory, wherein the possibility of contestation arising in the diffusion of world culture is not anticipated. Second, "norm promoters" require some kind of *organizational platform*. This can either be an established international body (World Bank, International Labour Organization) or one created specifically for the purpose of promoting the norm (Greenpeace, International Red Cross).

Once established, the norm spreads across the globe until it acquires a taken-for-granted quality. In the second stage, it "cascades" (Sunstein, 1997) through the community of states. Finnemore and Sikkink do not elaborate on the sociological nature of the diffusion process, variously suggesting that it follows a "dynamic of imitation" or takes the form of a "contagion." The dominant mechanisms here are said to be socialization, demonstration, and institutionalization. To their credit, the authors do recognize that the successful completion of the "norm life cycle" is not inevitable. Indeed, many emergent norms fail to reach a tipping point.

How do *transnational civil society* actors[4] succeed in changing hegemonic norms and practices and in creating new structures of power and meaning? Richard Price (2003) concludes that the key here is firmly establishing a sense of "authority." He further asserts that transnational activists derive their authority from three principal sources: expertise, moral influence, and a claim to political legitimacy. Expertise is exercised by *epistemic communities*, coalitions of scientist-activists and policymakers – usually transnational in scope – who share a common understanding of the nature of a problem and the appropriate solution (Young, 1994: 96).

World polity institutionalism and normative socialization theory each propose some ideas that are helpful in explaining the long, winding path taken by the international politics of disaster, but neither is fully adequate. World polity institutionalism situates the genesis of new values, principles, standards, and norms with civil society actors, most specifically INGOs. In a second stage, these new cultural conceptions are unwrapped at international conferences, and universally proclaimed through multilateral conventions, agreements, and treaties. Finally, "world culture" is institutionalized in the form of permanent intergovernmental organizations.

This model loosely describes the evolution of new paradigms of natural disaster, but it wraps things up much too neatly and abruptly. To date, a steady proliferation of congresses, conferences, agendas, strategies, plans of action, and even a designated International Decade for Natural Disaster Reduction, convened under the *imprimatur* of the United Nations, have not been sufficient to produce a binding treaty comparable to the Montreal Protocol on Ozone Depletion or an officially struck "consensus organization" such as the Intergovernmental Panel on Climate Change (IPCC). Whereas world culture is framed as a progressive diffusion of core principles, the culture of disaster reduction is more stop and go, frequently contested and contingent. Commitment to DRR remains very uneven, even in those countries identified as "disaster hotspots."

Normative socialization theory more adequately captures the dynamics of change. First and foremost, it acknowledges that the international system is *concurrently* composed of national states, continually engaged in self-interested, strategic game playing; and transnational advocacy networks, who adopt a more altruistic focus.

Additionally, normative socialization theory proposes that new ideas emerge in a highly contested "normative space" where they continually clash. This is very much the case with disaster paradigms. In particular, the disaster reduction paradigm has challenged embedded principles and regimes of humanitarian relief for nearly three decades. Note, however, that multiple frames may compete within the *same* discursive field (Steensland, 2008: 1031). In the case of disaster reduction, this is illustrated by the intermittent tension between seismologists, volcanologists, geologists, engineers, and others who adopt a technical orientation to disaster risk; and human geographers, political ecologists, and overseas development workers who prefer an approach that puts social vulnerability front and center. As Steensland (2008: 1029) makes clear, "People can share a frame while holding different substantive policy preferences."

Coordinative versus Communicative Discourse

Schmidt (2008) has distinguished between two fundamental forms of discourse in the realm of politics: the *coordinative discourse* among policy actors, and the *communicative discourse* between policy actors and the public. In the policy sphere, coordinative discourse refers to:

individuals and groups at the center of policy construction who are involved in the creation, elaboration, and justification of policy and programmatic ideas. These are the policy actors – the civil servants, elected officials, experts, organized interests and activists, among others – who seek to coordinate agreement among themselves on policy ideas (2008: 310).

Communicative discourse occurs in the political rather than the policy sphere. It consists of individuals and groups involved in the presentation, deliberation, and legitimation of political ideas to the general public. In addition to politicians and civil servants representing the governing regime, other participants in communicative discourse are members of opposition parties, the media, pundits, community leaders, social activists, public intellectuals, experts, think tanks, organized interests, and social movements. Tracing discursive processes of coordination and communication, Schmidt tells us, is a way of showing why ideas may succeed or fail. "What makes for a successful discourse, in fact, encompasses a lot of the same things that make for successful ideas: relevance to the issues at hand, adequacy, applicability, appropriateness and resonance" (Schmidt, 2008: 311).

In the global policy field of natural disasters, most ongoing dialog takes the form of coordinative, as opposed to communicative, discourse. With an occasional exception (rebuilding New Orleans after Hurricane Katrina; energy futures in the wake of the Japanese earthquake, tsunami, and nuclear crisis), policies, programs, and philosophies that resonate within disaster politics consistently fail to engage the aspirations and ideals of the general public. As Schmidt (2008: 308) observes, meeting the test of appropriateness means not just the presence of sound cognitive ideas capable of satisfying policymakers that a given approach will provide robust solutions; it also "depends on the presence of complementary normative ideas capable of satisfying policy makers and citizens alike that those solutions also serve the underlying values of the polity."

Most state-of-the-art interpretations of natural disasters that stress the importance of understanding vulnerability, risk reduction, and adaptation only weakly resonate in the public sphere. Although significant progress has been made in recent years, nevertheless, there has not been a complete paradigm shift in disaster research and policy either. As Pelling (2003: 240) observed nearly a decade ago, "Despite 30 years of technical research and a plethora of engineering-based solutions, joined more recently by efforts to reduce social vulnerability, the disaster-development relationship remains dominated by disaster response."

One source of the failure of DRR discourse to punch through into public consciousness lies in the origins and early years of disaster reduction (see chapter 4). Rather than originate in a critique formulated by transnational social movements and networks, DRR first emerged in an epistemic community composed primarily of earthquake engineers and supported by meteorologists. By the time the International Decade for Natural Disaster Reduction had been declared in 1990, the seismic scientists were giving way to a bevy of United Nations careerists and consultants whose roots were in the fields of humanitarian relief, international development, and social justice. This has some of the attributes of a social movement, but it also differs in some important ways.

Referring to transnational civil society generally, Florini and Simmons (1999: 8) distinguish between NGO service providers such as CARE and Doctors Without Borders (Médecins sans Frontières), celebrated for their humanitarian relief efforts and development work in poor countries, and members of advocacy networks or coalitions, who form the backbone of transnational civil society and are the main drivers of normative and value change. The two overlap, the authors say, but are not identical. Following the path carved in the 1990s, one of the distinguishing features of the global policy field of natural disasters is that service providers (Red Cross, Oxfam), along with epistemic communities of scientists, continue to act as the main sources of advocacy, rather than social movement activists.

Another professional overlap is between service providers and the state. In her recent book, *The Women's Movement: Inside and Outside of the State*, Lee Ann Banaszak (2010) argues that social movements cannot be assumed to be "outside" the state, but rather activists link social movements and the state by operating both within and outside of government service. If this is the case, then "the extent to which state actors and social movement activists constitute separate groups becomes an empirical question rather than a conceptual distinction" (Beckwith, 2011: 1064).

It is not unusual to find individual actors in the global policy field of disasters effortlessly moving back and forth between government, IGOs, and NGOs. Consider, for example, the career of the late Julia Vadala Taft. Taft was an early and outspoken advocate for putting social vulnerability at the epicenter of disaster risk reduction. From 1986 to 1989, she served as Director of the United States Office of Foreign Disaster Assistance, where she coordinated the federal government's response to earthquakes, floods, famine, and locust infestations around the world (Hevesi, 2008). In the 1990s, Taft moved on to the presidency of Interaction, a coalition of more than 150 NGOs that work on international aid and development. By decade's end, she had shifted back into government, serving as Assistant Secretary of State for Population, Refugees and Migration in the Clinton Administration. Taft finished her career at the United Nations, taking on several senior assignments, including that of Director of the UN Bureau for Crisis Prevention and Recovery (2001–4). Although not a member of a social movement organization per se, Julia Taft could nevertheless be considered an activist in the sense that Banaszak intends.

Another reason that "there may be no arrows between the coordinative and communicative discourses" (Schmidt, 2008: 311) in the global policy field of natural disasters is an overwhelming lack of popular knowledge of and interest in disaster risk reduction. Partly this reflects the absence of the kind of dramatic and topical media images that are so emblematic of humanitarian relief discourse. Even as I am writing this paragraph, the CBC newsreader is talking about starving children and dying cattle in the Horn of Africa as being a result of the recurrence of a killer famine. As Simon Levine of the Overseas Development Institute recently blogged, we have been here before (1999/2000, 2002/3, 2005/6, 2008/9) and will be again. Each time we have had ample warning but the humanitarian system inevitably responds too late and to the wrong signals, as do governments in the region. Crucially, areas that are supposed to be reserved for grazing during droughts have been taken over for settlements, irrigation schemes, and private investors. Meanwhile, "the spectre of famine" reappears on our television screens and in our newspapers, with urgent public appeals for help (Levine, 2011). Of course, as we saw in chapter 7, this "CNN effect" rarely creates an inevitable pressure on national governments to deliver vast quantities of aid; at best, it may be one factor among many bearing on the situation. But media preoccupation with crisis and humanitarian response dominates communicative discourse in the public sphere, leaving little room for any discussion of mitigation and prevention.

Disaster risk management does not make it easy for ordinary folk in the developed countries of the North "to do something to help out" in the more vulnerable countries of the South. Unlike with humanitarian appeals in the aftermath of disaster, you cannot just go online or call a toll-free number to make a donation, or volunteer your time to bundle up blankets or clothing for shipment to overseas victims of a flood or hurricane. Similarly, there is no equivalent to reducing your "carbon footprint" by consuming less or more wisely, as is the case with climate change reduction activism.

Risk-reductive activities such as lobbying local municipalities for tighter zoning regulations in flood plains or mandatory use of earthquake-resistant construction materials may be terrifically important but they barely resonate at a popular level. While a discourse of vulnerability and risk reduction as social justice is potentially powerful, too often it devolves into professional development jargon where the methodologies and language are much too technical to capture the sustained interest of the public. While this type of approach is undoubtedly helpful to disaster reduction planners and practitioners, it ensures that DRR will remain inaccessible, embedded "in closed debates out of public view" (Schmidt, 2008: 311).

One potential solution to this dilemma has been to link DRR discourse with that of climate change adaptation. In the sport of inline skating, *drafting* means following closely behind another skater in order to benefit from the resulting decrease in wind resistance. You can conserve energy by engaging in drafting, but doing it successfully requires good communication between skaters. To a certain extent, *discursive drafting* is comparable to David Snow's well-known concept of "frame alignment." In the latter case, social movement strategists craft social movement organization frames so that they are compatible with broader culture themes in society. With discursive drafting, policy actors attempt to skate in the slipstream of other competing policy communities whose discursive offerings generate a greater degree of popular legitimacy and recognition.

The recent flirtation of DRR with the global climate change community is an example of discursive drafting. As I noted in chapter 5, despite some significant political setbacks, climate change as an issue still has the political and popular attention that DRR lacks. For example, more than six million people are estimated to have tuned into Al Gore's "Climate Reality Project," a live video broadcast online for 24 hours in 24 time zones. On their part, climate change activists recognize that they need to ratchet up the rhetorical pressure, supplementing clips of polar bears and crumbling icebergs with footage of natural disasters. Thus, the Climate Reality Project site "showed images of dramatic weather events that advocates say are directly linked to climate change: a woman fleeing from a forest fire in Russia, a man in Brazil holding a rope during a mudslide, a dried-up lake in Switzerland" (Stone, 2011: A18). Gore's video presentation does not directly promote the idea of disaster risk reduction, but it does create an opportunity for DRR advocates to adopt the tactic of discursive drafting. But caution is required. In the sport of inline skating, forcing your way into a line can make the other skater and all the skaters behind fall down (Fry, 2011). So too, riding the climate change draft can be perilous, especially if communication between the discursive skaters is poor.

Conclusion

While much of what transpires in the international politics of disaster is explainable using a realist perspective, this alone is insufficient to account for the tremendous upsurge in humanitarian concern and response since World War Two. To do so, we must turn to a "constructivist" approach that features the analysis of discourse – a broad system of communication that conveys ideas. In the early twenty-first century, the most dynamic discourse in the global policy field of disasters is that of disaster risk reduction (DRR). Rather than stand alone, DRR is located at the interstices of four *discursive realms* – hazard, risk, and safety; humanitarian aid; international development; and environmentalism and climate change.

Despite having diffused widely within the disaster management sector, DRR remains marginal to mainstream international development, as well as resonating only faintly with the public-at-large. In this, it neither follows world polity institutionalism nor normative socialization theory, two perspectives within sociology and political science that seek to account for the global diffusion of new ideas, norms, and institutions. A major difficulty here is that within the global policy field of natural disasters, most ongoing dialog takes the form of coordinative rather than communicative discourse. That is, it occurs within the policy rather than the political or public sphere.

One potential solution to this problem has been to engage in the process of what I call discursive drafting, flowing in the slipstream of another, more popular discursive offering. DRR proponents have made tentative attempts to link up with the better funded and more publicly recognized global climate change community, specifically proponents of climate change adaptation (CCA). However, as discussed in chapter 5, this carries with it certain risks, most notably that DRR will be co-opted or transformed by CCA, which is informed by a rather different set of assumptions and priorities.

Further Reading

Martha Finnemore and Kathryn Sikkink (1998) International norm dynamics and political change. *International Organization*, 52, 887–917.

Lisa Schipper and Mark Pelling (2006) Disaster risk, climate change and international development: scope for, and challenges to, integration. *Disasters*, 30, 19–38.

Vivian A. Schmidt (2008) Discourse institutionalism: the explanatory power of ideas and discourse. *Annual Review of Political Science*, 11, 303–26.

CHAPTER NINE

Conclusion

Nearly four decades ago, fellow Canadian disaster researcher Rod Kueneman and I took to the field to study the community response to springtime flooding in southern Manitoba. We spent the first day hanging around the situation room, orienting ourselves to the flood threat, and the governmental handling of it. At one point during the afternoon, a provincial disaster manager became rather agitated. The official disaster plan stipulated that all information about flood levels was to be channeled exclusively through the command center, before being released to the public. A caller to a Winnipeg open-line radio show had unknowingly challenged that monopoly by spreading "rumors" that suggested existing control measures were proving insufficient to hold back the waters in one city neighborhood. We weren't sure whether the emergency manager was piqued because he thought that the caller was recklessly spreading panic in the community, or because, to him, this constituted an unanticipated and unauthorized breach of a disciplined, self-contained disaster response system.

In a command and control model of disaster management such as this, novelty and uncertainty have no place. Both the nature of the disaster agent, and how best to respond to the threat it poses, are treated as identifiable and actionable. If things go wrong – and they sometimes do – this is interpreted as a matter of poor communication, coordination, or leadership; and the proper steps are subsequently taken to remedy the situation.

Leonard and Howitt (2007) note that this style of responding to disasters is characteristic of *routine* or *familiar* emergencies, those that arise regularly and are closely related to others that have come before. By contrast, they say, some of the emergencies that have arisen in recent years are *not* like those we have previously experienced. These *crisis* or *novel* emergencies are distinguished from more familiar emergencies by virtue of "unusual scale, a previously unknown cause, or an atypical combination of sources" (2007: 4). Some examples are the 2004 Indian Ocean tsunami in Banda Aceh; Hurricane Katrina with its novel combinations of flooding and infrastructure loss; the 2005 earthquake in Pakistan; and the 2003 SARS (Severe Acute Respiratory Syndrome) scare in Hong Kong and Toronto. No doubt, if they were given an opportunity to update their chapter, the authors would cite the 2011 Japanese earthquake and tsunami that has presented challenges never before faced, most notably the potentially catastrophic damage to the nuclear plant prompted by the tsunami. In a crisis emergency:

> [t]he presence of significant novelty implies that understanding of the situation, at least at the outset, will be relatively low, and that there will be no executable script or routine that is known or identifiable and that provides a comprehensive, reliable, and fully adequate response. Existing routines are inadequate or even counterproductive (Leonard and Howitt, 2007: 7).

Emergent Institutionalism

One innovative attempt to understand socially constructed responses to uncertain risks is Ansell and Gingrich's (2007) concept of *emergent institutionalism*. The two British researchers first introduced this in a chapter they wrote on the BSE ("mad cow") epidemic in the United Kingdom in the 1980s.

The authors begin with Karl Weick's (1995) concept of "sense making." By sense making, Weick, a noted organizational scholar, means "a response to events in which people develop some sort of sense regarding what they are up against, what their own position is relative to what they sense, and what they need to do" (Weick, 1999: 42). Whereas framing emphasizes the external, strategic process of creating specific meaning in line with political interests, sense making stresses the internal, self-conscious process of developing a coherent account of what is going on (Fiss and Hirsch, 2005: 31).

In an "emergent problem" such as the BSE case, where no one is quite sure what it is they are dealing with, much of what happens subsequently depends on who initially does the interpreting. Once jurisdiction is effectively claimed over a developing problem, other subsequent attempts at sense making tend to be rebuffed, even when new information that contradicts the original interpretation becomes available. In the BSE case, this resulted in sticking too long to the notion that what scientists were dealing with was exclusively an animal health risk rather than a human health concern. What may occur then is *a serious mismatch between emergent problems and emergent institutions*. The term "emergent" here refers to "a problem-specific constellation of resources, relationships, authority and expertise" (Ansell and Gingrich, 2007: 172). Sheila Jasanoff, a leading policy scholar, on issues relating to science, technology, and risk, makes a similar point. As was the case with both Hurricane Katrina and the Boxing Day tsunami, the solution to a perceived social problem depends on the adequacy of its original framing: "If a problem is framed too narrowly, too broadly, or simply in the wrong terms, the solution will suffer from the same defects" (Jasanoff, 2010: 31). What Jasanoff does not mention is the importance of who claims the right to do the initial framing of the problem.

Ansell and Gingrich's discussion is pitched at a micro-institutional level. Following from Philip Selznick's (1957) classic discussion, they conceptualize institutions as "incipient communities" or "communities on the fly."

> ## Box 9.1 Ansell and Gingrich's Emergent Institutionalism Model: Key Points
>
> - Public problems arise in conditions of uncertainty, and are characterized by an incomplete and not fully understood pattern of clues and symptoms. This demands an *emergent response*, that is, an identification and analysis of the problem that develops concurrently with the presentation of problem symptoms.
> - The emergence of a new problem requires the mobilization of a particular and possibly unique configuration of people, knowledge, and resources. Once an incipient institution has crystallized around an interpretation of a problem, it claims jurisdiction and rebuffs other attempts to engage in sense making.
> - This can lead to a poor fit between emergent problems and emergent institutions, especially where new information becomes available making an early interpretation of a problem wrong or inadequate.

Nevertheless, the researchers make an important point that can be applied to a broader context. It is wrong, they point out, to "think of the relationship between problems and institutions in serial terms, with problems defined by pre-existing institutions or, conversely, with institutions created to solve predefined problems" (2007: 195). Emergence, institutionalization, and sense making, they argue, can optimally be viewed as *coevolving* in a mutually interdependent fashion.

Ansell and Gingrich's model can be compressed into three bulleted points (see box 9.1).

Emergent Institutionalism and the Politics of Natural Disasters

Sense making and emergent institutionalism are not restricted to government responses to poorly understood health risks such as BSE or SARS. This applies equally well to the broader landscape of international disaster politics, where things have often been in a state of flux, especially in recent times. In the past, Christoplos (2003) argues, disaster management was relatively straightforward, or at least, it appeared so. There were clear-cut "normal" roles for the state, the private sector, and civil society. Disaster mitigation and preparedness were narrowly technical in scope, but at least "the goal posts were not in question." This is no longer the case:

> In recent years, however, changes in the nature of disasters, the structure of international aid architecture and in the discourse on humanitarian response have compelled us to reflect critically on who should be doing what before, during and after a disaster strikes. The implications of globalization and structural adjustment have introduced a growing ambiguity into what had been seen as self-evident set-piece roles for states, non-governmental organizations (NGOs), and the private sector (Christoplos, 2003: 95).

The traditional view of natural disasters, then, has been changing. One reason for this has been the increasing blurring between humanitarianism and politics. As Fidler (2005) points out, the political nature of natural disasters is being significantly reframed so that policy for such disasters connects directly to the systemic interests states have in international relations. The most aggressive case of this is "militant humanitarianism" (see chapter 6), but it is happening all over.

Another factor is the widespread perception that natural disasters are significantly increasing in frequency and magnitude, probably in response to global climate change. Political leaders, who previously were content to relegate disasters to the care of the humanitarian relief sector and a small core of UN bureaucrats, now have begun to view disasters as impinging on national security.

Third, the institutional landscape of disaster management has been characterized by escalating participation by international financial organizations such as the World Bank, and by private sector players. In the case of the insurance industry, this clearly reflects concern over the increasing frequency of natural disasters. Interviewed immediately after Hurricane Irene pounded the Eastern seaboard of the United States and Canada in August 2011, Henry Blumenthal, vice-president and chief underwriter for TD Insurance, noted that there is a sense in the industry that natural disasters are more frequent: "Environmentalists will tell you clearly we see more large events happening and some of them are more significant than before. [Hurricane] Irene is just one example" (Marr, 2011: FP7).

The SCPQ Configuration

In the future, we could witness the advent of a realigned global policy field of natural disasters wherein a new constellation of resources, relationships, authority, and expertise (Ansell and Gingrich, 2007: 172) emerges. I have labeled this the **SCPQ** (securitization, catastrophe scenario building and modeling, privatization, and quantification) **configuration**.

Securitization

As I have noted at various points in this book, in the past, politicians and generals have not shied away from co-opting the machinery of humanitarianism and disaster relief when it suits them. Nonetheless, the militarization of humanitarianism and disaster management has accelerated in recent years. Recall, if you will, Walden Bello's take on this:

> In sum, a sea change has occurred in disaster relief and post-conflict reconstruction work. The old image of the United Nations raising the funds and managing the aid effort while the Red Cross tended to the hurt and the sick with studied neutrality no longer

reflects contemporary realities. Disaster relief and post-conflict reconstruction are increasingly driven by the same dynamics, reflecting the intersection of strategic interest, ideologically motivated economics and muscular humanitarianism (Bello, 2006: 294).

As is the case with the insurance industry, a major driver here is the perception that global climate change represents a major threat to prosperity and security. Since climate change affects the distribution and availability of critical natural resources, it can act as a "threat multiplier" by causing mass migrations and exacerbating conditions that can lead to social unrest and armed conflict. The destabilizing potential of climate-induced natural disasters is summarized in this excerpt from the *2010 Joint Operating Environment* *(JOE)*, an annual exercise in crystal ball gazing released by the United States Joint Forces Command:

> Tsunamis, typhoons, hurricanes, tornadoes, earthquakes and other natural catastrophes have been and will continue to be a concern of Joint Force commanders. In particular, where natural disasters collide with growing urban sprawl, widespread human misery could be the final straw that breaks the back of a weak state (United States Joint Forces Command, 2010: 33).

This being so, the US military views its intervention in disaster-ravaged nations as offering a valuable payoff:

> In the 2030s, as in the past, the ability of U.S. military forces to relieve the victims of natural disasters will impact the reputation of the United States in the world. For example, the contribution of U.S. and partner forces to relieve the distress caused by the catastrophic Pacific tsunami of December 2004 reversed the perceptions of America held by many Indonesians. Perhaps no other mission performed by the Joint Force provides so much benefit to the interests of the United States at so little cost (United States Joint Forces Command, 2010: 33).

This outlook is becoming paradigmatic in the defense policy community. For example, the Center for New American Security (CNAS), a Washington think tank, has been hosting a feature on its website entitled "Natural Security Blog" that highlights the impact of climate events and natural disasters on US national security issues. In one post from August 26, 2010, Alex Stark, a research intern at CNAS, comments on the implications of the August 2010 flooding in Pakistan for the United States. In the short run, Stark points out, the floods have disrupted the main supply lines for NATO and US forces in Afghanistan. Longer term, the floods could destabilize the country, especially if Islamist charities fill the humanitarian aid vacuum left by a seemingly indifferent President (see page 105). He concludes:

> The floods in Pakistan are a prime example of one of these issues that defies the traditional boundaries of security studies, and provides an example of the ways that traditional conceptions of what constitutes a threat to the United States will have to

evolve to match the increasingly tangled and complex nature and overwhelming scope of these new issues.

Stark's point is echoed in Robert Kaplan's book *Monsoon: The Indian Ocean and the Future of American Power* (2011). Kaplan, a best-selling author, is foreign correspondent for *The Atlantic* magazine and senior fellow at CNAS. In the twenty-first century, Kaplan argues, the geopolitical focus will shift from the Western Hemisphere to Monsoon Asia: India, Pakistan, China, Indonesia, Burma, Oman, Sri Lanka, Bangladesh, and Tanzania. This represents a strategic realignment in the post-Cold War world, wherein regions once regarded as having limited importance have been re-inscribed with value. One arena where this will especially play out is the politics of natural disasters. Bangladesh, in particular, is vulnerable to serious flooding: "The US Navy may be destined for a grand power balancing game with China in the Indian and Pacific oceans, but it is more likely to be deployed on account of an environmental emergency, which is what makes Bangladesh and its problems so urgent" (Kaplan, 2011: 139).

Catastrophic Scenario Building and Risk Modeling

As the German sociologist Ute Tellmann (2009: 17) recently suggested, "we are witnessing a much more widespread shift in the ways in which the future is imagined, rationalised and acted upon that goes beyond previous conceptualisations of risk." To cope with the specter of an inherently uncertain future, a wide spectrum of practitioners – academics, bankers, insurance companies, the military – are increasingly engaging in the process of imagining the future through constructing catastrophic scenarios. According to Tellmann, scenarios are "essentially 'plot lines'" that order events according to certain narratological structures (Tellmann, 2009: 18). Scenarios are not predictions, only plausible stories about the future, but they promise a knowledgeable sense of risk in an uncertain world (Schwartz, 1990; Tellmann, 2009: 18).

Catastrophic scenario building, of course, is scarcely new. During the Cold War, futurist Herman Kahn and his colleagues at RAND Corporation became renowned for their doomsday scenarios of nuclear attack and survival. In the late 1960s and early 1970s, the nascent environmental movement was no stranger to scenarios of global collapse. Two familiar examples of this can be found in Paul and Anne Ehrlich's bestselling demographic fright book, *The Population Bomb* (Ehrlich and Ehrlich, 1970), and in the influential Club of Rome study, *The Limits of Growth* (Meadows et al., 1972).

In the contemporary version, one common narrative is that of "sudden emergence and emergencies" (Tellmann, 2009: 18). As an illustration of this, Tellmann cites a 2003 Pentagon study about climate change undertaken for the US government by two well-known scenario planning specialists, Peter

Schwartz and Doug Randall, wherein the consultants warn that world climate will change abruptly, rather than gradually, making this a US national security concern rather than just the subject of a scientific debate. Catastrophic scenarios like that proposed by Schwartz and Randall, Tellmann says, are increasingly being used by "insurance and security discourses" (Tellmann, 2009: 17). For example, earthquake risk models are now available for most of the world's most seismically active regions where earthquake insurance premiums are sold (Johnson, 2000).

Collier (2008) has argued that, contrary to Ulrich Beck's (1992) "insurability thesis," which claims that contemporary societies increasingly face "catastrophe" risks such as nuclear accidents or large-scale terrorism that cannot be covered by private insurance and are beyond rational assessment and calculated mitigation, insurance companies today are using new technologies that use sophisticated catastrophe modeling. In the United States, the field was catalyzed by a series of major disasters in the late 1980s and early 1990s that shocked the insurance industry – Hurricane Andrew in 1992 evidently left nine insurance companies insolvent (Collier, 2008). According to one well-known catastrophe model, the four basic components of a catastrophe model are hazard, inventory, vulnerability, and loss.

By and large, this type of insurance is still restricted to Northern countries that are not included on the list of natural disaster "hotspots." For example, in the United States, about half of the costs of natural disasters are covered by insurance, as against less than 2 percent in the countries of the South. However, this is starting to change. In part, it reflects the aggressive move of large private insurers into the virgin territory of Asia and Latin America where a strong insurance culture has previously been a foreign concept. It can also be seen in a series of pilot projects in Southern countries supported by the World Bank that have included catastrophe bonds, index-based insurance, catastrophe models to facilitate coverage, work through microfinance institutions, contingency lines of credit, and the creation of a catastrophe insurance pool (Parker, 2006: 35). While some of these projects operate outside the private insurance market, nevertheless, the methods of risk estimation are similar.

Three leading firms, AIR, EQECat, and RMS, dominate the market for the modeling of catastrophic risk (Michel-Kerjan, 2005). AIR Worldwide (AIR), a company headquartered in Boston, founded the catastrophe modeling "industry" in the late 1980s. Today, it claims to model the risk from natural catastrophes and terrorism in more than 90 countries and supply software and services to 400 insurance, reinsurance, financial, corporate, and government clients. AIR has two main competitors: RMS (Risk Management Solutions, Inc.) and EQECat. Additionally, there are regional catastrophe modelers, for example, the Institute for Catastrophe Risk Management (ICRM) at Nanyang Technological University in Singapore. These catastrophe modelers do not claim to be able to completely eliminate uncertainty but, by parameterizing it, they hope to help their clients understand it better. In a recent interview with Insurance ERM, an online risk management website, Bill Keogh, president of EQECat, described the classification system that his firm has borrowed from former US defense secretary Donald Rumsfeld: "There are the 'known knowns,' the 'known unknowns,' and the 'unknown unknowns,' so every time an event happens it adds to this first category of the 'known knowns' and we learn a lot" ("Eqecat's Keogh stresses the limitations of models," 2011). Operating as they do in the private sphere, catastrophe modelers are not likely to face the unhappy fate of the six seismologists and one government official currently on trial in an Italian court on charges of manslaughter for failing to properly evaluate the potential danger to people living in the high-risk seismic zone of L'Aquila, where 300 people died in an earthquake in April 2009 (Thompson, 2011).

Privatization

Craig Calhoun, an American sociologist, recently appointed Director of the London School of Economics and Political Science, has written extensively on the changing landscape of disasters and global emergencies. Calhoun, you will recall, earlier proposed that the construction of a new rhetoric of "emergencies" in a global society offers a way of coping with risk and uncertainty beyond simply treating them as matters of fate. Humanitarian intervention thus represents a way of "managing" global affairs. For this to work, however, disasters (Calhoun is thinking mainly of complex humanitarian emergencies, but the same holds true for natural disasters) must be treated as brief, abnormal, and unpredictable. To illustrate this, Calhoun employs a medical metaphor. Global processes usually function normally and smoothly, but, occasionally, special cases emerge where something goes wrong – a buildup of plaque in the global arteries that causes a stroke (2004: 376). When this happens, quick action by external actors is needed. This is not how Calhoun himself thinks of this, but it is the outlook that what is required is humanitarian action by tens of thousands of paid workers and volunteers through the United Nations, aid agencies, and NGOs. Emergencies, therefore, shape "the way in which we understand and respond to specific events, and the limits to what we think are possible actions and implications" (Calhoun, 2004: 376).

Calhoun (2006: 258) has observed that at the same time as the rhetoric of a "world of emergencies" has thrived globally, the early twenty-first century "has seen a concerted effort to limit protections and privatize risk, to roll back provision of public goods, and to restructure public communications on the basis of private property rights rather than any broader conception of communicative rights." Citing the inept handling of Hurricane Katrina, Calhoun argues that the inadequate government response stemmed not only from incompetence but also from official policies that reduce the provision of public goods in favor of reliance on private markets and market opportunities. In this spirit, the libertarian Congressman and Republican presidential candidate from Texas, Ron Paul, argued recently (August 30, 2011) on Anderson Cooper's evening television program that the US federal government should totally withdraw from providing assistance in domestic disasters such as that provoked by Hurricanes Katrina and Irene. A major problem with this trend to privatization, Calhoun points out, is that the loss and suffering from disasters is unequally distributed across the population. Wealth often shapes who suffers most. Those who are better off financially can buy the mitigation of risk. But they are less than enthusiastic about the cost of loss and suffering from disasters being equally distributed.

Subsequent to his 2006 essay, Calhoun, in collaboration with Jacob Lasker, led a Social Science Research Council (SSRC) project on "The Privatization of Risk" that "considers the ways in which the distribution and management of collective risks has changed over recent decades. It analyzes the social and economic effects of efforts to replace public institutions with market mechanisms, shifting the burden of risk to those without substantial private wealth" (Lakoff, 2010b: 3).

SSRC, in conjunction with the Columbia University Press, has undertaken to publish a series on the privatization of risk. One of the first volumes to appear is *Disaster and the Politics of Intervention*, edited by Andrew Lakoff (2010a). Disaster here is given a broad definition, and includes catastrophic natural disasters such as Hurricane Katrina, complex humanitarian disasters, the HIV/AIDS pandemic, the threat of anthropogenic climate change, and even the global financial crisis. Private sector participation can range from constructing a "cap-and-trade" carbon emissions system to providing private security services in a disaster situation, as occurred during the 2007 Southern California wildfires when American International Group (AIG) sent in their own crews to protect houses belonging to members of their private client group.

Lakoff states that one insight that emerges from the book is that managing catastrophic risk will require the development of *new regulatory norms and organizational forms*. With regard to the privatization of risk, he concludes, "while it is clear that purely market-based approaches cannot be depended upon to provide collective health and security, it may be that market experiments in combination with government regulation can be part of a broad effort to create sustainable practices of collective security" (Lakoff, 2010b: 10).

Quantification

A fourth feature of this emerging institutional field is increasing quantification. According to a report released by the Institut Veolia Environnement, a nonprofit think tank created by a French water and energy corporation, "The occurrence of particularly devastating and large-scale natural disasters since the end of the 1980s has encouraged a growing number of stakeholders to recognize that there is a need for developing new methods of quantification to measure the impact and likelihood of such disasters" (Michel-Kerjan, 2005). In particular, insurance companies embraced this during the 1990s as a way of measuring their portfolio exposure to these hazards.

As I have already noted, quantification is a defining characteristic of catastrophe modeling. For example, in the aftermath of the 1999 Kocaeli (Turkey) earthquake, RMS developed a "shaking intensity map" which relies on a "quantitative technique" that permits "a more quantitative understanding of the location and extent of losses and generate(s) a loss estimate for the insurance industry" (Johnson, 2000). University of Malaya economist Mario Arturo Ruiz Estrada has recently proposed a "natural disasters vulnerability evaluation model (NDVE)" that purports to demonstrate how the GDP growth rate is directly connected to natural disaster events. He proposes three new indicators that are derived from historical disaster data: the natural disasters vulnerability propensity rate, the natural disaster devastation magnitude rate, and the *economic desgrowth rate*. The latter is designed to permit the analyst to observe the final impact of any natural disaster on GDP growth rate over a fixed period of time (Ruiz Estrada, 2011).

Pelling (2011: 47–8) has distinguished between two bases for evaluating between climate change adaptive choices: economic costs and human rights. In the former case, an increasingly popular tool is cost-benefit analysis (CBA). CBA is most familiar in the policy field of global climate change, but it "has also been used effectively to argue for proactive adaptation through investment in disaster risk reduction as an alternative to managing disaster risk through emergency response and reconstruction." Pelling tends to discount economic assessment tools such as CBA on the grounds that they do not allow estimation of costs for specific investments before disaster strikes. However, it is instructive to look at whom he cites as using and/or referencing this toolkit in connection with DRR: World Bank, DFID, US Geological Survey.

In similar fashion, DRR has increasingly taken a sharp turn in the direction of quantitative economic appraisal. In their series of guidance notes, *Tools for Mainstreaming Disaster Risk Reduction*, Charlotte Benson and John Twigg (2007) include a chapter on "Economic Analysis" that is primarily intended for use by economists working in development organizations. Cost-benefit and related economic appraisal approaches, they say, are applied to determine the highest return to investment in a project. In hazard-prone countries, it is easy to squander large sums by financing development projects whose physical infrastructure and capital equipment are destroyed in an instant by a flood, hurricane, or earthquake. Such losses are not inevitable, however, and "there can be potentially high returns to disaster risk reduction investments in hazard-prone areas" (Benson and Twigg, 2007: 91). To maximize returns, they review seven "basic steps in merging disaster risk concerns into economic analysis." This includes the use of "probability curves" and "worked cost-benefit analyses."

Benson, who wrote this guidance note, acknowledges receiving advice from colleagues at DFID, the Inter-American Development Bank, and the International Institute for Applied Systems Analysis. While acknowledging that the link between macroeconomic vulnerability to natural hazards and poverty alleviation and individual disaster risk reduction measures is not easily established, nonetheless, Benson and Twigg (2007: 92) advise that the macroeconomic impacts of disasters "may be an important consideration in determining a development organization's broader strategic areas of focus in hazard-prone countries."

Quantification can be detected in the "bottom line" criteria that donors use to assess the success of disaster development programs. You will recall, for example, the UK 2011 DFID Multilateral Aid Review that rated recipient agencies on the basis of "deliverables," that is, hard data on services provided such as the number of people fed or vaccinations given, as against activities such as planning and coordination that are more difficult to quantify (see chapter 4). This is consistent with the views of some development economists who believe that greater accountability must be built into foreign aid disbursements.

Viyajendra Rao of the World Bank's Development Research Group argues that, "it's critical to track funds and the performance of functionaries and assess changes in the lives of beneficiaries." This is only possible, he concluded, if you have "good monitoring data" (Rao, 2012). Unfortunately, aid agencies do not always pay attention to data and often rely on faulty "experiential information" gathered by senior project managers during their field visits. In a similar fashion, recent attempts to introduce a higher level of standardization and coordination into disaster risk management have put a premium on quantification. This has met with some resistance. As I note in chapter 2, Médecins sans Frontières has criticized the Sphere project on the grounds that it reduces humanitarian response to its technical aspects, leaving no room for non-quantifiable aspects of humanitarian action such as ethics and solidarity building.

Finally, quantitative data gathering is pivotal to a vision for the future of natural disaster management that features the toolkit of remote sensing. In the past, policymakers, emergency managers, first responders, aid agencies, and scientists have utilized remote sensing data in several ways: to form comprehensive risk assessments for pre-disaster planning; to map the effects of an event for post-disaster response; and for early warning in order to protect lives and property (Shiro, 2008).

Most recently, data sensing has been incorporated into the field of geospatial information gathering and intelligence. One key player here is the National Geospatial-Intelligence Agency (NGA). NGA, a little-known branch of the (US) Defense Department, uses some of the country's most sophisticated aerial imaging equipment, and has as its mission the collecting, analyzing, and distributing of geospatial intelligence in support of national security. In its investigative series, "Top Secret America," the *Washington Post* includes a section on NGA which it characterizes as a "combat support agency and a member of the national intelligence community." NGA was said to have played a vital role in tracking down Osama bin Laden at his compound in Pakistan, providing key data and intelligence (Ambinder, 2011).

Among its services, NGA provides an array of disaster data. For example, the agency supported Hurricane Katrina relief efforts by providing geospatial information to FEMA and other government agencies. Most recently, NGA purchased a system called Enhanced View Hosting Service from Geo-Eye, Inc., the world's largest space imaging corporation. Enhanced View makes high-resolution satellite imagery available to licensed federal customers across the National System for Geospatial Intelligence. It has been used domestically and in Japan to improve emergency response to natural disasters.

It would be easy to assert that the rise of SCPQ will inevitably lead to the colonization of the global field of international disaster politics by the corporate titans of "disaster capitalism" or "shock capitalism." Bello (2006) implies as much in his discussion of the rise of a new RRC (relief and reconstruction) establishment that has as its central players the US military and political command, the World Bank, and NGOs. With its volatile mixture of strategic concerns, bureaucratic imperatives, profitmaking, and partisan humanitarianism, RRC, Bello says, aggressively and narrowly advances the institutional interests of its stakeholders.

However, I think the situation is less cut and dried than that. Commenting on British philosopher Roger Scruton's (2012) assertion that only a new wave of "green conservatism" can reverse ecological destruction and save the planet, Julian Baggini (2012) observes that Scruton would be well advised to accept "that the environment is a large messy problem that requires a large mess of solutions, big and small, conservative and radical." So too, the management of natural disasters worldwide will continue to attract a wide variety of actors ranging from the humanitarian community to the national security establishment.

What is more likely to happen is that projects that provide quantifiable estimations or models of risk and/or mitigation measures for catastrophic-scale hazards will increasingly be privileged over those that do not. Hard data will crowd out soft data. Privatized security and disaster response services will continue to flourish in selected settings. Insurance logic will replace humanitarian concern. Resilience will trump transformation. The language of disaster management will shift, with phrases like accountability, era of results, measurable outcomes, economic viability, cost efficiency, return on disaster risk reduction investments, disaster proofing, and willingness to pay becoming paramount. Remote sensing will almost certainly become a standard tool in natural hazard monitoring and risk assessment, possibly in tandem with geospatial intelligence in support of national security.

In its 2009 report, "The Right to Survive," Oxfam International describes the humanitarian challenge of the twenty-first century as "an increasing total of largely local catastrophic events, increasing numbers of people vulnerable to them, too many governments failing to prevent or respond to them, and an international humanitarian system unable to cope" (Oxfam International, 2009: 8). This demands a *new humanitarian framework* wherein international aid agencies, working alongside local governments, civil society organizations, religious groups, and private companies, focus on strengthening the local community's ability to prevent, prepare for, and respond to natural disasters (Oxfam International, 2009: 105).

SCPQ does not fit comfortably within this new humanitarian framework. For example, reliance on catastrophic modeling and gathering remote sensing data reinforces the view that natural disasters are essentially hazard based rather than community based, and so, therefore, are the solutions. As Magrath (2009) points out, the prevailing task in the humanitarian/development community over the last 20 years has been to contradict the view widespread in the 1970s and 1980s that disasters are inevitable acts of God. Rather, natural events should be treated as a "trigger." Whether a hazard turns into a disaster or not depends on such measures as early warning coupled with effective communication, improved urban planning, tougher building regulations and construction standards, prohibitions against building in certain areas, and more effective grassroots community mobilization.

During and after the 2004 Indian Ocean tsunami, these measures were accorded a lower priority than a loot bag of initiatives that had more to do with politics and technology. First World nations such as the United States and Australia were motivated by the prospect of earning diplomatic kudos at the same time as enhancing regional security. Recall, for example, the problem-plagued project to build a coastal highway in Aceh, Indonesia (see box 6.3) where speed, tourism development, and American engineering expertise overshadowed local concerns.

At the January 2005 World Conference on Disaster Reduction (Hyogo Conference) the prime directive was to create a sophisticated tsunami early warning system for the Indian Ocean, moving disaster reduction down, if not off, the agenda (see chapter 4).

Employing Ansell and Gingrich's (1997) terminology, in the twenty-first century rapidly emerging problems involving disaster, poverty, and climate change show every indication of fitting poorly with a newly emergent set of institutions based on securitization, catastrophic modeling, privatization, and quantification.

Notes

Chapter 1

1 Clarke and Chess (2008) first introduced this notion of "elite panic." Tierney (2008: 131) claims that there is growing evidence that elite panic was quite evident in the aftermath of Hurricane Katrina. This was evidenced, she says, by "media and public officials' obsessions with looting and lawlessness, the issuing of shoot-to-kill orders arising primarily out of a concern with property crime, and the rush to act upon rumors that circulated regarding the 'savage' behavior of lower-class community residents, immigrants, and people of color."

2 United Nations Resolutions 43–131 ("Humanitarian assistance to victims of natural disasters and similar emergency situations") and 46–182 legally spell this out.

3 One exception is the ongoing collaboration between Quarantelli and Ian Davis. Now retired, Davis remains a respected figure in international disaster planning and management. In 2002 he was selected as one of four witnesses to appear in front of the (Parliamentary) Select Committee on International Development to discuss disasters. When Davis came to the United States in the spring of 1973 en route to the devastated city of Managua, Nicaragua, following the 1972 earthquake, he visited Quarantelli and co-director Russell Dynes at the Disaster Research Center seeking advice on what he might expect to observe in Managua (Davis, 2004: 130–1). A commonly shared interest in the popular culture of disaster has recently been consummated with the joint publication of a monograph (Quarantelli and Davis, 2011).

Chapter 2

1 In the twentieth century, there were only two multilateral treaties, separated by 71 years, that directly concern disaster response. The *Convention and Statute Establishing an International Relief Union*, enacted in 1932, ultimately failed completely (see chapter 3). The *Tampere Convention on the Provision of Telecommunications Resources for Disaster Mitigation and Relief Operations*, which entered into force on January 8, 2005, still applies, but it is limited in scope and deals entirely with technical issues related to the provision of emergency telecommunications assistance (Fidler, 2005). Note also the *International Charter on Space and Major Disasters*, an agreement signed by 10 space agencies to make available satellite resources and data that otherwise are subject to data policy restric-

tions without delay in the wake of a disaster. The Charter, which is not a legally binding treaty as such, has been activated several hundred times since it came into force in 2000, mostly in flood situations (50%), hurricanes (10%), and volcanoes (6%) (Shiro, 2008).

2 According to Schipper and Pelling (2006: 24), the term "disaster risk management" refers to both disaster risk reduction (prevention, preparedness, and mitigation) *and* humanitarian and development action (emergency response, relief, and reconstruction). This should not be confused with "emergency management," which is a profession that has traditionally dealt with disaster mitigation and hazard management.

3 I have deliberately opted to describe these as "organizational" rather than "institutional" actors or players. In so doing, I am following Young's (1994: 3–4) distinction between institutions and organizations, "Whereas institutions are sets of rules of the game or codes of conduct defining social practices, organizations are material entities possessing offices, personnel, budgets, equipment, and, more often than not, legal personality."

4 DFID was established in 1997 by the newly elected Labour government, replacing the former Overseas Development Administration, which used to be part of the Foreign and Commonwealth Office (Galperin, 2002: 17).

5 I am grateful to one of the appraisers of an earlier draft of this book for pointing this out.

6 West (2001: 20) notes that the ICRC "has been viewed an exception in the international humanitarian system; it has been considered neither an NGO nor an IGO." In similar fashion, Walker and Maxwell (2009: 108–9) suggest, "In some ways, it [the Red Cross and Red Crescent Movement] sits between intergovernmental organizations like the UN agencies and NGOs." Measured by number of employees, total budget, and volunteers, the three components of the Red Cross/Red Crescent are undeniably the largest force in the global field of natural disasters. However, in terms of influence, its role is more difficult to judge. One reason for this is that the ICRC, which adheres religiously to its charter as an independent neutral organization, regularly declines to formally join any joint initiatives, for example, the Humanitarian Network in Canada, the United Nations-led "clustering" initiative, and the Sphere Project.

7 For example, WE ADVANCE, a grassroots health movement with a mission to empower Haitian women living in Wharf Jeremy and Cité Soleil, among the poorest slums in the Western hemisphere, was co-founded by Maria Bello, the American film and television actress and women's rights activist. At this writing, Bello has been tweeting about the actions taken by WE ADVANCE staff on the ground in Haiti in preparation for the onset of Hurricane Emily, notably securing tents, jeeps, and extra medical staff.

8 As of August 2011, the total sum of public contributions by Canadians to assist in the famine in East Africa is roughly the same for World Vision Canada as it is for the entire Humanitarian Coalition.

9 Whereas the ProVention Consortium aims primarily to improve global awareness and knowledge of hazards, the GFDRR is designed to address hazard risk management, specifically by providing "technical assistance to assist the 86 high risk countries in the task of mainstreaming hazard risk management in

development strategies and investment grants for immediate recovery" (World Bank, Global Program Review, The ProVention Consortium, 2006: xii).

10 A prominent contributor here is the non-profit group, GeoHazards International, whose current projects include improving school and hospital earthquake safety in India, South Asia, and rural Peru.

11 For example, membership rolls on the writing teams for the International Panel on Climate Change (IPCC), Fifth Assessment Report, Working Group II (Impacts, Adaptation and Vulnerability) include such well-known names in DRR circles as Mark Pelling and Omar-Dario Cardona (urban areas), Tom Mitchell (livelihood and poverty), Lisa Schipper (regional context), and Ian Burton (climate-resilient pathways).

12 According to Hicks and Pappas (2006), there were a number of reasons for this. Of particular importance was the authoritative and independent role taken by the Pakistani military, which was well organized internally but divorced from the UN-led cluster-sectoral system. Furthermore, Pakistan lacked a national disaster plan or central authority for integrated disaster management. On its part, the UN-led coordination effort was understaffed, fragmented by sector, and missing both a clear implementation plan and the incorporation of lessons learned from previous earthquakes about coordinating relief efforts in the field. In its postmortem, ActionAid International (2006) provides some specific examples. Pakistani NGOs regarded the cluster meetings as gatherings of an elite group of foreigners. Cluster meetings were always held in English with no Urdu translators present. Local knowledge and views often went unnoticed, and local government structures were by-passed. For example, the shelter cluster lead ignored advice from a local Kashmiri NGO that tents would not stand up to the winter snowfall; predictably, the tents collapsed after the first snowfall (ActionAid International, 2006). By and large, local NGOs felt that the UN treated them as implementing partners, who needed to be "policed" rather than giving them input into conceptual thinking.

13 Sphere was jointly sponsored by InterAction, a coalition of 165 US-based humanitarian groups, and SCHR (Steering Committee for Humanitarian Response), composed of representatives from major NGOs such as CARE International, Oxfam, Save the Children, and two of the three Red Cross organizations – the International Committee of the Red Cross (ICRC) participated only as an observer.

Chapter 3

1 This comment is included in briefing notes from Alexander Cadogan, head of the League of Nations section at the Foreign Office, to Austen Chamberlain, prior to the League of Nations council meeting in December 1934. Cited in Hutchison (2001: 254).

2 The convention was signed by 42 states and ultimately ratified by 30. Opposing votes came from South Africa, India, Sweden, Norway, and the British Empire.

3 The "Great Kanto Earthquake" struck on the morning of September 1, 1923, killing between 100,000 and 140,000 people, mainly in Tokyo and Yokohama.

In addition to the hands-off attitude of the international community, to which Gorgé refers, another negative aspect of the event was a series of unprovoked and murderous mass attacks on Koreans and Chinese residents in these two cities. The attacks were evidently fueled by false rumors that Koreans were taking advantage of the disorder that ensued in the aftermath of the quake in order to commit arson and robbery.

4 The Oxford sanitation unit is an "innovative though controversial system for collecting and storing excreta in refugee camp situations" (Cuny, 1983: 122). According to one development primer, "This portable design can be used by 500 people and can be assembled in one day. It was first installed in Bangladesh and is ideal under special circumstances, such as for hospitals and refugee camps, where acceptance is more or less assured." ("Sanitation technology," Humanity Development Library 2.0, downloaded at http://www.greenstone.org/greenstone3/nzdl?a=d&d=HASH8546566458fc9f9b669.9.4 on July 27, 2011.)

5 In this, CARE (unknowingly) anticipated the current politics of disaster relief funding, wherein quantifying evaluation has become the flavor of the day.

6 According to the enabling resolution passed by the United Nations General Assembly on December 14, 1971, UNDRO's mandate was "to mobilize, direct and coordinate the relief activities of the United Nations system and coordinate the assistance with that given by other inter-governmental and non-governmental organizations."

7 Evaluation of the Office of the United Nations Disaster Relief Coordinator, Joint Inspection Unit, JIU/REP/80/11 (Geneva, United Nations, October 1980).

8 Later on, this was modified further, with 50 percent allocated to disaster relief and 50 percent to preparedness/prevention.

Chapter 4

1 Obasi indicates that extreme meteorological and hydrological events account for 62 percent of all events recorded as natural disasters. This figure rises to 85 percent if those associated with weather events (avalanches, landslides, epidemics, etc.) are included.

2 These data were provided by the Centre for Research on the Epidemiology of Disasters (CRED) in Louvain, Belgium.

3 According to Housner (1989: 47), the change in terminology from "Hazard" to "Disaster" seems to have been made in order to mesh with standard United Nations terminology.

4 As it happens, both Russell Dynes and E.L. (Henry) Quarantelli, the co-directors of the Disaster Research Center at The Ohio State University, had both objected to the absence of social scientists, even before the Decade was formalized.

5 The Overseas Development Institute also publishes *Disasters*, the leading journal in the disasters-development area.

6 Estimates of attendance vary considerably. Davis and Myers (1994) thought there were 2,000+ in attendance. Handmer (1995: 35) put this at 3,000, but pointed out that, according to a senior UN conference official, there were nearly 5,000 participants on the busiest day.

7 In this regard, James P. Bruce, Chair of the IDNDR Scientific and Technical Committee, complained in 1994 that underfunding meant "The STC has had difficulty pursuing a public information strategy" (Bruce, 1994).
8 The team consisted of Yasemin Aysan, whose experience consists primarily of working with the Red Cross, the United Nations Development Programme, and a number of inter-agency task forces related to the IDNDR and ISDR; Alexandra Galperin, who specializes in capacity building, and policy evaluation for disaster reduction in transitional economies; and Ian Christoplos, an academic and consultant at several Swedish universities and the Overseas Development Institute whose research focuses on risk, poverty alleviation, natural disasters, and complex political emergencies.
9 Three of these meetings have been held in Geneva at three-year intervals: June 5–7, 2007; June 16–19, 2009; June 8–13, 2011.
10 This represents 7 percent of ISDR's total budget.

Chapter 5

1 Pelling (2011: 7) notes, "Outside of the imaginary worlds of computer models it is yet impossible to determine the proportion of any hydrological or meteorological event that is attributable to climate change;" but a few sentences later asserts, "We may never understand the precise contribution of anthropocentric climate change to these events and trends but we can be certain that climate change is a decisive contributing factor and that vulnerability exists, demanding action."
2 CRED's database contains more than 12,000 records of disaster from 1900 to the present, compiled from multiple sources. The Red Cross publishes recent CRED statistics on natural disasters annually in its widely read *World Disasters Report*.
3 Note that property damage is not universally accepted as the most accurate measure of climate-related losses. Thus, Parks and Roberts (2005) argue that using monetary damage estimates as a proxy for climate-related risk is highly misleading because it underestimates the *real* economic costs borne by developing countries. For example, use of this method privileges the luxury consumption losses incurred by the wealthy, such as the destruction of a beachfront property. Parks and Roberts believe that a more appropriate way of measuring climate-related losses is to "tally the number of people killed, made homeless, or otherwise affected by climate-related disasters in individual countries."
4 Jim Bruce, formerly Deputy Secretary-General, the second highest-ranking position, at the World Meteorological Association, was a key player in founding the Intergovernmental Panel on Climate Change. According to British science writer Fred Pearce (2010: 34), Bruce pressed hard for a political follow-up statement from the landmark International Conference on the Assessment of the Role of Carbon Dioxide and other Greenhouse Gases in Climate Variations and Associated Impacts, held in Villach, Austria in October 1985, and first conceived of the idea of a new body to assess climate science. During the 1990s, Bruce served as Chair of the Scientific and Technical Committee of the IDNDR.

5 Burton, an emeritus professor of geography at the University of Toronto, first came to notice in the 1960s and 1970s as a leading member of the "Chicago School of Natural Hazards Research." His book, *The Environment as Hazard* (written with Robert Kates and Gilbert White), is considered a seminal contribution (Burton et al., 1993). By the 1990s, he had re-emerged as a consultant in the areas of meteorology, environment, and sustainable development. Burton has been a contributor to IPCC Working Group II (Impacts, Adaptation and Vulnerability) for both the Fourth and Fifth Assessment Reports) and is a member of the PPCR (Pilot Program for Climate Resilience) Expert Group.

6 In 1980, 133 disasters were reported, whereas in recent years it has become the norm for 350 disasters to be reported annually. This represents an average increase of 4.1 percent per year for the sample of countries that have a first disaster reported from 1980 onwards. For countries whose first report was from 1990 or earlier, the number is slightly higher – 4.9 percent.

7 McKibben is the founder of global climate campaign 350.org.

8 To take just one example, as of May 2011, the Pilot Program for Climate Resilience (PPCR), administered by the World Bank, listed US$986 million in pledges, of which US$647 million was on deposit. By May 2011, US$27 million had been distributed – US$14 million on projects and US$13 million on administrative fees ("Pilot program for climate resilience," 2011).

9 According to an internal evaluation carried out in 2006, only one of the 60 activities identified in Bank-supported projects has taken less than three years to implement, on average. This guarantees that the types of activities that can have the greatest impact on reducing vulnerability are not included in ERL projects because they cannot be completed in the three years allotted (IEG-World Bank, 2006: xxi).

10 The countries include: Bangladesh, Bolivia, Cambodia, Mozambique, Nepal, Niger, Tajikistan, Yemen, Zambia, Dominica, Grenada, Haiti, Jamaica, Saint Lucia, Saint Vincent and the Grenadines, Papua New Guinea, Samoa, and Tonga (World Development Movement, 2011).

Chapter 6

1 *The Lancet* editorial provoked a flurry of letters from readers, some of whom seemed to be rather upset. For example, Jeremy Shoham, Fiona Watson, and Marie McGrath, workers in the emergency nutrition sector, challenge the journal editors to provide evidence of lack of coordination in health and nutrition in the response to the earthquake. In particular, they point to contributions in Haiti by the Nutrition Cluster led by UNICEF and blame any shortcomings on the scale and rapid onset of the crisis. "Such tabloid sensationalism and poorly researched Editorials have no place in *The Lancet*," they complain (Shoham et al., 2010).

2 According to O'Neill (2009: 9), the three primary traditions within the mainstream of the international relations field are realism (or neo-realism), liberal institutionalism, and, most recently, cognitivism (sometimes called constructivism). These are based respectively on power, institutions, and ideas. Most

mainstream research on the international politics of natural disasters has been undertaken from a realist perspective.

3 As Dynes (2005) explains, at mid-eighteenth century, Anglo–Portuguese relations were stable, but potentially strained. The British Factory, an association of English merchants with favorable trade agreements with Brazil and Paraguay, increasingly threatened Portuguese colonial interests in South America.

4 Tavares (2008: 6) notes that because FTS reporting is strictly voluntary, the data are far from comprehensive.

5 Exceptions to this are states that are politically isolated from the international community, for example, Cuba, Libya, and South Africa during Apartheid. In such cases, the national government is compelled to invest in disaster prevention and response to avoid post-disaster unrest (see Cohen and Werker, 2008). In the case of Cuba, the excellence of its disaster management system is even a source of national pride (Pelling and Dill, 2010: 26).

6 The junta was more open to receiving supplies from humanitarian organizations, which were perceived as less threatening. For example, it was reported that the International Rescue Committee sent more than 11 tonnes of plastic sheeting, water containers, and health and hygiene supplies to devastated villages in Myanmar (Hrywna, 2008).

7 The 7.2-magnitude Great Hanshin Earthquake, which hit the Kobe area on January 17, 1995, resulted in 5,200 deaths, 300,000 homeless, and 110,000 buildings being damaged.

8 This statement is not entirely correct. Evidently, the 1906 San Francisco earthquake generated millions of dollars in foreign aid. Japan, the largest donor, contributed a quarter of a million dollars. Furthermore, in a telegram dated April 26, 1906, to Elihu Root, Secretary of State, W.W. Rockell of the American Legation in Peking reports that 40,000 taels was being sent to the Chinese Minister in Washington for the relief of Chinese residents in San Francisco and a further 100,000 taels was to follow as the personal contribution of the Chinese Empress Dowager ("Relieving the Japanese and Chinese," n.d.).

9 However, the effectiveness of imprinting these logos is questionable. For example, in African nations the State Department eagle is seen as militaristic, while the red ribbon "confuses Africans who don't instinctively connect lethal diseases with fabric trimming" (McNeil, 2010).

10 It seems Bush unwisely borrowed the phrase from governor Haley Barbour of Mississippi, who had assured him minutes before that Brown was performing well.

11 Speculation was rife that Zardari's 21-year-old son Bilawi Bhutto Zardari, the current chairman of the PPP (Pakistan People's Party), would join him at the rally, where the latter would formally launch his political career. Instead Bhutto Zardari chose to open a donation point for flood victims in London. "This is not a time to play politics," he insisted. "We need to do what is necessary to help our brothers and sisters in Pakistan."

12 Measuring 7.4 on the Richter scale, the Marmara earthquake struck 90 miles from the Turkish capital, Istanbul, on August 17, 1999. It left 20,000 dead, 48,901 injured, and 377,897 buildings damaged or destroyed (Pelling and Dill, 2010: 31–2).

Chapter 7

1 Anderson Cooper's disaster reporting has not been universally acclaimed. For example, in a recent article in *The New Yorker* entitled "The Gulf War," Cooper is depicted as rather naïve for repeatedly giving an open pulpit to Billy Nungessen, the president of Plaquemines Parish (Louisiana) in the aftermath of the BP oil spill. CNN framed Billy as symbolizing the anger and frustration of Gulf fishing communities in the face of official bungling, especially by the Coast Guard. However, *The New Yorker* piece paints a portrait of Nungessen as continually pushing cleanup schemes that were more populist grandstanding than technically feasible. At one point, an irritated President Obama is quoted as telling Billy, "If you can't get it done through the chain of command, you pick up the phone and call the White House ... If you can't get me on the phone, then you can go call Anderson Cooper" (Khatchadourian, 2011).

2 The disasters were selected from the Emergency Events Database (EM-DAT). Following the standard EM-DAT definitions and classifications, Jeong and Lee defined a disaster as a situation or event which overwhelms local capacity, necessitating a request for external assistance, in which 70 or more people are reported killed, or an economic loss of US$1 million or more is sustained.

3 Like Jeong and Lee (2010), the researchers utilized data on natural disasters culled from the Emergency Events Database (EM-DAT) as provided by the Centre for Research on the Epidemiology of Disasters (CRED). Complex emergencies and technological disasters were excluded. Floods (32 percent) caused the majority of these disaster events, followed by storms (23 percent), and epidemics (14 percent).

Chapter 8

1 From the late 1980s to the mid-1990s, the proportion of emergency-related expenditure in Overseas Development Assistance (ODA) in the UK increased substantially – from 3 percent in 1988 to almost 10 percent at its height in 1994 (Macrae and Leader, 2000: 15; cited in Galperin, 2002: 4).

2 Kalder (2003) treats "transnational civic networks" such as that dedicated to the removal of landmines as a *type* of global civil society actor identified primarily with the late 1980s and 1990s.

3 Tarrow (2005: 75) cautions that the global justice frame has not entirely succeeded in creating a unified strategic repertoire of collective action among various activist factions, for example, between social movements from Northern and Southern countries.

4 In his review article on seven books on normative international theory, including *Activists Beyond Borders*, Price (2003: 580) chooses *transnational civil society* as an umbrella term to describe a variety of similar phenomena: non-state actors, transnational advocacy networks, transnational or global civil society. It refers to "self-organized advocacy groups that undertake voluntary collective action across state borders in pursuit of what they deem the wider public interest."

References

A Safer Future: Reducing the Impacts of Natural Disasters (1991) Commission on Geosciences, Environment and Resources, US National Committee for the Decade of Natural Disaster Reduction. National Academies Press, Washington, DC.

ABC International/Radio Australia (2011) Australia announces flood tax levy, January 28.

Abney, G. and Hill, L. (1966) Natural disasters as a political variable: the effects of a hurricane on an urban election. *American Political Science Review*, 60, 974–81.

ActionAid International (2006) Lifting the lid on the UN's cluster approach to disaster preparedness, May 25. Accessed at <www.actionaid.org.uk/100411/lifting_the_lid_on_the_uns_cluster_approach_to_disaster_preparedness.html>.

Adams, W.C. (1986) Whose lives count? TV coverage of natural disasters. *Journal of Communication*, 36, 113–22.

Adger, W.N., Eakin, H. and Winkels, A. (2009) Nested and teleconnected vulnerabilities to environmental change. *Frontiers in Ecology and the Environment*, 7, 150–7.

Adinolfi, C., Bassouni, D.S., Lauritzsen, H.F. and Williams, H.R. (2005) *Humanitarian Response Review*. Commissioned by the United Nations Emergency Relief Coordinator and Under-Secretary-General for Humanitarian Affairs. New York and Geneva, August. Accessed at <http://oneresponse.info/Coordination/ClusterApproach/Documents/Humanitarian%20Response%20Review.pdf>.

Agence France Press (2005) Outspoken relief chief says "newly rich" countries not donating enough, January 18. Reprinted in *Media Monitoring Report (2005)*. Accessed at <http://www.unisdr.org/2005/wcdr/media/wcdr-media-monitoring.pdf>.

Allen, E. (1994) Political responses to flood disaster: the example of Rio de Janeiro. In Varley, A. (ed.) *Disasters, Development and Environment*. John Wiley & Sons, Chichester, pp. 99–108.

Altay, N. and Labonte, M. (2011) Humanitarian logistics and the cluster approach: global shifts and the US perspective. In Christopher, M. and Tatham, P. (eds.) *Humanitarian Logistics: Meeting the Challenge of Preparing for and Responding to Disasters*. Kogan Page, London, pp. 85–101.

Ambinder, M. (2011) In raid on bin Laden little-known geospatial agency played a vital role. *National Journal*, May 5. Accessed at <nationaljournal.com/whitehouse/in-raid-on-bin-laden-little-known-geospatial-agency-played-vital-role-20110505>.

Ansell, C. and Gingrich, J. (2007) Emergent institutionalism: the United Kingdom's response to the BSE epidemic. In Gibbons, D.E. (ed.) *Communicable Crises: Prevention, Response, and Recovery in the Global Arena*. Information Age Publishing, Charlotte, NC, pp. 169–202.

Aspinall, W. (1989) Guest editorial: The International Decade for Natural Hazard Reduction: a challenge for SECED in Britain. *The Society for Earthquake and Civil Engineering Dynamics (SECED) Newsletter*, Vol. 3, No. 3, October.

Audit Report (2010) Audit Report: Governance and organizational structure of the inter-agency secretariat to the United Nations International Strategy for Disaster Risk Reduction (ISDR). United Nations Office of Internal Oversight Services, Internal Audit Division, July 28. Accessed at <http://www.unisdr.org/files/14946 _1000672FinalReportAN200938701Audito.pdf>.

Baggini, J. (2012) Shades of green (Review of Scruton, 2012). *Financial Times*, December 31/January 1, p. 11 (Life and Arts).

Banaszak, L.A. (2010) *The Women's Movement: Inside and Outside the State*. Cambridge University Press, New York.

Bankoff, G. (2001) Rendering the world unsafe: "vulnerability" as Western discourse. *Disasters*, 25, 19–35.

Bankoff, G. (2002) *Cultures of Disaster: Society and Natural Hazard in the Philippines*. RoutledgeCurzon, London and New York.

Barnett, M. (2008) Humanitarianism as a scholarly vocation. In Barnett, M. and Weiss, T.G. (eds.) *Humanitarianism in Question: Politics, Power, Ethics*. Cornell University Press, Ithaca, NY, pp. 235–63.

Barthel, F. and Neumayer, E. (2012) A trend analysis of normalized insured damage from natural disasters. *Climatic Change*, forthcoming. DOI: 10.1007/s10584-011-0331-2. Electronic copy available at <http://ssrn.com/abstract=1831633>.

Barton, A.H. (1969) *Communities in Disaster: A Sociological Analysis of Collective Stress Situations*. Doubleday, New York.

Barzelay, M. and Gallego, R. (2006) From "new institutionalism" to "institutional processualism": addressing knowledge about public management and policy change. *Governance*, 19, 531–57.

Bates, F.L. and Killian, C.D. (1982) Changes in housing in Guatemala following the 1976 earthquake: With special reference to earthen structures and how they are perceived by disaster victims. *Disasters*, 6, 92–100.

Beck, U. (1992) *Risk Society*. Sage, London.

Beckwith, K. (2011) Review of Banaszak (2010). *Social Forces*, 89, 1064–6.

Bello, W. (2006) The rise of the relief-and-reconstruction complex. *Journal of International Affairs*, 59, 281–97.

Benini, A. (1999) Network without centre? A case study of an organizational network responding to an earthquake. *Journal of Contingencies and Crisis Management*, 7, 38–47.

Benson, C. and Twigg, J. (2007) Tools for Mainstreaming Disaster Risk Reduction: Guidance Notes for Development Organisations. ProVention Consortium, Geneva.

Benson, C., Twigg, J. and Myers, M. (2001) NGO initiatives in risk reduction: an interview. *Disasters*, 25, 199–215.

Best, J. (1987) Rhetoric in claims-making: Constructing the missing children problem. *Social Problems*, 34, 101–21.

Bisaux, A., Carrell, R., Kohler, P., Schipper, L. and Vavilov, A. (2005) United Nations Conference on Disaster Reduction: Summary and Analyses. *Earth Negotiations Bulletin* (International Institute for Sustainable Development), 26 (9), January 24. Accessed at <http://www.iisd.ca/isdr/wcdri>.

Black, M. (1992) *A Cause for Our Times: Oxfam the First 50 Years*. Oxfam and Oxford University Press, Oxford.

Blyth, M. (2002) *Great Transformations: Economic Ideas and Institutional Change in the Twentieth Century*. Cambridge University Press, Cambridge.

Board on Natural Disasters, National Research Council, Washington, DC (1999) Mitigation emerges as major strategy for reducing losses caused by natural disasters. *Science*, 284 (5422), 1943–7.

Boli, J. and Thomas, G.M. (1997) World culture in the world polity: a century of international non-governmental organization. *American Sociological Review*, 62, 171–90.

Boli, J. and Thomas, G.M. (1999) *Constructing World Culture: International Nongovernmental Organizations since 1875*. Stanford University Press, Stanford, CA.

Boli, J., Loya, T.A. and Loftin, T. (1999) National participation in world-polity organization. In Boli and Thomas (eds.) *Constructing World Culture: International Nongovernmental Organizations since 1875*. Stanford University Press, Stanford, CA, pp. 50–77.

Bolin, R. with Stanford, L. (1998) *The Northridge Earthquake: Vulnerability and Disaster*. Routledge, New York.

Boullé, P. (1999) Disaster reduction as a central element of government policy. Presentation to the EIIP Virtual Forum, June 23. Accessed at <http://www. emforum.org>.

Brookings Institution (2002) The "CNN effect": how 24-hour news coverage affects government decisions and public opinion. Brookings/Harvard Forum Press Coverage and the War on Terrorism, January 23.

Bruce, J.P. (1994) The Fifth Session of the IDNDR Scientific and Technical Committee. *Natural Hazards Observer*, XVIII (4), March, 6–7.

Bruce, J., Burton, I. and Egener, M. (1999) Disaster mitigation and preparedness in a changing climate. A synthesis paper prepared for Emergency Preparedness Canada, the Insurance Bureau of Canada and the Institute of Catastrophe Loss Reduction. Global Change Strategies, Inc., Ottawa.

Brûlé, T. (2011) Still time to catch the blossom. *Financial Times Weekend*, April 16–17, Life & Arts, p. 20.

Buchanan-Smith, M. (2003) How the Sphere Project came into being: a case study of policy-making in the humanitarian aid sector and the relative influence of research. Working Paper 215, Overseas Development Institute, London.

Burton, I., Kates, R.W. and White, G.W. (1993) *The Environment as Hazard*, 2nd edn. The Guilford Press, New York.

Buttel, F.H. (2000) World society, the nation state, and environmental protection. *American Sociological Review*, 65, 117–21.

"Cable disaster coverage gets low marks" (2008) Reuters.com, May 27.

Calhoun, C. (2004) A world of emergencies: fear, intervention, and the limits of cosmopolitan order. *The Canadian Review of Sociology and Anthropology*, 41, 373–95.

Calhoun, C. (2006) The privatization of risk. *Public Culture*, 18, 257–63.

Calhoun, C. (2010) The idea of emergency: humanitarian action and global (dis)order. In Fassin, D. and Pandolfi, M. (eds.) *Contemporary States of Emergency: The Politics of Military and Humanitarian Interventions.* Zone Books, New York, pp. 29–58.

Cannon, T. (1994) Vulnerability analysis and the explanation of "natural disasters." In Varley, A. (ed.) *Disasters, Development and Environment.* John Wiley & Sons, Chichester.

Cardona, O.D. (2004) The need for rethinking concepts of vulnerability and risk from a holistic perspective: a necessary review and criticism for effective risk management. In Bankoff, G., Frerks, G. and Hilhorst, D. (eds.) *Mapping Vulnerability: Disasters, Development and People.* Earthscan, London, pp. 37–51.

Cate, F.H. (1994) Media, disaster relief and images of the developing world: Strategies for rapid, accurate and effective coverage of complex stories from around the globe. In Cate, F.H. (ed.) *International Disaster Communications: Harnessing the Power of Communications to Avert Disasters and Save Lives.* The Annenberg Washington Program in Communications Policy Studies at Northwestern University, Washington, DC.

Chabbott, C. (1999) Development INGOs. In Boli, J. and Thomas, G.M. (eds.) *Constructing World Culture: International Nongovernmental Organizations since 1875.* Stanford University Press, Stanford, CA, pp. 222–48.

Challenges of the IDNDR (1989) Report and Summary of Proceedings of the International Symposium on "Challenges of the IDNDR." Yokohama, Japan, April 13. United Nations Centre for Regional Development, Nagaya, Japan. Accessed at <http://www.hyogo.uncrd.or.jp/publication/pdf/Proceedings/1989intlSymposium.pdf>.

Chandler, D. (2001) The road to military humanitarianism: How the human rights NGOs shaped a new humanitarian agenda. *Human Rights Quarterly*, 23, 678–700.

Charnovitz, S. (1997) Two centuries of participation: NGOs and international governance. *Michigan Journal of International Law*, 18, 183–286.

Christoplos, I. (2003) Actors in risk. In Pelling, M. (ed.) *Natural Disasters and Development in a Globalizing World.* Routledge, London and New York, pp. 95–109.

Christoplos, I. (2008) The Oslo Policy Forum on changing the way we develop: dealing with disasters and climate change. Report on the findings of the conference. Norwegian Ministry for Foreign Affairs/ProVention Consortium/United Nations Development Programme, Oslo.

Christoplos, I., Liljelund, A. and Mitchell, J. (2001) Re-framing risk: the changing context of disaster mitigation and preparedness. *Disasters*, 25, 185–98.

Christoplos, I., Aysan, Y. and Galperin, A. (2005) *External Evaluation of the Inter-Agency Secretariat of the International Strategy for Disaster Reduction.* UN ISDR, Geneva.

Clarke, L. (2006) *Worst Cases: Terror and Catastrophe in the Popular Imagination.* University of Chicago Press, Chicago, IL and London.

Clarke, L. and Chess, C. (2008) Elites and panic: more to fear than fear itself. *Social Forces*, 87, 993–1014.

CNN (2005) US receives aid offers from around the world. CNN International.com, September 4. Accessed at <http://edition.cnn.com/2005/US/09/04/katrina.world.aid/>.

Cohen, C. and Werker, E.D. (2008) The political economy of "natural" disasters. Unpublished manuscript, Department of Economics, Cambridge, and Harvard Business School, Harvard University, Boston, MA.

Collier, S.J. (2008) Enacting catastrophe: preparedness, insurance, budgetary rationalization. *Economy and Society*, 37, 224–50.

Comfort, L.K. (2007) Asymmetric information processes in extreme events: the December 26, 2004 Sumatran earthquake and tsunami. In Gibbons, D.E. (ed.) *Communicable Crises: Prevention, Response, and Recovery in the Global Arena.* Information Age Publishing, Charlotte, NC, pp. 137–68.

Coppola, D.P. (2011) *Introduction to International Disaster Management*, 2nd edn. Elsevier, Amsterdam.

Cuny, F.C. (1983) *Disasters and Development*. Oxford University Press/Oxfam America, New York.

Dagge, J. (2011) Australia floods pose a political test not all pass. *The Christian Science Monitor*, January 14.

Dahlgren, P. and Chakrapani, S. (1982) The third world on TV news: Western ways of seeing the other. In Adams, W.C. (ed.) *Television Coverage of International Affairs*. Ablex, Norwood, NJ.

Davis, I. (2004) Progress in analysis of social vulnerability and capacity. In Bankoff, G., Frerks, G. and Hilhorst, D. (eds.) *Mapping Vulnerability: Disasters, Development and People*. Earthscan, London, pp. 128–44.

Davis, I. and Myers, M. (1994) Observations on the Yokohama World Conference on Natural Disaster Reduction, May 23–27, 1994. *Disasters*, 18, 368–81.

Davis, M. (1975) *Civil Wars and the Politics of International Relief: Africa, South Asia and the Caribbean*. Praeger, New York.

de Ville de Goyet, C. (2008) Information gaps in relief, recovery, and reconstruction in the aftermath of natural disasters. In Amin, S. and Goldstein, M. (eds.) *Data against Natural Disasters: Establishing Effective Systems for Relief, Recovery, and Reconstruction*. World Bank, Washington, DC, pp. 23–58.

de Waal, A. (1997) *Famine Crimes: Politics and the Disaster Relief Industry*. James Curry in association with African Rights, Oxford.

de Waal, A. (2006) Towards a comparative political ethnography of disaster prevention. *Journal of International Affairs*, 59, 129–52.

"Developing countries ratcheting up action on climate change" (2011) Climate change updates, World Bank, Washington, DC. Accessed at <http://climatechange.worldbank.org/climatechange/content/developing-countries-ratcheting-up-action>.

DFID (UK Department for International Development) (2011) *Multilateral Aid Review*, April. Accessed at <http://www.dfid.gov.uk/Documents/publications1/mar/multilateral_aid_review.pdf>.

DHL Express (2010) DHL and the One Laptop per Child Foundation to deliver thousands of computers to Haitian school children. Press release, March 23.

Dilley, M., Chen, R.S., Deichman, U., Lerner Lam, A.L. and Arnold, M. (2005) *Natural Disaster Hotspots: A Global Risk Analysis*. World Bank, Washington, DC.

DiMaggio, P.J. and Powell, W.W. (1983) The iron cage revisited: institutional isomorphism and collective rationality in organizational fields. *American Sociological Review*, 48, 147–60.

Dougherty, J.E. and Pfaltzgraff, R.L. Jr. (1981) *Conflicting Theories of International Relations: A Comprehensive Theory*. Harper & Row, New York.

Drury, A.C. and Olson, R.S. (1998) Disasters and political unrest: an empirical investigation. *Journal of Contingencies and Crisis Management*, 6, 153–61.

Drury, A.C., Olson, R.S. and Van Belle, D.A. (2005) The politics of humanitarian aid: U.S. foreign disaster assistance, 1964–1995. *The Journal of Politics*, 57, 454–73.

Duffield, M. (1994) Complex emergencies and the crisis of developmentalism. *IDS Bulletin*, 25, 37–45.

Dynes, R. (2004) Expanding the horizons of disaster research. *Natural Hazards Observer*, 28, 1–2.

Dynes, R. (2005) The Lisbon earthquake in 1755: the first modern disaster. In Braun, T. and Radner, J. (eds.) *The Lisbon Earthquake of 1755: Representations and Reactions*. Voltaire Foundation, Oxford, pp. 34–49.

Eakin, H. and Luers, A.L. (2006) Assessing the vulnerability of social-environmental systems. *Annual Review of Environment and Resources*, 31, 365–94.

Edwards, P.N. (2006) Meteorology as infrastructural globalism. *OSIRIS*, 21, 229–50.

Ehrlich, P. and Ehrlich, A. (1968) *The Population Bomb*. Ballantine Books, New York.

Eisensee, T. and Strömberg, D. (2007) News droughts, news floods, and US disaster relief. *The Quarterly Journal of Economics*, 122, 693–728.

ENN (Emergency Nutrition Network) (2007) Evaluation of cluster approach in Mozambique. *Field Exchange*, Issue 31 (September), p. 24. Accessed at <http://fex.ennonline.net/31/clusterapproach.aspx>.

"Eqecat's Keogh stresses the limitations of models" (2011) *Insurance ERM*, June 27. Accessed at <http://www.insuranceerm.com/analysis/Eqecats-Keogh-stresses-the-limitations-of-models.html?searched=limitations+of+models&advsearch=exact phrase&highlight=ajaxSearch_highlight+ajaxSearch_highlight1>.

Etkin, D., Medalye, J. and Higuchi, K. (2011) Climate warming and natural disaster management: an exploration of the issues. *Climatic Change*. Published online, November 1, 2011. Accessed at <http://www.springerlink.com/content/46761/qw660885087/fulltext.pdf>.

Fagen, P.W. (2008) Natural disasters in Latin America and the Caribbean: national, regional and international interactions. HPG Working Paper, Overseas Development Institute, London.

Fassin, D. (2010) Heart of humaneness: the moral economy of humanitarian intervention. In Fassin, D. and Pandolfi, M. (eds.) *Contemporary States of Emergency: The Politics of Military and Humanitarian Interventions*. Zone Books, New York, pp. 265–93.

Feldman, I. (2010) The humanitarian circuit: relief work, development assistance and CARE in Gaza, 1955–1967. In Bornstein, E. and Redfield, P. (eds.) *Forces of Compassion: Humanitarianism between Ethics and Politics*. School for Advanced Research Press, Santa Fe, NM, pp. 203–26.

Ferree, M.M. and Merrill, D.A. (2000) Hot movements, cold cognition: thinking about social movements in gendered frames. *Contemporary Sociology*, 29, 454–62.

Fick, J. and Prada, P. (2011) Nearly 500 are dead in Brazil flooding. *The Wall Street Journal*, January 14.

Fidler, D.P. (2005) Disaster relief and governance after the Indian Ocean tsunami: What role for international law? *Melbourne Journal of International Law*, 6, 458–73.

Finnemore, M. (1999) Rules of war and wars of rules: the International Red Cross and the restraint of state violence. In Boli, J. and Thomas, G.M. (eds.) *Constructing World Culture: International Nongovernmental Organizations since 1875*. Stanford University Press, Stanford, CA, pp. 149–68.

Finnemore, M. and Sikkink, K. (1998) International norm dynamics and political change. *International Organization*, 52, 887–917.

Fiss, P.C. and Hirsch, P.M. (2005) The discovery of globalization: framing and sensemaking of an emerging concept. *American Sociological Review*, 70, 29–52.

Florini, A.M. and Simmons, P.J. (1999) What the world needs now. In Florini, A. (ed.) *The Third Force: The Rise of Transnational Civil Society*. Japan Center for International Change and Carnegie Endowment for International Peace, Tokyo and Washington, DC, pp. 1–15.

Fordham, M. (2003) Gender, disaster and development: the necessity for integration. In Pelling, M. (ed.) *Natural Disasters and Development in a Globalizing World*. Routledge, London and New York, pp. 57–74.

Forsythe, D.P. (2005) *The Humanitarians: The International Committee of the Red Cross*. Cambridge University Press, Cambridge.

Forsythe, D.P. (2009) Contemporary humanitarianism: the global and the local. In Wilson, R.A. and Brown, R.D. (eds.) *Humanitarianism and Suffering: The Mobilization of Empathy*. Cambridge University Press, Cambridge, pp. 58–87.

Frank, D.J. (2002) The origins question: building global institutions to protect nature. In Hoffman, A.J. and Ventresca, M.J. (eds.) *Organizations, Policy and the Natural Environment*. Stanford University Press, Stanford, CA, pp. 41–56.

Fry, K. (ed.) (2011) How to draft another skater. Inline skating and roller-skating. Accessed at <http://www.skatelog.com/speed/how-to-draft.htm>.

Fuentes, V.E. (2009) Post-disaster reconstruction: an opportunity for political change. In Ensor, M.O. (ed.) *The Legacy of Hurricane Mitch: Lessons from Post-Disaster Reconstruction in Honduras*. The University of Arizona Press, Tucson, AZ, pp. 100–28.

Fukushima, G.S. (1995) The Great Hanshin Earthquake. Japan Policy Research Institute, University of San Francisco Center for the Pacific Rim, Occasional Paper No. 2, March.

Galperin, A. (2002) Discourses of Disaster, Discourses of Relief and DFID's Humanitarian Aid Policy. Working Paper No. 02-28, Development Studies Institute, London School of Economics and Political Science, London.

Gans, H.J. (1980) *Deciding What's News: A Study of CBS Evening News, NBC Nightly News, Newsweek and Time*. Vintage, New York.

Garrett, T.A. and Sobel, R.S. (2003) The political economy of disaster payments. *Economic Inquiry*, 41, 496–509.

Gelling, P. (2009) Indonesian project shows obstacles after tsunami. *New York Times*, December 26.

Gershman, J., Fleisher, L. and Banjo, S. (2011) 3 Governors, 3 strategies in flood fight. *The Wall Street Journal*, September 3. Available at: <http://online.wsj.com/article/SB10001424053111904583204576547102408402770.html>.

Gibbs, D. (2000) Realpolitik and humanitarian intervention: The case of Somalia. *International Politics*, 37, 41–55.

Gilboa, E. (2005) THE CNN effect: the search for a communication theory of international relations. *Political Communication*, 22, 27–44.

Glennie, J. (2011) The rise of the "south-south" aid agencies. *The Guardian Weekly*, March 4, p. 44.

Globe and Mail [Toronto] (2012) Merkel sans frontiers. *Globe and Mail*, January 31, A12.

Goodspeed, P. (2011) Why is this happening again? After 60 years and $1 trillion in development and aid, famine returns to Africa. *National Post* (Toronto), July 25, A15.

Gorgé, C. (1938) *The International Relief Union: Its Origins, Aims, Means, and Future.* International Relief Union, Geneva.

Green, D. (2008) Shocks and change. From poverty to power: a conversational blog, Oxfam International, June 29. Accessed at <http://www.oxfamblogs.org/fp2p/>.

Green, S. (1977) *International Disaster Relief: Towards a Responsive System.* McGraw-Hill/Council on Foreign Relations, New York.

Grieco, J.M. (1988) Realist theory and the problem of international cooperation: analysis with an amended prisoner's dilemma model. *The Journal of Politics*, 50, 600–24.

Haas, P. (1989) Do regimes matter? Epistemic communities and Mediterranean pollution control. *International Organization*, 43, 377–403.

Haas, P. (1990) *Saving the Mediterranean: The Politics of International Environmental Cooperation.* Columbia University Press, New York.

Hake, T. (2011) Death toll from floods and mudslides in Brazil approaches 700. *Natural Disasters Examiner*, January 18.

Hall, P.A. (1993) Policy paradigms, social learning and the state – the case of economic policymaking in Britain. *Comparative Politics*, 29, 275–96.

Handmer, J. (1995) A safer world for the 21st century? The Yokohama World Conference on Natural Disaster Reduction. *Journal of Contingencies and Crisis Management*, 3, 35–7.

Hannigan, J. (1976) Newspaper conflict and cooperation content after disaster: an exploratory analysis. Preliminary Paper #27, Disaster Research Center, The Ohio State University/University of Delaware, February.

Hannigan, J. (2006) *Environmental Sociology*, 2nd edn. Routledge, London and New York.

Hannigan, J. (2010) The emergence model of environment and society. In Redclift, M.R. and Woodgate, G. (eds.) *The International Handbook of Environmental Sociology*, 2nd edn. Edward Elgar, Cheltenham, pp. 164–78.

Hay, C. (2004) Ideas, interests and institutions in the comparative political economy of great transformations. *Review of International Political Economy*, 11, 204–26.

Hayter, T. (1971) *Aid as Imperialism.* Penguin, Harmondsworth.

Hehir, A. (2010) *Humanitarian Intervention: An Introduction.* Palgrave Macmillan, Basingstoke.

Hevesi, D. (2008) Julia Vadala Taft, official who led relief efforts, is dead at 65. *New York Times*, March 18.

Hewitt, K. (ed.) (1983) *Interpretations of Calamity from the Viewpoint of Human Ecology.* Allen and Unwin, London.

Hicks, E. and Pappas, G. (2006) Coordinating disaster relief after the South Asian earthquake. *Society*, 43 (5), 42–50.

Hoffman, A.J. (1999) Institutional evolution and change: environmentalism and the US chemical industry. *The Academy of Management Journal*, 42, 351–71.

Holloway, A. (2003) Disaster risk reduction in Southern Africa: hot rhetoric–cold reality. *African Security Review*, 12, 29–38.

Homeland Security News Wire (2011) Economic, infrastructure damage of floods in Australia, Brazil staggering, January 21.

Höppe, P. (2007) Natural hazards: the increasing importance of insurance for the poorest of the poor. Munich Re Archive: Climate Change and Insurance, January 5. Accessed at <http://www.munichre.com/en/group/focus/climate_change/archive/default.aspx>.

Horwitz, S. (2008) Making hurricane response more effective: lessons from the private sector and the Coast Guard during Katrina. Mercatus Center, George Mason University. Accessed at <http://www.mercatus.org/uploadedFiles/Mercatus/Pub...>.

Horwitz, S. (2009) Best responders: post Katrina innovation and improvisation by Wal-Mart and the U.S. Coast Guard. *Innovations*, 4, 93–9.

Housner, G.W. (1989) An International Decade of Natural Disaster Reduction: 1990–2000. *Natural Hazards*, 2, 45–75.

Hrywna, M. (2008) Fundraising fizzles for Myanmar and China. *The Non-Profit Times*, June 15.

Hulme, M., Barrow, E.M., Arnell, N.W., Harrison, P.A., Johns, T.C. and Downing, T.E. (1999) Relative impacts of human-induced climate change and natural climate variability. *Nature*, 397, 688–91.

Humanitarian Practice Network (Overseas Development Institute) (1994) The IDNDR – for the initiated. *Humanitarian Exchange Magazine*, Issue 1 (March).

Hutchison, J.F. (2001) Disasters and the international order – II: The International Relief Union. *The International History Review*, xxiii, 253–304.

IEG-World Bank (Independent Evaluation Group-World Bank) (2006) *Hazards of Nature, Risks to Development: An IEG Evaluation of World Bank Assistance for Natural Disasters*. The World Bank, Washington, DC.

"Into the inferno" (2010) *The Economist*, August 14, p. 39.

IPCC (Intergovernmental Panel on Climate Change) (2007) *Fourth Assessment Report*. Cambridge University Press, Cambridge.

IRIN Humanitarian News and Analysis (2005) Disaster reduction and the human cost of disaster. UN Office for the Coordination of Humanitarian Affairs, June. Accessed at <http://www.irinnews.org/report.aspx?reportid=62452>.

Jackson, J.H. (2011) Envisioning disaster in the 1910 Paris Flood. *Journal of Urban History*, 37, 176–207.

Jasanoff, S. (2010) Beyond calculation: a democratic response to risk. In Lakoff, A. (ed.) *Disaster and the Politics of Intervention*. Columbia University Press, New York, pp. 14–40.

Jayasuriya, S. and McCawley, P. (2010) *The Asian Tsunami: Aid and Reconstruction after a Disaster*. Edward Elgar, Cheltenham.

Jeggle, T. (1994) Is the IDNDR a slow-onset disaster in the making? *Natural Hazards Observer*, 18(4), 1–2.

Jennings, S. (2011) *Time's Bitter Flood: Trends in the Number of Reported Natural Disasters*. Oxfam Research Report, Oxfam GB, May 27.

Jeong, Y. and Lee, S. (2010) A study on the news values of international disasters: change of determinants on news coverage of international disasters in the US news media. Presented at the Annual Meeting of the International Communication Association, Suntec City, Singapore, June 22.

Jervis, R. (1988) Realism, game theory, and cooperation. *World Politics*, 40, 317–49.

Johnson, L.A. (2000) Earthquake loss modeling applications for disaster management: lessons from the 1999 Turkey, Greece, and Taiwan earthquakes. Presented at the EuroConference on global change and catastrophe risk management: earthquake risks in Europe, International Institute for Applied Systems Analysis, Laxenberg, Austria, July 7.

Joint Inspection Unit (1980) Evaluation of the Office of the United Nations Disaster Relief Coordinator, JIU/REP/80/11. United Nations, Geneva, October.

Juneja, S. (2008) Disasters and poverty: the risk nexus. Background Paper for the 2009 ISDR Global Assessment Report on Disaster Risk Reduction. United Nations International Strategy for Disaster Reduction, Geneva, August. Accessed at <http://www.preventionweb.net/English/hyogo/gar/background-papers/documents/Chap4/Juneja-disasters-and-poverty-the-risk-nexus.doc>.

Kalder, M. (2003) *Global Civil Society: An Answer to War*. Polity Press, Cambridge.

Kaplan, R.D. (2011) *Monsoon: The Indian Ocean and the Future of American Power*. Random House, New York.

Kates, R.W. (2000) Cautionary tales: adaptation and the global poor. *Climatic Change*, 45, 5–17.

Keck, M.E. and Sikkink, K. (1998) *Activists Beyond Borders: Advocacy Networks in International Politics*. Cornell University Press, Ithaca, NY.

Keen, D. (2008) *Complex Emergencies*. Polity Press, Cambridge.

Kelly, P.M. and Adger, W.N. (2000) Theory and practice in assessing vulnerability to climate change and facilitating adaptation. *Climatic Change*, 47, 325–52.

Kelman, I. (2003) Beyond disaster, beyond diplomacy. In Pelling, M. (ed.) *Natural Disasters and Development in a Globalizing World*. Routledge, London and New York, pp. 110–23.

Kelman, I. (2007) Hurricane Katrina disaster diplomacy. *Disasters*, 31, 288–309.

Kelman, I. (2011) *Disaster Diplomacy: How Disasters Affect Peace and Conflict*. Routledge, London and New York.

Kelman, I. and Koukis, T. (2000) Disaster diplomacy. *Cambridge Review of International Affairs*, XIV, 214–94.

Kelman, I. and Warnaar, M. (2004) Typology of disaster diplomacy. *Radix: Radical Interpretations of and Solutions for Disaster*, December 21. Accessed at <http://www.disasterdiplomacy.org/projects.html>.

Kent, R.C. (1983) Reflecting upon a decade of disasters: the evolving response of the international community. *International Affairs*, 59, 693–711.

Kent, R.C. (1987) *Anatomy of Disaster Relief: The International Network in Action*. Pinter Publishers, London.

Ker-Lindsay, J. (2000) Greek-Turkish rapprochement: the impact of "disaster diplomacy"? *Cambridge Review of International Affairs*, 14, 215–32.

Khatchadourian, R. (2011) The Gulf War. *The New Yorker*, March 14. Accessed at <http://www.newyorker.com/reporting/2011/03/14/110314fa_fact_khatchadourian?currentPage=1>.

King, R.J. (2006) *Big, Easy Money: Disaster Profiteering on the American Gulf Coast.* CorpWatch, Oakland, CA.

Kingdon, J.W. (1984) *Agendas, Alternatives and Public Policies.* Little, Brown, Boston, MA.

Klein, N. (2005) The rise of disaster capitalism. *Nation*, May 2.

Klingaman, S. (2010) Why we lurch from disaster to disaster and how to fix it. Open Salon blog, May 20. Accessed at <http://open.salon.com/blog/steve_klingaman>.

Korten, D.C. (1990) *Getting to the 21st Century: Voluntary Action and the Global Agenda.* Kumarian Press, West Hartford, CT.

Kuhn, T.S. (1996 [1962]) *The Structure of Scientific Revolutions.* University of Chicago Press, Chicago, IL.

Kurlantzick, J. (2008) Destructive power. Boston.com (*The Boston Globe*), May 11. Accessed at <http://www.boston.com/bostonglobe/ideas/articles/2008/05/11/destructive_power/>.

Lakoff, A. (2010a) *Disaster and the Politics of Intervention.* Columbia University Press, New York.

Lakoff, A. (2010b) Introduction. In Lakoff, A. (ed.) *Disaster and the Politics of Intervention.* Columbia University Press, New York, pp. 1–12.

The Lancet (2010) Growth of aid and the decline of humanitarianism. *The Lancet*, 375, No. 9711, 253.

Laqueur, T.W. (2009) Mourning, pity, and the work of narrative in the making of "humanity." In Wilson, R.A. and Brown, R.D. (eds.) *Humanitarianism and Suffering: The Mobilization of Empathy.* Cambridge University Press, Cambridge, pp. 31–57.

Laurent, P. (1999) The humanitarian impasse. In Pirotte, C., Husson, B. and Grunewald, F. (eds.) *Responding to Emergencies and Fostering Development: The Dilemmas of Humanitarian Aid.* Zed Books, London and New York, pp. 27–9.

Leader, N. (1999) Codes of conduct: who needs them? *Relief and Rehabilitation Network Newsletter*, 13, Overseas Development Institute, London.

Leonard, H.B. and Howitt, A.M. (2007) Against desperate peril: high performance in emergency preparation and response. In Gibbons, D.E. (ed.) *Communicable Crises: Prevention, Response, and Recovery in the Global Arena.* Information Age Publishing, Charlotte, NC, pp. 1–25.

Lessig, L. (1995) The regulation of social meaning. *University of Chicago Law Review*, 62 (3), 944–1045.

Letukas, L., Olofsson, A. and Barnshaw, J. (2009) Solidarity trumps catastrophe? An empirical and theoretical analysis of post-tsunami media in two Western nations. Preliminary Paper #363, Disaster Research Center, University of Delaware.

Levine, S. (2011) Here we go again: famine in the Horn of Africa. Overseas Development Institute, July 6. Accessed at <http://blogs.odi.org.uk/blogs/main/archive/2011/07/06/horn_of_africa_famine_2011_humanitarian_system.aspx>.

Lewis, D. and Kanji, N. (2009) *Non-Governmental Organizations and Development.* Routledge, London and New York.

Lies, E. (Reuters) (2005) Disaster conference to end with little in hand. Cited in *Media Monitoring Report*, World Conference on Disaster Reduction.

Lin, B., Perfecto, I. and Vandermeer, J. (2008) Synergies between agricultural intensification and climate change could create surprising vulnerabilities for crops. *BioScience*, 58 (9), 847–54.

Linnerooth-Bayer, J. (2007) Insurance for reducing vulnerability to climate-related disasters. Presented at the Research and Policy Workshop on Climate Change, Humanitarian Disasters and International Development: Linking Vulnerability, Risk Reduction and Response Capacity. Oslo Center for International Climate and Environmental Research, April 27.

Liu, Junhong (2008) Time for Asian system to fight back disasters. *China Daily*, April 6.

Liverman, D. (1990) Drought impacts in Mexico: climate, agriculture, technology and land tenure in Sonora and Puebla. *Annals of the Association of American Geographers*, 80, 49–72.

McAllister, I. (1993) *Sustaining Relief with Development: Strategic Issues for the Red Cross and Red Crescent*. Martinus Nijhoff Publishers, Dordrecht.

McCleary, R.M. (2009) *Global Compassion*. Oxford University Press, New York.

McDonald, B. and Gordon, P. (2008) United Nations' efforts to strengthen information management for disaster preparedness and response. In Amin, S. and Goldstein, M. (eds.) *Data against Natural Disasters: Establishing Effective Systems for Relief, Recovery and Reconstruction*. World Bank, Washington, DC, pp. 59–81.

McEntire, D.A. (2005) International relations and disasters: illustrating the relevance of the discipline to the study and profession of emergency management. Unpublished paper. Accessed at <http://training.fema.gov/emiweb/downloads/Chapter%20-%20International%20Studies.pdf>.

McKibben, B. (2011) What should we make of all these natural disasters? *Washington Post*, May 25.

McNeil, Jr., D. (2010) Disaster strategy: the soft heart and the hard sell. *New York Times*, August 22, WK3.

McNicoll, T. (2010) After and before the flood. *The Daily Beast*, January 19. Accessed at <http://www.thedailybeast.com/newsweek/2010/01/19/after-and-before-the-flood.html>.

Macrae, J. and Leader, N. (2000) Shifting sands and the search for coherence between political and humanitarian responses to complex emergencies. Humanitarian Policy Group, Report no. 8, Overseas Development Institute, London.

Magrath, J. (2009) Comment on Stan Lewis, "Spotlight on satellites for disaster management," *SciDev Net*, November 11. Accessed at <http://www.scidev.net/en/editorials/spotlight-on-satellites-for-disaster-management-1.html>.

Mandel, R. (2002) Security and natural disasters. *Journal of Conflict Studies*, XXXII, 118–43.

Margesson, R. (2007) International Crises and Disasters: US Humanitarian Assistance, Budget Trends, and Issues for Congress (CRS Report for Congress), May 3.

Marr, G. (2011) You didn't escape disaster toll: Natural disasters to raise insurance premiums. *National Post* (Toronto), August 31, FP1, FP7.

Maskrey, A. and Jegillos, S. (1997) Promoting community-based approaches in disaster management. *Asian Disaster Management News*, 3 (2), June. Accessed at <http://www.adpc.net/infores/newsletter/1997/theme-2.html>.

Mason, A. and Wheeler, N. (1996) Realist objections to humanitarian intervention. In Holden, B. (ed.) *The Ethical Dimensions of Global Change*. Macmillan, Basingstoke, pp. 94–110.

Meadows, D.L., Meadows, D.H., Randers, J. and Behrens, W.W. (1972) *The Limits to Growth*. Earth Island, London.

Media Monitoring Report (2005) World Conference on Disaster Reduction, January 18–22, Kobe, Hyogo, Japan. Accessed at <http://www.unisdr.org/2005/wcdr/media/wcdr-media-monitoring.pdf>.

Mercer, J. (2010) Disaster risk reduction or climate change adaptation: Are we reinventing the wheel? *Journal of International Development*, 22, 247–64.

Meyer, J.W., Frank, D.J., Hironka, A. and Tuma, N.B. (1997) The structuring of a world environmental regime, 1870–1990. *International Organization*, 51, 623–9.

Michel-Kerjan, E. (2005) Financial protection of critical infrastructure: uncertain insurability and terrorism risk. Report No. 3, Institut Veolia Environnement, Paris, June.

Middleton, N. and O'Keefe, P. (1998) *Disasters and Development: The Politics of Humanitarian Aid*. Pluto Press, London.

Miller, C. (2001) Scientific internationalism in American foreign policy: the case of meteorology, 1947–1958. In Miller, C. and Edwards, P.N. (eds.) *Changing the Atmosphere: Expert Knowledge and Environmental Governance*. The MIT Press, Cambridge, MA.

Mills, K. (1998) *Human Rights in the Emerging Global Order: A New Sovereignty?* Macmillan, Basingstoke.

Minear, L., Scott, C. and Weiss, T. (1996) *The News Media, Civil War, and Humanitarian Action*. Lynne Rienner, Boulder, CO.

Minkel, J.R. (2008) Pandemic hot spots map a path to prevention. *Scientific American*, February 22, p. 5.

Mitchell, T. (2011) Climate conversations – Why is Britain ending support to UNISDR? *AlertNet*, March 7.

Mitchell, T. and van Aalst, M. (2008) Convergence of disaster risk reduction and climate change adaptation: A review for DFID, October 31. Accessed at <http://www.preventionweb.net/files/7853_ConvergenceofDRRandCCA1.pdf>.

Moeller, S. (1999) *Compassion Fatigue: How the Media Sells Disease, Famine, War and Death*. Routledge, New York and London.

Morrill, C. and Owen-Smith, J. (2002) The emergence of environmental conflict resolution: subversive stories and the construction of collective action frames and organizational fields. In Hoffman, A.J. and Ventresca, M. (eds.) *Organizations, Policy and Strategic Perspectives*. Stanford University Press, Stanford, CA, pp. 90–118.

Mowforth, M. (2001) *Storm Warnings: Hurricanes Georges and Mitch and the Lessons for Development*. CIIR, London.

Munich Re (1973) *Flood/Inundation*. Munich Re, Munich.

Munich Re (2000) *Topics*. Munich Re, Munich.

Nadelmann, E. (1990) Global prohibition regimes: the evolution of norms in international society. *International Organization*, 44, 479–526.

Nelson, T. (2008) International politics of disaster aid refusal. Presented at the Annual Meeting of the Midwest Political Science Association, Chicago, April 6. Accessed at <http://www.gpoaccess.gov/congress/Index.html>.

Nelson, T. (2010) Rejecting the gift horse: international politics of disaster and refusal. *Conflict, Security and Development*, 10, 379–402.

Newell, P. (2006) *Climate for Change: Non-State Actors and the Global Politics of the Greenhouse*. Cambridge University Press, Cambridge.

Nishikawa, Y. (2005) *Japan's Changing Role in Humanitarian Crises*. Routledge, London and New York.

Norris, J. (2007) *The Disaster Gypsies*. Praeger, Westport, CT.

Obasi, G.O.P. (1994) WMO's role in the International Decade for Natural Disaster Reduction. *Bulletin of the American Meteorological Society*, 75, 1655–61.

"Oblique strategies" (2010) *The Economist*, May 11.

O'Brien, G., O'Keefe, P., Rose, J. and Wisner, B. (2006) Climate change and disaster management. *Disasters*, 30, 64–80.

OCHA (United Nations Office for the Coordination of Humanitarian Affairs) (2008) OCHA 2008: Part III: Performance. Accessed at <http://ochaonline.un.org/OCHA2008AR/part3a-goal1.html>.

O'Donnell, I. (2011) Protecting development gains – the role of integrated disaster risk management. Asian Development Bank. *Knowledge Management and Learning*, July.

OHDACA (Overseas Humanitarian, Disaster, and Civic Aid) (2000/2001) Biennial Budget Estimates.

Oliver, J. (1977) Climate change and meteorologically induced hazards. *Natural Hazards Observer*, 2 (1), 3.

Oliver-Smith, A. (1996) Anthropological research on hazards and disasters. *Annual Review of Anthropology*, 25, 303–28.

Oliver-Smith, A. (1998a) What is a disaster? Anthropological perspectives on a persistent question. In Oliver-Smith, A. and Hoffman, S.H. (eds.) *The Angry Earth: Disaster in Anthropological Perspective*. Routledge, London and New York, pp. 18–34.

Oliver-Smith, A. (1998b) Peru's five-hundred-year earthquake: vulnerability in historical context. In Oliver-Smith, A. and Hoffman, S.H. (eds.) *The Angry Earth: Disaster in Anthropological Perspective*. Routledge, London and New York, pp. 74–88.

O'Neill, K. (2009) *The Environment and International Relations*. Cambridge University Press, Cambridge.

Oxfam International (2008) OI Policy Compendium Note on Humanitarian Coordination, July.

Oxfam International (2009) The Right to Survive: The Humanitarian Challenge for the Twenty-first Century, April.

Oxfam International (2011) Climate change investment through the Pilot Program for Climate Resilience in Tajikistan, January 24. Accessed at <http://www.oxfam.org/sites/www.oxfam.org/files/climate-resilience-tajikistan-240111-en.pdf>.

Ozerdem, A. (2003) Disaster as a manifestation of unresolved development challenges: the Marmara earthquake, Turkey. In Pelling, M. (ed.) *Natural Disasters and Development in a Globalizing World*. Routledge, London and New York, pp. 199–213.

Parker, R.S. (2006) *Hazards of Nature, Risks to Development: An IEG Evaluation of World Bank Assistance for Natural Disasters*. The World Bank, Washington, DC.

Parks, B. and Roberts, J.T. (2005) Understanding vulnerability to disasters: a cross-national analysis of 4,000 climate-related disasters. Paper presented at the Annual Meeting, American Sociological Association, August.

Parks, B. and Roberts, J.T. (2010) Climate change, social theory and justice. *Theory, Culture & Society*, 27, 134–66.

Pearce, F. (2010) *The Climate Files: The Battle for Truth about Global Warming*. Guardian Books, London.

Pelling, M. (2003) Emerging concerns. In Pelling, M. (ed.) *Natural Disasters and Development in a Globalizing World*. Routledge, London and New York, pp. 233–43.

Pelling, M. (2011) *Adaptation to Climate Change: From Resilience to Transformation*. Routledge, London and New York.

Pelling, M. and Dill, K. (2006) "Natural disasters" as catalysts of political action. ISP/NSC briefing paper 06/01. Chatham House, London.

Pelling, M. and Dill, K. (2007) "Natural" disasters as catalysts of political action. World Association for Christian Communication. Accessed at <http://waccglobal.org/en/20064-communication-and-disaster/607-Natural-disasters-as-catalysts-of-political-action.html>.

Pelling, M. and Dill, K. (2010) Disaster politics: tipping points for change in the adaptation of sociopolitical regimes. *Progress in Human Geography*, 34, 21–37.

Pelling, M. and Wisner, B. (2009) Reducing urban disaster risk in Africa. In Pelling, M. and Wisner, B. (eds.) *Disaster Risk Reduction: Cases from Urban Africa*. Earthscan, London.

Perlez, J. (2006) After tsunami, intentions to build no road yet. *New York Times*, October 9.

Picou, J.S., Marshall, B.K. and Gill, D.A. (2004) Disaster, litigation and the corrosive community. *Social Forces*, 82, 1493–522.

Pielke, R.A., Jr. (1998) Rethinking the role of adaptation in climate policy. *Global Environmental Change*, 8, 159–70.

Pieterse, J.N. (1998) Sociology of humanitarian intervention: Bosnia, Rwanda and Somalia compared. In Pieterse, J.N. (ed.) *World Orders in the Making: Humanitarian Intervention and Beyond*. London: Macmillan Press/Institute of Social Studies, pp. 230–65.

Pieterse, J.N. (2010) *Development Theory*, 2nd edn. Sage, Thousand Oaks, CA.

Pilling, D. (2005) UN moves to forge worldwide tsunami alert plan. *Financial Times*, January 19.

"Pilot program for climate resilience" (2011) Climate Funds Update, Heinrich Böll Stiftung/Overseas Development Institute. Accessed at <http://www.climatefundsupdate.org/listing/pilot-program-for-climate-resilience>.

Plate, E.J. and Kron, W. (1994) The International Decade for Natural Disaster Reduction (IDNDR): a challenge to science. *Soil Dynamics and Earthquake Engineering*, 13, 45–8.

Platt, R.H. (1999) *Disasters and Democracy: The Politics of Extreme Natural Events*. Island Press, Washington, DC.

Potter, D. and Van Belle, D. (2007) The impact of news coverage on Japanese foreign disaster aid: a comparative example of bureaucratic responsiveness to the news media. Paper presented at the American Political Science Association Annual Meeting, Chicago, August 30. Accessed at <http://www.allacademic.com/mete/p210816_index.html>.

Price, R. (2003) Review article: Transnational civil society and advocacy in world politics. *World Politics*, 55, 579–606.

Prins, G., Galiana, I., Green, C., Grundmann, R., Hulme, M., Korhola, A., Laird, F., Nordhaus, T., Pielke Jr, R., Rayner, S., Sarewitz, D., Shellenberger, M., Stehr, N. and Tezuka, H. (2010) *The Hartwell Paper: A new direction for climate policy after the crash of 2009.* Institute for Science, Innovation and Society, University of Oxford and LSE Makinder Programme, London School of Economics, Oxford and London, May. Accessed at <http://eprints.lse.ac.uk/27939/1/HartwellPaper_English_version.pdf>.

ProVention Consortium (2008) *Annual Report 2007: Working in Partnership to Build Safer Communities and Reduce Disaster Risk.* Geneva. Accessed at <http://www.preventionweb.net/files/9675_ProVentionannualreport071.pdf>.

Quarantelli, E.L. (ed.) (1998a) *What is a Disaster? Perspectives on the Question.* Routledge, London and New York.

Quarantelli, E.L. (1998b) Epilogue: Where we have been and where we might go: putting the elephant together, blowing soap bubbles, and having singular insights. In Quarantelli, E.L. (ed.) *What is a Disaster? Perspectives on the Question.* Routledge, London and New York, pp. 234–73.

Quarantelli, E.L. and Davis, I. (2011) An Exploratory Research Agenda for Studying the Popular Culture of Disasters (PCD): Its Characteristics, Conditions and Consequences. Disaster Research Center, Newark, DE.

Quarantelli, E.L. and Dynes, R.R. (1976) Community conflict: its absence and its presence in natural disasters. *International Journal of Mass Emergencies and Disasters*, 1, 139–52.

Rajaram, P.K. (2002) Humanitarianism and representations of the refugee. *Journal of Refugee Studies*, 15, 247–64.

Rao, V. (2012) With foreign aid, failure is essential to learning. *Globe and Mail* (Toronto), January 23, A-11.

reliefweb (2011) World humanitarian consortium releases revamped industry standards – The Sphere Handbook 2011. UN Office for the Coordination of Humanitarian Affairs, April 14. Accessed at <http://reliefweb.int/node/396396>.

"Relieving the Japanese and Chinese" (n.d.) Virtual Museum of the City of San Francisco. Accessed at <http://www.sfmuseum.net/conflag/relief1.html>.

"Revitalizing Humanitarian Reform" (2011) Interaction, Washington, DC, April 12. Accessed at <http://www.interaction.org/document/revitalizing-humanitarian-reform>.

Rhinard, M. and Sundelius, B. (2010) The limits of self-reliance: international cooperation as a source of resilience. In Comfort, L.K., Boin, A. and Demchak, C.C. (eds.), *Designing Resilience: Preparing for Extreme Events.* University of Pittsburgh Press, Pittsburgh, PA, pp. 196–219.

Richter, R. (1995) *Utopia Lost: The United Nations and World Order.* The Twentieth Century Fund Press, New York.

Risk and Poverty in a Changing Climate (2009) Summary and Recommendations: 2009 Global Assessment Report on Disaster Risk Reduction. United Nations.

Roberts, A. (1993) Humanitarian war: military intervention and human rights. *International Affairs*, 69, 429–49.

Rocha, J.L. and Christoplos, I. (1999) NGOs and natural disasters: gaps and opportunities. *Revista Envio*, 220, November.

Rodda, J.C. (2000) Meteorology, hydrology and the geosciences. Lectures presented at the Fiftieth Session of the WMO Executive Council. World Meteorological Organization, Geneva.

Rourke, A. (2011) Australian floods kill nine as waters threaten Brisbane. *The Guardian*, January 11.

RTÉ (Raidió Teilifís Éireann) (2011) Hundreds killed in Brazil floods and mudslides. *RTÉ News*, January 13.

Ruiz Estrada, M.A. (2011) The Natural Disasters Vulnerability Evaluation (NDVE) Model. *SciTopics*, June 20. Accessed January 4, 2012, from <http://www.scitopics.com/The_Natural_Disasters_Vulnerability_Evaluation_NDVE_Model.html>.

Salt, J.E. (2003) The insurance industry: Can it cope with catastrophe? In Pelling, M. (ed.) *Natural Disasters and Development in a Globalizing World*. Routledge, London and New York, pp. 124–38.

Schipper, E.L.F. (2006) Conceptual history of adaptation to climate change under the UNFCCC. *Review of European Community and International Environmental Law*, 15, 82–92.

Schipper, E.L.F. (2009) Meeting at the crossroads? Exploring the linkages between climate change adaptation and disaster risk reduction. *Climate and Development*, 1, 16–30.

Schipper, L. and Pelling, M. (2006) Disaster risk, climate change and international development: scope for, and challenges to, integration. *Disasters*, 30, 19–38.

Schmidt, V.A. (2008) Discourse institutionalism: the explanatory power of ideas and discourse. *Annual Review of Political Science*, 11, 303–26.

Schwartz, P. (1990) Accepting risk in forecasting. *New York Times*, FORUM, September 2.

Scruton, R. (2012) *Green Philosophy: How to Think Seriously About the Planet*. Atlantic Books, London.

Seipel, J. (2011) The impossible interface? Combining humanitarian logistics and military supply chain capabilities. In Christopher, M. and Tatham, P. (eds.) *Humanitarian Logistics: Meeting the Challenge of Preparing for and Responding to Disasters*. Kogan Page, London, pp. 215–30.

Select Committee on International Development (UK) (2002) *Minutes of Evidence*, February 12. Accessed at <http://www.publications.parliament.uk/pa/cm200102/cmselect/cmintdev/519/2021206.htm>.

Selznick, P. (1957) *Leadership in Administration: A Sociological Interpretation*. Harper & Row, New York.

Sen, A. (1981) Ingredients of famine analysis: availability and entitlements. *Quarterly Journal of Economics*, 96, 433–64.

Sen, A. (1985) *Commodities and Capabilities*. Oxford University Press, Oxford.

Shah, A. (2005) Media and natural disasters. *Global Issues*, October 23. Accessed at <http://www.globalissues.org/article/568/media-and-natural-disasters>.

Sham, P. (1990) Reduction in weather-related disasters in Southeast Asia and the Western Pacific – a response to IDNDR. Presented to the Fourth World Congress on Tall Buildings and Urban Habitat, Hong Kong, November 5–9.

Shelter Centre (2011) The Sphere Handbook 2011: Humanitarian Charter and Minimum Standards in Disaster Response (library resources). Shelter Centre, Geneva. Accessed at <http://sheltercentre.org/library>.

Shiro, B. (2008) Remote sensing for natural disaster management, December 17. Accessed at <http://www.scribd.com/doc/44773212/Remote-Sensing-for-Natural-Disaster-Management>.

Shohan, J., Watson, F. and McGrath, M. (2010) Humanitarian disaster response (letter). *The Lancet*, 375, No. 9718, 891.

Sikkink, K. (1998) Traditional politics, international relations theory, and human rights. *PS: Political Science and Politics*, 31, 516–23.

Silva, J.A. (2010) Nature as a sword of Damacles. INS (Inter Press Service), May 25. Accessed at <http://www.ipsnews.net/news.asp?idnews=51577>.

Silva, K. (2010) Race, nation and ideology: CNN in Sri Lanka for Tsunami 2004. In Fuller, L.K. (ed.) *Tsunami Communication*. Hampton Press, Cresskill, NJ, pp. 133–46.

Siméant, J. (2005) What is going global? The internalization of French NGOs "without borders." *Review of International Political Economy*, 12, 851–83.

Skelton, T. (2006) A Case Study of British Media Discourses of the Indian Ocean Tsunami: the December 2004 Coverage. Asian Meta Centre Research Paper Series No. 21, National University of Singapore, June. Accessed at <http://www.populationasia.org/Publications/Research_Papers.htm>.

Skogstad, G. and Schmidt, V.A. (2012) Introduction: paradigm development, transnationalism and domestic politics. In Skogstad, G. (ed.) *Policy Paradigms, Transnationalism and Domestic Politics*. University of Toronto Press, Toronto.

Smirl, L. (2008) Building the other, constructing ourselves: spatial dimensions of international humanitarian response. *International Political Sociology*, 2, 236–53.

Snow, D.A. (2004) Framing processes, ideology and discursive fields. In Snow, D.A., Soule, S.A. and Kriesi, H. (eds.) *The Blackwell Companion to Social Movements*. Blackwell, Malden, MA, pp. 380–412.

Solnit, R. (2009) *A Paradise Built in Hell: The Extraordinary Communities That Arise in Disaster*. Viking, New York.

Spillman, L. (1995) Culture, social structure and discursive fields. *Current Perspectives in Social Theory*, 15, 129–54.

Sridhar, V. (2006) Partners in rebuilding. *Frontline*, 22, January. Accessed at <http://www.flonnet.com/fl2227/stories/20060113007100400.htm>.

Stamatov, P. (2010) Activist religion, empire, and the emergence of modern long-distance advocacy networks. *American Sociological Review*, 75, 607–28.

Steensland, B. (2008) Why do policy frames change? Actor-idea coevolution in debates over welfare reform. *Social Forces*, 86, 1027–54.

Steinberg, F. (2011) Rebuilding lives and homes in Aceh and Nias: a retrospective. In Steinberg, F. and Smidt, P. (eds.) *Rebuilding Lives and Homes in Aceh and Nias, Indonesia*. Asian Development Bank, Mandaluyong City, Philippines, pp. 1–19. Accessed at <http://www2.adb.org/documents/books/rebuilding-aceh-nias/rebuilding-aceh-nias.pdf>.

Stephens, T. (1978) *The United Nations Disaster Relief Office: The Politics and Administration of International Relief Assistance*. University Press of America, Washington, DC.

Stockholm Plan of Action (2007) *Stockholm Plan of Action for Integrating Disaster Risks and Climate Change Impacts in Poverty Reduction*. Stockholm, Sweden, October 24. Accessed at <http://www.unisdr.org/files/1441_StockholmPlanOfAction WBSIDAISDR.pdf>.

Stoddard, A. (2006) *Humanitarian Alert: NGO Information and its Impact on US Foreign Policy*. Kumarian Press, Bloomfield, CT.

Stone, L. (2011) Gore's climate case hits cyber space. *Toronto Star*, September 16, A18.

Strobel, W.P. (1996) The CNN effect. *American Journalism Review*, May. Accessed at <http://www.ajr.org/Article.asp?id=3572>.

"The summer of acid rain" (2007) *The Economist*, December 19, pp. 133–5.

Sunstein, C.R. (1997) Social norms and social roles. In Sunstein, C. (ed.) *Free Markets and Social Justice*. Oxford University Press, New York, pp. 32–69.

Susman, P., O'Keefe, P. and Wisner, B. (1983) Global disasters: a radical interpretation. In Hewitt, K. (ed.) *Interpretations of Calamity from the Viewpoint of Human Ecology*. Allen and Unwin, London.

Susskind, L.E. (1994) *Environmental Diplomacy: Negotiating More Effective Global Agreements*. Oxford University Press, Oxford.

Tarrow, S. (2005) *The New Transnational Activism*. Cambridge University Press, New York.

Tavares, S.C. (2008) Do more corrupt countries receive less disaster relief? Visiting scholar lecture, Department of Economics, Bar-Ilan University, Israel, January 20. Accessed at <http://www.biu.ac.il/SOC/ec/events/visiting_lectures.htm>.

Taylor, J.B., Zurcher, L.A. and Key, W.H. (1970) *Tornado: A Community Response to Disaster*. University of Washington Press, Seattle.

Telford, J., Cosgrave, J. and Houghton, R. (2006) Joint Evaluation of the International Response to the Indian Ocean Tsunami: Synthesis Report. Tsunami Evaluation Coalition, London.

Tellmann, U. (2009) Imagining catastrophe: scenario planning and the striving for epistemic security. *economic sociology: the european electronic newsletter*, 10 (2), 17–21.

"Thai floods to cost up to $11B: Insurer" (2011) *Metro* (Toronto), December 2, p. 12.

Thomalla, F., Downing, T., Spanger-Siegfried, E., Han, G. and Rockström, J. (2006) Reducing hazard vulnerability: towards a common approach between disaster risk reduction and climate adaptation. *Disasters*, 30, 39–45.

Thompson, J. (2011) Quake case sends tremors through scientists. *Globe and Mail*, September 20, p. A15.

Tierney, K. (2008) Hurricane Katrina: catastrophic impacts and alarming lessons. In Quigley, J.M. and Rosenthal, L.A. (eds.) *Risking House and Home: Disasters, Cities, Public Policy*. Berkeley Public Policy Press/Institute of Governmental Studies, Berkeley, CA, pp. 119–36.

Tong, J. (2004) Questionable accountability: MSF and Sphere in 2003. *Disasters*, 28, 176–89.

Toosi, N. (2010) Floods expose civilian-military divide in Pakistan. Boston.com (*Boston Globe*), August 20. Accessed at <http://www.boston.com/news/world/asia/articles/2010/08/20/pakistan_accepts_indian_aid_for_flood_relief/>.

Townsend, F.F. (2006) *The Federal Response to Hurricane Katrina: Lessons Learned*. Office of the Assistant to the President for Homeland Security and Counterterrorism, Washington, DC.

"Unable to help Myanmar relief efforts, U.S. Navy vessels sailing away" (2008) The Associated Press, June 4. Accessed at <http://www.burmalivechat.com/>.

United States Government Accountability Office (2006) Hurricane Katrina: comprehensive politics and procedures are needed to ensure appropriate use of and accountability for international assistance. GAO, Washington, DC.

United States Joint Forces Command (2010) *2010 Joint Operating Environment* (JOE), Suffolk, VA, February. Accessed at <http://www.fas.org/man/eprint/joe2010.pdf>.

Van Belle, D.A. (2000) New York Times and network TV news coverage of foreign disasters: the significance of the insignificant variables. *Journalism & Mass Communications Quarterly*, 77, 50–70.

Van Belle, D.A. (2009) Media agenda-setting and donor aid. In Norris, P. (ed.) *Public Sentinel: News Media & Governance Reform*. The World Bank, Washington, DC.

Van Belle, D.A., Rioux, J.S. and Potter, D.M. (2004) *Media, Bureaucracies and Foreign Aid: A Comparative Analysis of the United States, Canada, France and Japan*. Palgrave Macmillan, New York.

van der Linde, D. (2008) The politics of disaster: a study into post-Katrina international aid. Accessed at <http://www.disasterdiplomacy.org/pbl/vanderlinde2008.pdf>.

van Niekerk, D. (2008) From disaster relief to disaster risk reduction: a consideration of the evolving international relief mechanism. *The Journal for Transdisciplinary Research in Southern Africa*, 4, 355–76.

Van Wassenhove, L.N. (2006) Humanitarian aid logistics: supply chain management in high gear. *Journal of the Operational Research Society*, 57, 475–89.

Ventresca, M.J. (2002) Global policy fields: conflicts and settlements in the emergence of organized international attention to official statistics, 1853–1947. Institute for Policy Research Working Paper WP-02-45, Northwestern University, October.

Vidal, J. (2011) Warning: extreme weather ahead. *The Guardian Weekly*, June 24, 28–9.

Views from the Frontline: a local perspective of progress toward implementation of the Hyogo Framework for Action (2009) Global Network of Civil Organisations for Disaster Reduction: Teddington, Middlesex, June 19. Accessed at <http://globalnetwork-dr.org/images/reports/vflfullreport0609.pdf>.

Volberg, T. (2005/6) The politicization of humanitarian aid and its effect on the principles of humanity, impartiality and neutrality. European Masters Thesis in International Humanitarian Assistance submitted to the Ruhr-University Bochum, Institute for International Law of Peace and Armed Conflict.

Walker, P. and Maxwell, D. (2009) *Shaping the Humanitarian World*. Routledge, London and New York.

Wal-Mart (2010) Disaster Relief Fact Sheet. Accessed at <http://www.walmartstores.com/media/factsheets/fs_2304.pdf>.

Watanabe, T. (1995) Angry Japan official rebuffs critics. *Los Angeles Times*, January 27.

Weaver, R. (2009) Linking climate change adaptation and disaster risk reduction. Tearfund, Middlesex, April 17.

Weick, K.E. (1995) *Sensemaking in Organizations*. Sage, Thousand Oaks, CA.

Weick, K.E. (1999) Sensemaking as an organizational dimension of change. In Cooperrider, D.L. and Dutton, J.E. (eds.) *Organizational Dimensions of Global Change*. Sage, Thousand Oaks, CA, pp. 39–56.

Welsh, I. (1996) Risk, governance and environmental politics. *Innovation*, 9, 407–20.

West, K. (2001) *Agents of Altruism: The Expansion of Humanitarian NGOs in Rwanda and Afghanistan*. Ashgate, Aldershot.

Wilson, R.A. and Brown, R.D. (2009) Introduction. In Wilson, R.A. and Brown, R.D. (eds.) *Humanitarianism and Suffering: The Mobilization of Empathy.* Cambridge University Press, Cambridge, pp. 1–28.

Wisner, B., Blaikie, P., Cannon, T. and Davis, I. (2004) *At Risk: Natural Hazards, People's Vulnerability and Disasters,* 3rd edn. Routledge, London and New York.

Worawongs, W.T., Wang, W. and Sims, A. (2007) US media coverage of natural disasters: a framing analysis of Hurricane Katrina and the tsunami. Presented at the Annual Meeting of the Association for Education in Journalism and Mass Communications, Washington, DC, August 8. Accessed at <http://www.allacademic.com/meta/p203908_index.html>.

World Bank (2006) Global Program Review: The ProVention Consortium. Independent Evaluation Group, Thematic and Global Evaluation Division. World Bank, Washington, DC, June 28.

World Development Movement (2011) "No" to climate loans: statement by civil society groups in the global south, June. Accessed at <http://www.wdm.org.uk/>.

Wuthnow, R. (1989) *Communities of Discourse.* Harvard University Press, Cambridge, MA.

Young, N. and Dugas, E. (2011) Representations of climate change in Canadian national print media: The banalization of global warming. *Canadian Review of Sociology,* 48, 1–22.

Young, O.R. (1994) *International Governance: Protecting the Environment in a Stateless Society.* Cornell University Press, Ithaca, NY.

Index